Inheritocracy

Inheritocracy

It's Time to Talk About the Bank of Mum and Dad

Eliza Filby

Biteback Publishing

First published in Great Britain in 2024 by
Biteback Publishing Ltd, London
Copyright © Eliza Filby 2024

ISBN 978-1-78590-858-3

10 9 8 7 6 5 4 3 2 1

A CIP catalogue record for this book is available from the British Library.

Set in Minion Pro and Obbligato

Printed and bound in Great Britain by
CPI Group (UK) Ltd, Croydon CR0 4YY

FSC
www.fsc.org
MIX
Paper | Supporting
responsible forestry
FSC® C171272

For my mother,
for the best type of inheritance: an example.

And for Christian, Chaplin and Amaryllis,
for bringing meaning to it all.

'Time and family are part of the same thing really; the generation is the actual unit of time by which humanity lives.'

JAMES MEEK

Contents

Chapter 1

Inheritocracy: The Family Tree

We were in the living room of the house that he had inherited from his parents. Perched in the only armchair that still offered comfort, my father rested his leg on a cushion in front of the open fire.

'Press record; let's get started,' he said. I was his middle daughter and had a PhD in history – two useful distinctions for the urgent task of recording the Filby family story, before it was lost. When he had first been diagnosed the previous year, I'd pledged to interview him about his past, but as hospital visits took their toll on both of us (I had been pregnant with my first child), it stretched into something we said we really must do, rather than something we did. Then, suddenly, it was now or never.

So, we sat together, ready to climb the family tree. My father's voice was weak; sometimes it drifted away entirely. Sometimes, he would screech as spasms of pain took hold. 'Whiskey,' he whispered. 'Get me a whiskey. You know, Sinatra *always* had a jar before a big show,' he smirked. I poured him a thimbleful, and, sipping, he returned to his story about my great-grandfather's horse and cart grocery business during the Great Depression. It was mostly about the horse.

Largely untouched by the two world wars or migration (unless you count a move from Bermondsey to Tooting), my family have lived in south London for two centuries and in the same house for eighty years. And perhaps this was what made us distinct: our *consistency*, especially as Londoners.

These recordings – which six years on I find impossible to listen to – had to be done, in my father's words, 'so that the Filby family history would not go with him'. But in his telling, there was a lack of spontaneity, verve and joy that should naturally accompany such childhood reminiscences and family legends. I wasn't fully present either; my attention divided between my restless one-year-old son rattling around in his playpen and my racing mind preoccupied with the morbid realisation that, before long, I'd be telling my son stories of a grandfather he had never known.

I'd always assumed that facing death freed you from the past. But in my father's case, it was the opposite. He was obsessed with his childhood and catalogued possessions in the house he had lived in his entire life: what was meaningful, what was worth holding on to and what could be 'flogged on that auction site'. But in telling his tale, and the various tentacles of our family history, my father had a particular aim: he was not seeking to preserve the memories of those long gone; rather, he was slotting himself into that timeline. It was about legacy. And these stories, like all family trees, had roots that are deeply interwoven within the grand sweep of history. It was, in short, an inheritance.

■　■　■

We live in an inheritance economy. If you're under forty-five, your life chances and opportunities are increasingly determined by your access to the Bank of Mum and Dad, not by what you earn or learn. Rather than a meritocracy – where hard work pays off – we live in an *inheritocracy*, where family wealth catalyses success.

The Bank of Mum and Dad dominates our economic system and especially our property market – operating best for those who can lean on parental support. Family wealth is now more than ever the condition for opportunity. You know it when you see it: it's your friend who never took out a student loan, who had their rent subsidised or who suddenly acquires the deposit for a flat. It's those who enjoy luxurious holidays in their twenties and thirties, multigenerational jaunts paid for by their parents. It's the friends who had the safety net of staying with Mum and Dad while they saved, upskilled and/or had a quarter-life crisis. But that's the stuff you can see. There's another layer of privilege that is even less detectable: it's those who enjoy a level of disposable income unburdened by major expenses such as student loans, rent, saving for a deposit or childcare. It's those who can afford the smaller, everyday luxuries to ease the pressures of modern life. Those who can take taxis more often, have a house cleaner, not think twice about going out for dinner. These conveniences, though seemingly small, collectively contribute to a more efficient, relaxed and high-performing lifestyle, providing more free time compared to those worrying about how on earth they can afford the big-ticket items in life.

Family wealth is the *real* economic story of the twenty-first century. Inheritance has, of course, always existed, but the extent to which young people now rely on it is a relatively recent development. The forces at play are structural and there are no signs of the inheritance economy abating, only increasing. Whether we are talking about wealth inequality, increasing gender equality, rising property and rent prices or delayed adulthood, inheritance is the story behind the story. Educational effort and graduate jobs are still necessary (probably more necessary than ever) but are not the guaranteed rewards we were told they would be. Instead, it's a trickling down of money, time and support from parents that is required for nailing the basics of adulthood, let alone any kind of conventional success or financial stability in today's world. But as much as this subject is a past and present force, it will profoundly shape our future: everything from caring for our parents in an ageing society to our work and retirement plans to the social division amongst our children and potentially our grandchildren.

We're going to do a deep dive into this overlooked story. But, to clarify, it's written with the beneficiaries of the inheritance economy in mind more than the benefactors. This one is for the kids, rather than the parents – millennials (1981–96) and Gen Z (1997–2010) rather than baby boomers (1942–65) or Gen X (1966–80). That means those under forty-five who have grown up in this inheritance era and whose life cycle, culture and economic circumstances have been shaped by these forces. Both those who've had access to the parental ATM and those who have not. That's because the backdrop to our generational story is an economy increasingly built on generational wealth.

Up until now, much of the debate has centred on how lucky the baby boomers were and how unlucky millennials are, often pitting parents against offspring. The generational war of boomers versus millennials, that familiar trope of intergenerational unfairness, has dominated public debate since the 2008 financial crisis. It's not just unhelpful; it's also increasingly untrue. An intergenerational duel conceals the deeper story of *intra*generational unfairness; some millennials have ridden on the coat-tails of their parents and are doing much better than those who have had no such advantage. This conflict has divided millennials from the point we entered adulthood. But it is more pronounced and urgent now as we enter mid-life and our parents begin to pass away. In short, it is time to put the whole family in the frame, rather than zooming in on one generation's wealth. This is because so much of our parents' money is tied up in property and, quite often, because the long-term rise in house prices is only one generation old: a legacy of Thatcher's Britain. The point is that in many families, this wealth will only be truly realised when our parents pass away.

I'm going to explore the origins, mutations and consequences of inheritocracy through my own story as a millennial, when our family was confronted with the inheritance issue after my father died. But it would be pointless to pretend that my story is representative; it is a privileged, London-centric and distinctly white, female wealth tale. Still, it reflects the need for a more nuanced debate, because familial wealth today is not confined to the global 1 per cent or even the professional upper middle class: the Bank of Mum and Dad involves upwardly mobile families like mine. In 2017, 74 per cent of people aged sixty-five years and over in England owned their own home outright.[1] In 2023, it was calculated that those aged over sixty-five owned a record estimated £2.5 trillion of net housing wealth.[2] In theory, that's a lot of money in property to pass down. Little wonder then that 80 per cent of millennials expect to receive some kind of inheritance in their lifetime.[3] Inheritance is not a minority issue affecting a rich few. The dilemmas and dynamics set out here affect more families in Britain than we realise or admit.

■　■　■

So, what is my story? How do I fit into the inheritance economy? What was the legacy that my father passed on to me during those last-minute sessions with the voice recorder?

My dad was an English working-class boy done good. He didn't have a good start. He failed the 11-plus – his generation's great determiner of opportunity – and ended up at a secondary modern school. It did not stump him chiefly because he came of age during the liberating thrills of swinging '60s London: when class and social shackles were coming off and the world was opening up for men like him. After an intense but short-lived experience at art school, he was kicked out for laziness and general misdemeanours. This was followed by a few more years of carefree exploration as an amateur film director in his twenties. He settled down in his thirties with a wife, three kids and a more conventional path – although not *that* conventional. He was a stay-at-home dad (very avant-garde in the 1980s) and a painter and decorator on the side.

This enabled my mother, who worked as an interior designer with the John Lewis Partnership, to push forward as the breadwinner. Despite living through an age of increasing meritocracy, it was not the education system that freed them. Instead, it was the social liberalism of the 1960s, followed by the tough but, for many, fortuitous circumstances of the Thatcher years. Their life was full of opportunities unavailable to their parents – the Second World War generation. Yet arguably these same chances have not been extended to their kids – the millennial generation. In short, the story of my parents' life would have been completely different had they lived thirty years earlier. But tellingly, their story would have been highly unlikely had they been born thirty years later, too.

The most important part of this tale is that it seems fortuitous only in hindsight. My mother and father transformed their fortunes in the 1980s but not in a way they, nor my two sisters and I, felt at the time. My parents were about as far from yuppie culture as you can imagine – antique-collecting, subversive punks whose working-class roots meant that the notion of 'getting ideas above your station' never fully wore off.

They were also from south London: Tooting, an area then deemed insalubrious but which today is an aspirational destination for middle-class graduates. If gentrification is a maturation process, then Tooting Broadway, when I was young, was stuck in its infancy years – transient occupants, run-down houses and petty crime. My father, an only child, grew up in a house that my grandfather, a compulsive gambler, had acquired through a bet. Wisely, he swiftly put the deeds in my grandmother's name, so he couldn't lose them just as fast as he'd won them. This story is the crucial one in the 'Filby family history'.

My childhood home was eclectic and eccentric. The house itself was always in a ramshackle state, with 1960s wallpaper and limited central heating. My parents, inspired by Thatcher's vision of a 'property-owning democracy', took the plunge and, first with relatives and then with friends, invested in two more houses in Tooting. And crucially they held on to them. Scraping through the market crash of the '80s and the repossession surge of the early '90s, by the turn of the millennium, they were sitting on a portfolio of properties that was gaining value at approximately 13 per cent each year. My mother signed her first mortgage just six years after the 1975 Sex Discrimination Act, which allowed women to apply for a mortgage independently. The loan she took out back then was only four times her annual income. Today, in contrast, most houses in London are nearly fifteen times the typical wage.[4]

By the early 2000s, Tooting Broadway began to change. It had entered its gentrification adolescence. Cafes sold cappuccinos; wine bars came with those chrome high stools. One pub, once notorious for its strip shows, began hosting a craft fair. Another, which in the 1980s used to have a 'last orders' collection box for the IRA, started putting on *James Bond* theme nights. Prices were rising, but it was only after the 2008 financial crash that it dawned on my sisters and me that we couldn't actually afford to live where we grew up. More absurdly, our well-heeled university friends aspired to rent a flat in our neighbourhood.

Despite the expansion in my parents' assets, my childhood was defined by scarcity rather than wealth. We weren't poor; we were homeowners after all. But we didn't go on holiday until I was about thirteen and everything was carefully budgeted. My parents certainly had no encounters with the sector that was then evolving to service their generation's considerable rise in personal wealth and assets. My parents did not know anyone who knew about finance, let alone seek advice on personal investments or private pensions. My father distrusted banks – preferring to literally hide cash under the stairs. Still, by the time the global financial crisis hit, and I reached the age I was expected to be financially independent – I was twenty-seven and wasn't – my parents had become paper millionaires.

Even at this monumental tipping point, they had little understanding of the implications of the wealth they had amassed over thirty years: what it was worth, what they should do with it or, even, how to gain access to it.

That was until, of course, my father's cancer diagnosis forced us to confront this legacy and its implications.

■ ■ ■

But let's back up a second. Is this *really* the true story? Or have I just fed you a 'working-class accidental millionaires' tale because that's how I, a millennial beneficiary of the Bank of Mum and Dad, attempt to justify my own exceedingly privileged position? Well, frankly, yes – and I'm not alone. One academic study interviewed several first-time homeowners in London who had bought property with help from their family. The researchers noticed a familiar narrative amongst the beneficiaries; a tendency to frame this financial windfall not in terms of their own individual privilege but as evidence of their parents' hard work and upward mobility.

In other words, I, and many others like me, legitimise access to the Bank of Mum and Dad by talking about *their* stories of struggle rather than *our* smooth path. This represents a shift from the past, where once parents lived vicariously through their children's achievements and opportunities. Now, children often define themselves through their parents' struggles. In today's climate of identity politics, being privileged and middle class, whether we like it or not, can lead to feelings of self-consciousness and even shame. According to Liz Moor and Sam Friedman, the authors of the study, when it comes to talking about inheritance or gifts from the Bank of Mum and Dad, therefore, we are more likely to reach 'back beyond the influence of one's own, often privileged background, to a more humble, and often working-class, multigenerational family history'.[5]

My reliance on the Bank of Mum and Dad, for example, is the only reason I've been able to stay living in the area I was born. For this and many other reasons, we are more likely to see a parental gift as a rightful flow of wealth within a family rather than what it has become: a powerful force reshaping our economy and influencing our society and its ideas of fairness and equality. Inheritance (and, frankly, all manner of familial support) is deemed a right by young and old alike. This is one of the major reasons why it is so difficult to make it a political issue. It is, as my father knew when he asked me to record his recollections, a deeply personal experience, where relationships, emotion and human connection converge with cold, hard economics.

In recent years, we have understandably and rightly sought to interrogate and widen the conversation about privilege in society. And yet how much do we interrogate one of the most obvious advantages experienced by anyone under forty-five: the presence or absence of a parental safety net? There's no denying that family privilege intersects with class, race, educational attainment and sexuality, and in a different way gender, as we shall see, but why is it that so many of us ignore or give a false impression of our parental springboard? We enjoy mocking the 'nepo babies' of the rich and famous, but we shy away from recognising ourselves as, perhaps on a lesser scale, being like them.

In the twentieth century, it was commonplace to speak of education as the key success metric. It is something I have been guilty of. I was the first person in my family to be awarded a university degree, but this gives an entirely false impression of my status and class in the twenty-first century. Culturally, I was raised in a working-class household; my great-aunt was a Pearly Queen, that iconic mascot of working-class London, and we really did stand around a piano bashing out 'Maybe It's Because I'm a Londoner'. But I was also raised on impressionist art and Waitrose food and in a house my family owned. I also had parents who offered a critical safety net and a lift-up when I needed it. This afforded me a degree of freedom and security that many never experience.

In some middle-class circles, all talk of the Bank of Mum and

Dad has become so normalised that it is the timing and amount of financial support that are the points debated, not whether there is any support at all. Does this display a certain level of blindness when it comes to economic advantage in our society? Frankly, yes.

Inheritance and the Bank of Mum and Dad are at the centre of our emotional, social and economic lives. And yet most people don't talk about it. This book sets out to start the conversation.

■　■　■

Over the past twenty years, the wealth divide amongst millennials has been shaped by this dynamic and it is only set to widen in the next twenty years as our parents' generation dies out. In the UK, approximately £5.5 trillion of family wealth will be passed down the generations.[6] In the US, the figure is estimated to be a sum anywhere between $15 trillion and $84 trillion.[7] We are looking at the largest transference of wealth in human history, with millennials being told that we are set to become the richest generation ever. These figures are hard to compute and certainly up for dispute. But the wider point is that inheritance is not a minority issue and not just a matter for the elderly to consider when they get their affairs in order. On the contrary, it is one that affects the recipient more than the giver. In short, it is the millennial story. We are a generation of heirs.

The French economist Thomas Piketty, whose 2013 book *Capital in the Twenty-First Century* became something of a manifesto for post-crash left-wing politics, saw the growth of the inheritance economy in the millennial generation as an echo of the 'patrimonial economy' of the nineteenth century: 'Inherited wealth comes close to being as decisive at the beginning of the twenty-first century as it was in the age of Balzac's *Père Goriot*.'[8] Piketty referenced the way in which inheritance formed the narrative backbone of many nineteenth-century novels. Indeed, divided families and last will and testaments are key plot devices in *Bleak House*, *Middlemarch* and *Pride and Prejudice*. Today, the HBO series *Succession*, in which a dysfunctional money-bags baby boomer plays puppet master to his desperate and dependent children, is, in the same way, a dynastic tale for our times. The assumption surrounding the show's popularity is that we enjoy being voyeurs of the mega-rich and lust for daughter Shiv's 'quiet luxury' fashion choices. But perhaps this outlandish story of inheritance speaks to the average person more than we might first think. In the twenty-first century, with the quiet massing of record levels of personal wealth through property, pensions and investments, the Bank of Mum and Dad has become one of the main drivers of the economy; reshaping family finances and relationships, widening wealth inequality and providing untold opportunity *for some*. Familial privilege isn't universal, but it has universal consequences.

■　■　■

My story is just one of many millennial lives we'll reflect on in *Inheritocracy*. We will hear from the voices of very different people, all of whom are caught, in very different ways, in the web of inheritocracy. These interviews show rich and varied life stories, demonstrating the breadth and variation of opportunity and costs of the Bank of Mum and Dad in Britain today. My hope is that they spark self-reflection, not just about your own family and circumstances but also about the potential ways in which your life and the lives of your friends have been shaped (and will continue to be) by the great economic force of the Bank of Mum and Dad – whether through its presence or its absence.

This book is not just about family and money; it is also about capturing and understanding growing up in the twenty-first century, because we need to look at this story in the round. We'll discover how millennials were sold the meritocratic educational myth, how our dating history fits into the inheritance economy, how delayed adulthood and millennial female milestone culture interlinks with the Bank of Mum and Dad, why class is now determined by family wealth not individual income, the complications that come with divorce and the rise of 'blended' families, what happens when you end up caring for your parents and the ultimate question, yes, will millennials become the richest generation in history? We will hear from cultural commentators, authors and economists, as well as politicians, wealth managers and personal financial advisors. I've also commissioned original polling by YouGov to get to the bottom of how we actually *feel* about parental gifts, inheritance, family wealth and privilege. Much of the polling up until now has narrowly focused on the right to inherit (which is pretty resounding) or the specifics of inheritance tax. It doesn't cover the deeply personal terrain that inheritance occupies.

I'm not fixated on political policies or the economics of the housing market – while important, these are not my areas of expertise. What is here is far from comprehensive; others can crunch the numbers, compose the policies and solutions and service the assets and wealth. I do not claim to have any answers. My focus is on people – families, individuals and society at large. Ultimately, I'm interested in how generational wealth is bringing families together but also how it is pulling society apart.

This book is not a definitive history of 21st-century inheritance. Instead, my hope is that it will be a conversation starter within our generation, within our families and across society. The aim isn't to flatten the experience as simply *generational* but to bring it to life as a phenomenon shaped by class, race, culture, financial literacy, circumstance, family, geography, economics and just plain luck. If we millennials and Gen Z feel we have been in the economic background up until now, we will soon be propelled into the forefront as our parents age and the power shifts. Gen X are already experiencing these forces, sandwiched as they are between looking after their kids and their elderly parents. Millennials will follow in their footsteps but with less personal wealth, and greater dependence on inheritance.

Whether you see all this as good fortune, perfectly justified or outrageously unfair, we need to untangle the many threads that, woven together, constitute the fabric of our inheritocracy. So, our first task is to understand how we got here. And our story begins not with the crash of 2008, not with the Right to Buy housing scheme of the 1980s, but with a very cool girl in 1940s Fulham, south-west London.

Chapter 2

The Backstory: The Making of the Boomers and the Origins of Inheritocracy

Aged thirteen, my mum joined the Young Communist League. She had the uniform: duffel coat and black polo neck, a well-thumbed copy of *The Communist Manifesto* poking out of one pocket. My grandmother was ashamed enough to cross the street if she saw her daughter out in public. By fourteen, my mum would sneak out of her bedroom window in Fulham to spend her nights in the coffee bars of Soho. At fifteen, she marched against the looming spectre of nuclear proliferation on the 'Ban the Bomb' protest from the home of Britain's nuclear deterrent, Aldermaston, all the way to Trafalgar Square. Over the weekend protest, she slept in church halls, befriended fellow pacifists and carried a banner that said, 'Soho says Noho'. At sixteen, she busked with a young Rod Stewart; she was no singer but would be the one who went round the crowds with a flat cap for donations. When she was seventeen, she went to the Lucie Clayton modelling school alongside famous '60s model Jean Shrimpton and got a job as a showroom girl. In her twenties, she met my father, and they lived a bohemian life – unmarried, lots of parties, surrounded by artists, musicians and writers. None of them was successful in any conventional sense, but they were successful in that they lived the lifestyle they chose, free from the constraints of past generations. In her thirties, Mum had her punk years, with Dr Martens and safety-pinned clothes and could be found in a headlock with my father pogo dancing to the Clash.

This was my mother before I knew her. My mother, immortalised in grainy photos, is always cool, beautiful and forever young.

My mum was (and very much still is) incredibly cool. But I'm not the only one who has a cool mum. I have friends whose mothers hitchhiked through Afghanistan in the '70s; one who emigrated from Jamaica and challenged racial and class barriers in the civil service; one, a Catholic, who defied convention and married a Protestant; another was a dancer with the Velvet Underground before becoming an editor on Fleet Street. Every act, self-conscious or otherwise, was one of subversion against the conservative status quo; from the skirts they wore to who they married (and especially divorced). Every one of them in small and big ways was a female pioneer. Their rebellions were immortalised in broader culture, too. It's not that our mothers were all Gloria Steinem, but we (and they) can't help but frame their lives within that feminist chronology.

Perhaps this all feels particularly prescient for me as I am now my mother's age in my earliest memories of her. I can recall her fortieth birthday party, which took place in the home where I now live. This was a time in her life when she was taking out a mortgage rather than rebelling against the world. And yet it is the life I can't personally recall that sticks. Compared to our parents' generational life story (however airbrushed and fantasised), ours seems frankly rudimental and mundane. Netflix binges during a global lockdown?

It doesn't have the same wow factor as busking with Rod Stewart. Nor do endless exams, hustle culture, unpaid internships, career ladders, networking on LinkedIn or even, frankly, city breaks. We fly; they hitchhiked. My mother agrees. 'Your generation are just so bloody boring,' she likes to remind me, on everything from sex to smoking. But is our generation restricted by a script our parents helped draft?

Many of us have no understanding of ourselves that is not in some fundamental way forged within their history. That is how parental heritage normally works, but it is also undeniable how the past seventy years of history have been seen through baby boomers' eyes. Crudely speaking, the 1950s were conservative but wholesome, the '60s were idealistic and disruptive, the '70s were disillusioning and debauched, the '80s were when the hippies became yuppies. Historians have done much to challenge this casual overriding narrative, but it is still surprising how much this perception conditions the modern mind. Its imprint is etched on their offspring's psyche.

In 1958, *Life* magazine's front page featured a dozen babies holding up a sign that read 'Kids: Built-in Recession Cure – How 4,000,000 a Year Make Billions in Business'. That was in the US, where the term 'baby boom' came to refer to the economic windfall synonymous with this demographic bulge. In the UK, though, the 'boom' was more a succession of bangs, with a significant peak immediately after the Second World War, followed by another in the early 1960s. Nor was there an immediate economic surge accompanying this swelling demographic. The baby boomers, however, would reshape our world over the course of the next eighty years. In short, there will probably never be a generation like them (in the west) again.

They are the only generational group whose label refers to their point of difference: their number. The generation after them, Gen

X, were at one time known as the 'baby busters', because of the decline in birth rates during this period and arguably have yielded far less influence as a result. When baby boomers were teenagers, the emerging life stage of adolescence crystallised. With growing affluence and disposable income, these teenagers became an economic force that has never waned. In their youth, they found that culture and politics swung to their beat. When baby boomers hit their maturing years, the policies and politics of Thatcherism served their economic interests – even though there were many for whom it didn't, of course. And as they entered retirement age in the 2000s, the sheer number of them (and their propensity to vote) meant that political priorities swung in their favour once again. Demographers like to compare the impact of this cohort to a pig being digested by a python. As it moves through society, so we contort our body to shoulder the impact.

Close your eyes and say the phrase 'baby boomer'. You will probably picture a wealthy white suburban man or woman, who has a mortgage-free home and plenty of spare rooms. It is true: they are the most homogenised generation within the UK in terms of wealth, culture, values and racial diversity – 92 per cent identify as white.[1] Yet these stereotypes are limiting; nearly 900,000 households headed by the over-55s are still renting, for example.[2] Many, like my parents, grew up with little affluence and a lot of austerity. And many are what can be termed 'first-generation wealth', defined by rising assets, decent pensions and savings accrued in their lifetime.

If there's one thing that characterises families with first-generation wealth, it is that the children often live in the shadow of their parents who made it. The children's path is eased as their parents provide them with all the opportunities they themselves did not have. The offspring then struggle to go it alone, faltering under the pressure to recreate or sustain that lifestyle and ambition. For millennials, this feels like the major plotline for our generation.

As this chapter will show, the UK's shift to an inheritocracy in the twenty-first century has its origins in the post-war period and in the baby boomers' generational narrative. It is the backstory to the story. If we are going to explore the impact of the Bank of Mum and Dad, we briefly need to understand how it was established. This is a broad tale with many aspects, but for our purposes the most important are threefold: firstly, the rupture in social values and how that affected their parenting. Secondly, the rupture in education, not only the system they endured but how they thought about education for their millennial kids. Thirdly, most obviously, the rupture in economics and their rising personal wealth, in short the foundations of the Bank of Mum and Dad.

The First Rupture: Values

Generations tend to be shaped by key moments as well as gradual trends. So, if there is a year that symbolises the youth culture of the swinging '60s, it is, of course, 1968. This was the moment when it appeared that the world's young students erupted into a mass orgy of protest, standing up against war, racism, sexism and more. People began to point to their generation as a key factor in their identity and many governments across the world listened, lowering the voting age from twenty-one to eighteen. This generation of youths were what sociologists like to call post-materialists. Many now had the luxury to ask: 'What do you care about when you don't have to worry about shelter and food?' The post-war generation in the UK may have been raised on rationing, outside loos and playing in deserted bomb sites, but they would come to be defined by the end of austerity and a growth in material conditions as they entered adulthood.

'They've created the greatest age of individualism in American history!' wrote journalist Tom Wolfe in his famous 1976 essay on what he christened the 'me' decade: 'All rules are broken!'[3] The collapse of deference that underpinned this cultural rupture meant that baby boomers were frequently the victims of age-bashing, routinely dismissed and criticised for being lazy, entitled and self-possessed. Sound familiar, millennials and Gen Z?

When John Lennon made his notorious comment that the Beatles were 'more popular than Jesus', it sparked outrage mainly because it was becoming true. Baby boomers, especially women, may have been raised cradle Christians, but they increasingly rejected organised religion, triggering an unstoppable wave of decline in mainstream Christianity in the UK. It's hard not to understate how revolutionary this was. We millennials may have been raised as cultural Christians – at a push we can probably recite the Lord's Prayer and 'All Things Bright and Beautiful' – but for most of us, we grew up in a world where traditional Christian expectations seemed truly archaic (especially for women), and we comfortably accepted the new thriving multireligious reality. In this and much else, baby boomers were the disruptors, triggering a generational culture war between old and young – and it's a dynamic that we have been watching on repeat ever since. They started life as its perpetrators, even if they now see themselves as its victims.

Baby boomers are now the elders in most families and arguably have earned the right to reprimand (however politely) anyone younger on how they are doing it all wrong. Such lectures are often peppered with some warped nostalgia of how difficult but how much more fun life used to be – whether it be coal fires or bad food, interest rates or workplace dynamics. Baby boomers, like generations before them, now play the role of society's sages in families, culture and businesses, and yet this conceals a blatant truth: baby boomers have struggled with a traditional transition into elderhood. The generation who invented youth was never supposed to get old.

Youth culture did not matter before the long 1960s and arguably no other youth culture has mattered to the same degree since. For a long time, if not still, the popular hits played at a wedding, the headliners at a royal celebration or the Pyramid Stage at Glastonbury belong to their era. A young Mick Jagger (an honorary boomer) once asserted: 'I'd rather be dead than sing "Satisfaction" when I'm forty-five.'[4] Well, Mick, you are selling out stadiums in your eighties and still apparently can't get no satisfaction.

The original youthful generation have inevitably come to redefine old age. Just look at the baby boomer woman's yearning for contemporary fashion. My 78-year-old mother shops in Zara, whereas when her mother was in her seventies in the 1990s, she continued to dress like a 1950s housewife. Gen X, with their twinning mother–daughter trends, are following the baby boomer lead. We can admire this consumer shift towards a more positive view of ageing, especially for women, but let's also remember that any greater recognition, representation or appreciation of the older woman by brands is also an economic calculation: this demographic have all the money right now. Look too at how baby boomers and Gen X ape the technological habits of their children – their taking over of Facebook, for instance. This influence is so profound that the Oxford Internet Institute has estimated that by 2070, profiles of the deceased will outnumber profiles of the living on that platform, such is the overwhelming weight of its older members.[5] Likewise the way in which baby boomers have embraced and redefined retirement away from golf courses and bridge clubs to adventure travel, entrepreneurship and increasingly a tech-fuelled life. Baby boomers spend as much time on their phones per day as millennials; commissioners at Netflix are now leaning into boomer boxset bingers; older female hosts dominate Airbnb.[6] There's also evidence that this generation is seeing the biggest rise in hospitalisations due to alcohol overconsumption and the greatest surge in sexually transmitted diseases while the abstemious youth are the new puritans.[7]

Culturally, politically and socially, baby boomers invented the modern world and continue to reinvent themselves in it. They may be today's conservative force, but in truth, they have always had more in common with their children than they ever did with their parents, the veterans of the Second World War to whom they directed most of their ire. One example of this is changing attitudes towards homosexuality. Two-thirds of people now agree that sex between two adults of the same sex is 'not wrong at all', a rise of almost fifty percentage points since the early 1980s, when the question was first asked.[8] All this is important because in today's inheritocracy, it helps if there is a synergy of values between parent and child. The idea is that we get on with them. Most of us aren't rebelling against our parents, not to the extent they did with theirs at any rate. Most of us do not need to. But more importantly, nor can we afford to.

The Second Rupture: Education

The critical scene in our parents' story is not the heated campus protests of the 1960s (which were always a minority sport) but the examination halls of English primary schools during the cut-throat era of the 11-plus system. If this generation were defined by a single piece of legislation, it was the 1944 Education Act. The legislation that extended secondary school provision fitted the idealistic spirit of the post-war age, which had also created the NHS.

Based on the 11-plus test result, pupils would be allocated a place at either a grammar school, technical college or secondary modern school. Central government, though, never found the resources to develop enough technical schools; meaning it was largely a two-school system in which you either passed the 11-plus and went to grammar school or failed and went to secondary modern. It was also a postcode lottery; in some areas nearly half went to grammar school whereas in others it was a fraction of that, with girls particularly disadvantaged.

It has been estimated that between 1944 and 1976, 30 million children took the test, and more than 20 million failed.[9] Can you imagine a government allowing such a failure rate today? Whether you passed, like my mother, or did not, like my father, this generation were nurtured from a young age on a somewhat curious but ruthless meritocratic ideal. On the one hand, it was social engineering, leading to what public intellectual Richard Hoggart optimistically called a new 'aristocracy of brains'.[10] But it was also confused, not least because the fee-paying private school system prevailed and because the 11-plus awarded places to predominantly middle-class kids. By the late 1950s, its failings were becoming clear. Social and intellectual segregation was reinforcing social division, but it was also disregarding large numbers of pupils, especially children of the increasingly affluent working class. The system was critiqued for rewarding combined privilege: those with money and merit. As we shall see, this is a dynamic that would be repeated in the twenty-first century.

The Labour government eventually threw its weight behind a comprehensive school system; however, it was not nationally enforced – only locally encouraged and took years to take hold. Grammar schools continued to be the barometer of middle-class aspiration and eventually a cause for the meritocratic matriarch Margaret Thatcher. By the time most Gen X and millennials had made their way through school, the 11-plus, although still evident in some areas, ceased to be a generational-defining experience as it had been for the baby boomers.

But what does the education system of the mid-twentieth century have to do with family wealth in the 2020s? Well, firstly, that experience of either passing or failing the 11-plus left an indelible mark on our parents' generation at a young age; just ask them. It elevated an important chunk of working-class and lower-middle-class baby boomers into the professions who were able to capitalise on multiple opportunities in terms of free training, wages and assets. Many of whom, such as retired teachers, are now living on a pension and in a lifestyle that today's millennial teachers can only dream of. It also pushed, although not equalised, many women and also high-achieving middle-class children to compete with the privately educated at university and in the professions. But more importantly, the experience of the 11-plus system – the conventional belief in merit, exams and brains – carried into the parenting and educational culture of the 1980s and 1990s. By the end of the century, university would become the central marker of aspirational baby boomer parenting.

There were, of course, many legitimate reasons for the expansion of tertiary education in the twenty-first century, but it is also true that baby boomers, more than any other generation, have a reverential view of formal education. This is especially true for the humanities subjects, which, up until very recently, have always been culturally elevated above STEM (science, technology, engineering and mathematics) subjects in the UK. It is common, for example, for a baby boomer, and even some Gen X graduates, to self-identify through an academic discipline: 'I'm a Classicist' or 'I'm a historian' they will say, when what they really mean is that they studied the subject at university decades ago. This is not something that a graduate under forty-five would ever say, especially as many more have a second degree – and a first they are still paying for. Not that this reverence is a negative trait; far from it. I remember when I was a university lecturer how many baby boomer mature students I taught on undergraduate, master's and PhD programmes. Most were there because they had missed out on pursuing this passion early on in their lives; many of whom had failed the 11-plus and saw this as their second chance. They were the most dedicated and committed of all my students.

The culture of elite intellectualism still holds for this generation in a way it doesn't for younger generations who grew up in a more comprehensive school system and with tech-enabled knowledge at their fingertips. For our parents' generation, institutionalised education and culture are both markers of social aspiration and civilised citizenship. This is why if you find yourself mid-week at lunchtime in an art gallery, theatre or bookshop, you will notice that it is the baby boomers who are keeping most of these industries and institutions alive right now. And it is not just because they have the time and money; they grew up in a world where education was aspiration and success. As we shall see, our generation – those who have lived through graduate saturation, expensive fees and the diluted power of one salary – have a much more complex relationship with education and qualifications. But perhaps the overriding fact worth remembering, as the historian Peter Mandler has stated, is that 'most baby boomers' parents did not go to secondary school … In contrast, the baby boomers themselves all went to secondary school and nearly half of *their* children have continued in education beyond eighteen.'[11] That is an extraordinary leap in educational status across three generations. Whether baby boomers failed the 11-plus or not, they grew up believing that educational meritocracy was as important as homeownership in defining family aspiration and ensuring success – a message their children ingested to the extent that it became almost an expectation.

The Third Rupture: Wealth

When we think about inheritance, our thoughts may immediately leap to our nation's historic families: its aristocracy and with it their declining influence. Netflix's *Saltburn*, *Downton Abbey*, Evelyn Waugh's *Brideshead Revisited*: there's a long line of tales of decrepit estates occupied by dysfunctional families in financial turmoil. The landed elite has become one of our great cultural outputs, but it only works because it is predicated on a narrative of decline, and it goes something like this. The British aristocracy experienced a slow death in the twentieth century where a combination of two world wars, expensive divorces, financial mismanagement, political change and some shambolic behaviour led to their gradual erosion, a drying up of their wealth and consequent loss of influence. The stately homes and the family silver were handed over to the National Trust, and over time and in various ways, a more meritocratic and democratic society emerged in Britain.

The central feature of this decline was the growing enforcement of tax and death duties on inherited wealth. By 1946, tax on estates was 75 per cent for amounts worth over £2 million. Between 1910 and 1950, private capital in the UK economy fell from 700 per cent of national income to 250 per cent.[12]

Today, as we pay our £50 for a family ticket to tour National Trust properties whose landscaped gardens are filled with toddler-friendly adventure parks, dedicated elderly volunteers and cafes selling over-priced Victoria sponge cakes, do we spare a thought for the low-key aristocrats reduced to an apartment in a private wing of their family's ancestral home? I doubt it.

But perhaps we should. Recently, two researchers from South Bank University, Julien Morton and Matthew Bond, delved into probate data for aristocratic families between 1858 and 2018. They discovered something surprising. Rather than a story of financial ruin, they found that a significant number of aristocratic families – 600 in fact – had seen their wealth grow substantially in recent years. The value of a hereditary title has increased four times since the 1980s and doubled between 2009 and 2019, namely since the financial crisis.[13] What was this resurgence of the British aristocracy due to? A new generation of savvy, spirited, entrepreneurial aristocrats taking the reins from their feckless ancestors? Well… no.

Morton and Bond uncovered that this turnaround wasn't down to design as such – rather, Britain's aristocrats have been benefiting from an asset- and inheritance-driven economy since the 1980s. 'As government policy becomes more conducive to wealth accumulation and inheritance, so wealthy aristocratic families do better,' they explained.

But these aristocrats are merely beneficiaries of an economic revolution that aided not just the minority elite but especially one generation: the baby boomers. The third rupture that we shall explore, then, concerns the rise of personal wealth unleashed by the Thatcher government in the 1980s.

If we think about the key elements of Thatcherism – the miners' strike, urban riots, privatisation of state industries, rising home-ownership, Section 28 – we understandably tend to focus on the class war, cultural divides and racial tension of that era. And yet it was also a period largely determined by changing demographics.

Demographics always act as an undercurrent in the ocean of political debate, pulling government spending in one direction or another: just look at the costs of pensions and social care in the 2020s. In the 1980s, Margaret Thatcher entered Downing Street just as the eldest baby boomers were building families and as the youngest were entering the workforce – two waves of the same generation that required Westminster to address their concerns.

In a complete inversion of recent times, back then, the government's emphasis was on helping its younger rather than older citizens. The Thatcherite policies of taking down the unions and privatising state industries disproportionately hit older men, for example, generating a rump of long-term unemployed, which left many to languish on benefits. The urban riots in 1981 and 1985 instead put the spotlight on unemployment amongst the young and fears of further social unrest immediately triggered a surge of government investment to tackle youth unemployment. Relative income of pensions also declined compared to wages. This too contrasts with modern times where the reverse has happened.[14] The 1980s saw a rise in pensioner poverty too, predominantly affecting the generation that had fought or shown sacrifice during the Second World War.

It was in housing where baby boomers benefited more than any other generation. The oldest baby boomer turned thirty-four when

Margaret Thatcher's government passed the transformative 1980 Housing Act, enabling millions of citizens over the course of the decade to buy their council house. We know the long-term impact of the Right to Buy policy: the selling off of council stock and not building more created a lack of decent homes that restricted social housing and pushed up house prices.

But the cultural transformation was broader than that. The goal was to create a 'property-owning democracy' and this ended up advantaging the baby boomers in particular. Of those born between 1931 and 1935, three-quarters ended up owning a home by the age of sixty, which sounds impressive were it not for the fact that 52 per cent were already homeowners well before Thatcher had come to power. In contrast, 70 per cent of those baby boomers born between 1956 and 1960 became homeowners by the age of forty.[15] This generation are not just luckier than their offspring; they are also considerably more fortunate than their elders. If we begin to see the Thatcher decade as a windfall for a particular demographic, it helps us realise why the next generation find it so hard to get on in life without their parents' support.

The person who knows this history better than most is former Conservative minister and now head of the Resolution Foundation think tank, Lord David Willetts. In 2006, at a fringe meeting of the Conservative Party conference, he broke ranks with his generation and made a statement that would start a very big conversation. Baby boomers, he noted, were the 'biggest, most powerful, most prosperous group in Britain today'. He continued:

We baby boomers haven't just bought our houses cheap and written off the borrowings with high inflation. We've then pulled up the ladder behind us … A young person could be forgiven for seeing Britain's economic and political structure as nothing less than a conspiracy by the baby boomers in our own interests.[16]

Willetts did not stop there. In 2010, he published *The Pinch: How the Baby Boomers Took Their Children's Future – And Why They Should Give It Back*, a book that would put him at the centre of an emerging debate about why the baby boomers were so advantaged and why their millennial kids were not being afforded the same opportunities.

I was keen to speak to Willetts; his telling of this story of intergenerational unfairness has become so ingrained in our national story over the past fifteen years as to go unquestioned and now acts as a collective point of self-identification for the millennial generation.

'How fair is it to say that baby boomers are an exceptional generation?' I asked him.

'Well, they were the beneficiaries of three advantages not as widely available to young people today. Firstly, and most obviously, homeownership.'

In the 1980s, the average purchase price was £47,488, with an average deposit of £2,955, and the average length of time saving up for this was just three years and one month.[17] These were the days when there was so much housing stock that properties were being sold at less than their rebuilding cost. When my mother bought her first home in Tooting, admittedly a wreck with no ceilings or bathrooms, one of the reasons she took the plunge was that at the time the local councils were giving out grants for new owners to renovate inhospitable dwellings. The government also encouraged homeownership through the mortgage interest relief that allowed households to deduct a portion of the interest paid on their mortgage from their taxable income. It was abolished in 2000.

'What was the second advantage?' I asked Willetts.

'Then, of course, you had rising wages,' he replied. Unless you worked in heavy industry, wages rose for baby boomers when they were in their prime earning years. Wages, however, have stalled since the 2008 financial crisis when millennials have been in theirs. There have been rises in earnings since the Covid pandemic, but these are far from being a corrective to the years of stagnation, not least as they have come at a time of rising inflation and sky-high living costs.

Willetts continued: 'But it wasn't just that, baby boomers were also the last generation to enjoy unfettered access to final salary pension schemes.' Willetts is pointing to the gap that exists in pension provisions between older retirees and younger employees – a switch that has long been in the making. In 1967, more than 8 million employees working for private companies had final salary pensions, along with 4 million state workers. Today, only 1 million working in private industry have access to such schemes, while the public sector still retains a generous system.[18] On this, many baby boomers found themselves sliding under a rapidly closing door as corporations abandoned their generous pension schemes from the late 1980s onwards. The real challenge was that people were living longer. When pension funds were first established, members were expected to be retired for an average of six to seven years; today it is more like twenty-five to thirty years.

Final salary pension schemes faded out and private pensions were encouraged as part of an overall transformation in how people saved and were allowed to invest in the 1980s. In 1984, only 3.5 per cent of British people owned shares; by 1989, it was reportedly a third of the population. You could pick up shares while shopping in Debenhams; the *Daily Mirror* even had its own dedicated hotline service so that readers could call to see whether their investments were up or down. Looking at this expansion in share ownership, historian Amy Edwards has shown how this was not as democratic as it looked. In 1963, shareholders accounted for 54 per cent of equity in the stock market; by 1990, it was down to 20 per cent.[19] The market became increasingly dominated by major pension funds. By 2006, 46 per cent of Britons held shares indirectly through their pension, with a further 15 per cent of the most affluent owning equities or investment funds privately managed by a new army of financial advisors and wealth managers. Edwards calls this process the 'institutionalisation of British investment culture' and it was one that would provide the necessary framework for an inheritocracy and the passing on of family wealth.[20]

The 1987 market crash reminded everyone of the inherent uncertainty and risks, but this was the era where our parents were told that the compounding effect of wealth over time was the eighth wonder of the world. Pensions have increased considerably over the past thirty years to six times the national income and roughly the same value as the baby boomers' housing wealth. The key difference is that most of these pensions, specifically the defined benefit pensions, aren't heritable, unlike property.

When we talk about the baby boomers' housing wealth, we tend to focus on how easy it was for them to buy a property but not reflect on how difficult it was for them to hold on to it. Those that did, benefited. But many struggled. In the early 1990s, the housing crash saw 34 per cent wiped off the value of homes and many fell into negative equity. Some had their houses repossessed. Repayments for first-time buyers reached 30 per cent of gross income in 1990 and house prices continued to fall. In 1995, valuations were still 37 per cent below the house price peak of 1989.[21] We need to remember that for our parents, boom, bust and risk defined their early experience of the property market. It is worth noting that it was only in the early twenty-first century that housing came to be seen as an investment as well as a home.

I wanted to know whether David Willetts thought the premise of my book had weight. I explained my thesis: 'You wrote that baby boomers stole their children's future through wealth accumulation, but so much of their property wealth in particular will only be realised as it trickles down to the next generation. So, should we be talking about the emerging inheritance divide? And what about the Bank of Mum and Dad now – that trickling of funds that so many parents provide for their kids well into adulthood? Shouldn't we therefore be talking about the intragenerational divide within millennials rather than an intergenerational divide between boomers and millennials?'

I was braced for a polite dismissal, so was relieved when he said: 'Yes, yes, that's it. It is such a powerful point. It is absolutely making the family more significant.' Willetts's language here was revealing. He had legitimately framed the topic as being about the importance of 'family' rather than the unfair privilege of birth.

Willetts had pointed to the major question that lies at the heart of this book: is the Bank of Mum and Dad, which is in essence a financial source built on generosity and love, inherently good or bad? Because as much as this is a story about policies and economics, at its heart, inheritance is ultimately an emotive issue. Behind the baby boomers' property privilege was a sense of duty and legacy, often sacrifice and hard work. Behind these stories of upward mobility, there was often a fear of disparity, a desire for their kids to avoid the struggles they had endured. Behind this wealth may even be feelings of guilt or compensation for the other ways they had potentially failed as parents. In some families, inheritance can be about enforcing financial control as much as freedom, expecting certain behaviours or imposing certain conditions. In other words, our inheritance stories are as much to do with the state of our familial bonds as the state of the housing market or inheritance thresholds.

The Birth of Inheritocracy

Back in 1997, only one town in Britain – Gerrards Cross in Buckinghamshire – had an average house price that hit the tax threshold for inheritance tax. By 2006, the *Daily Mail* calculated that millions of households were now falling into what they dubbed the 'inheritance tax trap'.[22] This reflected the fact that property values were beginning to surge, rising by 130 per cent between 1997 and 2004. Inheritance tax was becoming a political issue. When he was Prime Minister, Tony Blair had reportedly wanted to abolish it, mainly because he realised the growing importance of property wealth for Britain's middle classes. Chancellor Gordon Brown vetoed it, but the government did increase the point at which the tax was levied on estates. At the time, a Treasury spokesperson stated: 'No government has ever linked the inheritance tax threshold to short-term movements in house prices or other asset prices.'[23] If that was true, it wouldn't be true for much longer. As properties rose in value and became increasingly central to families' understanding of their wealth, so subsequent governments came to fear any accusation they would tax the family home when it was passed down.

But as property wealth increased, unsurprisingly, homeownership started to decline. Levels peaked at 71 per cent in 2003, but from then on, it began to reverse.[24] In the years leading up to the 2008 financial crisis, the first cohort of baby boomers started to draw their pension, symbolising (for many) a shift of that generation from predominantly wage earners to wealth owners. Their interests would be solidified after 2008, as the Conservatives increasingly turned to defending the policies that protected the wealth and assets of retirees to the detriment of employees, mostly the young.

House prices may have been growing steadily, and baby boomers may have felt richer, but at the turn of the millennium, our generation, whose name was born out of this new era, was being serenaded by a different song, and the chorus was 'Education, Education, Education'.

Chapter 3

Education, Education, Education: The Illusion of a Meritocracy

I went to an all-girls, inner-city comprehensive, but like most labels that description is misleading. It was based in St James's, London SW1, a former grammar, church school whose origins dated back to 1698, with Westminster Abbey our local place of worship. It was the kind of state school that politicians liked to send their offspring to. That is to say that, apart from its funding model, there was very little that was 'comprehensive' about our school.

I was there from the early to late '90s, when female education was undergoing a cultural transformation. Back in the 1970s, feminists had decried the underinvestment, underperformance and the lack of ambition of girls at school. But by the 1980s, policy-makers had started to notice that girls were, in fact, outperforming boys in the newly formed GCSEs. As it turned out, it wasn't that female students had lacked ability; quite the opposite: the system hadn't catered for them nor encouraged them. By the late 1990s, domestic science, needlework and prepping women for certain roles – receptionist, nurse or mother – were out. When I was taking my exams, women's educational achievements seemed unstoppable. Every year on GCSE or A-level results day, the broadsheets would have pictures of leaping, joyous girls – often white, always pretty, frequently state-educated – gaining all those A grades. Coincidentally, this was also the era when the right-wing press and Tory politicians would regularly denigrate teenage mothers as reckless, immoral state dependents. I remember countless lectures at school on the dangers of getting pregnant too young. Here was seemingly the alternative, those leaping teenage girls elevating themselves. Education *was* female aspiration. By the year 2000, my first year of university, women already outnumbered men on UK campuses.

So, even though my mother left school at sixteen, and my older sister had gone straight to work after her A-levels, it was always expected that I would apply to university. By the late 1990s, getting pupils into tertiary institutions became the barometer of success on which schools were judged. Each year, on prize day, our school would compile the list of leavers and their university places. Even within the cohort that went, there was a distinct hierarchy. At the top, of course, was Oxford and Cambridge. Potentials had been hand-picked and advised on which subjects and colleges provided the likeliest route to success. They were given bespoke coaching and mock interviews. The school roped in one of the governors who had connections. Even in a distinguished school like ours in the centre of London, Oxbridge felt like an improbable leap.

I was boxed as enthusiastic but not exceptional, and my teachers were split on whether I was Oxbridge calibre. At one point, I found myself having an uncomfortable conversation with both my history and English teachers trying to convince them to predict me As rather than Bs so that I could submit the application. I was also fighting pressure at home: my father was determined that I applied.

It was a confusing mix of encouragement and disparagement at that age. All I needed was an interview, I thought.

Up I went to Cambridge in late November 1998, accompanied by my dad for moral support. I entered the interview room alone and facing me was a female professor who I very quickly realised had written *the* book on my coursework subject of Victorian republicanism. She looked like Maggie Smith in the *Harry Potter* movies, with a hawk's gaze, infrequently peering up from her reading glasses with a bothered expression. She had read my submitted piece. Her initial salvo felt immediately hostile: 'Do you not think that you've misstated the republican threat to Queen Victoria here?'

Uncomfortable pause. 'Could you elaborate?' I slowly replied; the only coherent thing I could think to say, my mind blanked by intimidation.

She was not impressed. 'Well, for example, you seem to overplay the role of Benjamin Disraeli,' she said, looking my words up and down and turning the pages dismissively. In hindsight, her strategy was obvious; she wanted a duel, a verbal joust, she was testing my mettle, seeing whether I was 'Cambridge material'. But I was unable to muster the self-belief or confidence that some innately have or are schooled in – I simply limped off the field. At that moment, I questioned everything I knew and couldn't defend anything I had written. I retreated into stutters, pauses, incoherent sentences and incessant apologies. My teachers had been right, I thought.

The interview continued painfully for another twenty minutes before she put me out of my misery. She gestured that the interview was over, and I stood up, said my thanks, and took the door opposite her desk. Except it wasn't the exit. I walked in and the door closed behind me before I realised that I was in the cloakroom. I couldn't see a thing; all I could feel was woollen coats and academic gowns. I stood there for far longer than was necessary wondering what to do. Like I had a choice? This unintended hideaway was not leading to Narnia. I started to hiccup-cry; the kind you can only do in public when acute embarrassment is the driving emotion. I tried to quash it but that just made the hiccups louder. My internal monologue turned nasty: I couldn't even make my way out of the room, how on earth did I think I could make it into this college? After what felt like twenty minutes, I finally opened the door and emerged back into her study. The hawk peered up from her glasses and looked surprised. 'Oops,' I managed to blurt out over my tears, curling my shoulders forward in embarrassment. I uttered yet another 'Sorry' and made my exit. This time through the right door.

My father was waiting outside in the grand quadrangle. 'How did it go?' he asked, expectantly.

'Well, I don't think I got in, Dad. I ended up in the cupboard.'

Sensing my distress, he simply said what I needed to hear: 'Never mind, kid. You did your best.'

I got over the rejection quickly, the interview sharply eliminating any romanticism I had about dreaming spires. But I do know someone who was so convinced she belonged there she applied three times – to no avail. I also have several friends who found that their time at Oxbridge was a particular kind of intensity and elevation they never really recovered from. I once went to a wedding where the father of the bride read out the marks of both the bride and groom's finals. Their results roused bigger cheers than the bridesmaids, florist and mother of the bride combined.

All this is to show the extent to which winning a place at either Oxford or Cambridge was then, and deservedly still is, the educational golden ticket. By the time I had applied in 1998, female undergraduates were attending in roughly equal numbers to their male counterparts. An extraordinary leap, given that in the 1970s women made up just 20 per cent of undergrads at Oxford and 12.9 per cent at Cambridge.[1] These institutions and their degree of accessible elitism serve as key litmus tests for British meritocracy – an indicator of whether we live in a country where brains count above all. This is why we exhaust column inches and airtime on their admission policies and their success. Undergraduates from state schools now account for around two-thirds of pupils at Oxbridge, although this still means that one-third are from private schools (which nationally make up around 6 per cent of school-leavers). This may be an unfinished revolution, but it is central to our belief that education equals opportunity and that the brightest can rise to the top. As this chapter reveals, this is something our parents believed in with vigour but we, as a generation, have become increasingly sceptical of. A degree for our generation went from aspiration to necessity – and an increasingly expensive one. It was an experience, too, that became increasingly bankrolled and defined by access to the Bank of Mum and Dad.

Turns out my teachers had been wrong on one thing: I scored higher than they or, frankly, I expected on my A-levels. Like a lot of Oxbridge rejects, I ended up at Durham University. Armed with two suitcases, I took the six-hour coach journey north in late September 1999. That freshers' week, while I was downing vodka shots and trying to make friends, Prime Minister Tony Blair, then at the height of his power and pumped full of end-of-century optimism, was addressing an adoring crowd at the Labour Party conference in the seaside town of Bournemouth. At the dawn of a new millennium, here was Blair outlining his pledge to 'renew British strength and confidence for the twenty-first century'. We were told that the next century would herald a meritocratic society. Millennials just needed to prioritise working with our heads rather than our hands:

We know what a 21st-century nation needs. A knowledge-based economy … The challenge is how? The answer is people … The liberation of human potential not just as workers but as citizens. Not power to the people but power to each person to make the most of what is within them. People are born with talent and everywhere it is in chains.

Then Blair pledged:

Talent is 21st-century wealth … In the eighteenth century, land was our resource. In the nineteenth and twentieth centuries, it was plant and capital. Today, it is people … So, today, I set a target of 50 per cent of young adults going into higher education in the next century.[2]

His commitment may have received a roaring cheer in the auditorium, but this wasn't as impressive as Blair made it sound. Between 1970 and 1988, university entrants had stalled at around 15 per cent, with a surge in the early 1990s when polytechnics were converted into universities, increasing student numbers to 30 per cent of school-leavers.[3] Still, 50 per cent was a symbolic goal, pledged to be met by the end of a second Labour term; in fact, it was reached twenty years later in 2019.[4]

Millennials grew up with the message that 'talent is 21st-century wealth'. In our parents' day, meritocracy had been centred on grammar school places; for our generation, it became about university places. That was the founding idea and sending as many people as possible to university was the goal. Very little provision, of course, was made for those left behind. With more employers expecting a graduate level of education, millennials became, in the words of

American writer Malcolm Harris, the first generation for whom a degree became a 'prerequisite, not a golden ticket'.[5] As this chapter will reveal, the price of a degree went up; but the value of a degree began to stall and then actually decline. We came to realise that opportunity was not just about our talents; it was also about our parents' capacity to invest in those talents. Increasingly, the truly privileged and successful were the ones who had both: merit and wealth. This realisation would, of course, come much later; now was the time for optimism. As Chancellor Gordon Brown reiterated: 'I say it is time to end the old Britain where what mattered was the privilege you were born to not the potential you were born with. Remove the old barriers, open our universities and let everyone move ahead.'[6] Future opportunity was apparently set. We just needed to work hard. And boy, did we do that.

A Protected and Productive Childhood

It is perhaps obvious, but one of the reasons I ended up hiccup-crying in that professor's cupboard was because that moment felt like the culmination of all my schooling (and therefore life) experiences up to that moment. That was in 1998. Educational pressure has only intensified since then. To discover its origins, we need to go back to the '80s and '90s – to our millennial and Gen Z childhoods.

Researcher Killian Mullan has examined time data records between 1975 and 2015 to identify changes in how children spend their time over this period. Her research reveals much about how childhood has evolved over the course of three decades. Children have spent more time at home, more time connected to a screen and more time doing homework. This came with a decline in children playing, especially freely without parental supervision. Any period spent outside the home was more likely to be structured and a paid activity. She discovered a gender distinction here, too. Girls tended to do more homework than boys, who spent more time on screens, sport and outdoor play. There was also a decline in hobbies by both boys and girls.[7] A similar story has been analysed by Sandra L. Hofferth who, collating American time data between 1981 and 2003, found that fewer hours were devoted to play, sport and religious activities and more was spent on studying and reading, with the biggest increase occurring for those aged six to eight. By 2003, six-year-olds were doing nearly as much studying as older children.[8]

It is worth stressing how new all this was. The 1970s and early 1980s had seen rising divorce rates and increasing numbers of mothers going out to work. The children of that decade became known as 'latchkey kids'. With parents at home less, the door would be left on the latch, or they would have their own key to let themselves in. But something started to happen to parent and child culture in the 1980s, which has only intensified since. A paranoia about child safety and 'stranger danger' warnings, combined with a growing sense of aspiration through education, all meant a tightening of the leash on childhood and children. Out went playing in the street; in came adult-supervised play indoors and eventually paid activities in safe environments which aided 'child development'. Out went concrete playgrounds; in came protective spongy floors. Out went children walking home on their own; in came the Green Cross Code and sex education. This transition from free to supervised play was partly down to family necessity: the number of households with both parents working doubled between 1990 and 2003. It was an evolution in parenting that our great-grandmothers probably would have found bizarre, and many modern experts now cite as one of the reasons for the current mental health crisis amongst young people.

The term 'helicopter parent' was first coined in the 1980s, but it was only in the 1990s and 2000s, as the new interventionist parenting culture went mainstream, that the term took hold. Back then, the phenomenon reflected a broader intergenerational conversation around expectations of parenthood, specifically motherhood. A fun game to play on this topic is: 'What did my mother let me do that children wouldn't be allowed to do today?' Aged ten, I went to and from primary school on the Underground into central London every day unsupervised and in charge of my seven-year-old sister. I would certainly hesitate to let my seven-year-old son do that now, given what we were exposed to on those journeys. But it was hardly exceptional back then. Similarly, my friend, aged fourteen, was put on a train by her mother and was expected to make her own way to Switzerland to stay with a family friend for three weeks in the summer holidays. Her mum waved her off at the Eurostar in Waterloo and she had to travel alone, criss-crossing the Parisian metro and on to Basel. This wasn't neglect, just different times. Hasn't every generation raised the bar on child safety? In the 1940s, our grandmothers sent their kids to live with strangers as part of the wartime evacuation programmes. Today, with GPS tracking, we are in the militaristic era of surveillance parenting. If anything, it's undoubtedly time the pendulum swung the other way.

As childhood became more structured in the 1980s, so school became more centred on exams. In the words of American historian Malcolm Harris, millennial kids were raised during a 'scholastic arms race' in which they were told that childhood was 'no longer a time to make mistakes' but when 'bad choices have the biggest impact'.[9] In the 1980s, competitive school culture mirrored the

geopolitical tussles of the Cold War but also the growing globalisation of capital and ultimately labour. Ranking was everywhere:
in international league tables on maths and reading, in schools
with their Ofsted ratings and streaming within classes all in the
name of standards. You could say that millennials and Gen Z have
been primed for the likes, clicks and ranks of social media since
childhood.

High-achieving, diligent girls adapted to this culture, perhaps too
well. It also made teachers more inclined to dismiss those who did
not conform, increasingly boys. Millennials were also caught in the
crossfire of the culture wars of the 1980s. Section 28, which outlawed
the 'promotion of homosexuality' in schools, was the Conservative
government's attempt to morally regulate content in the classrooms.
The homophobic clause, under which no one was ever prosecuted,
would have huge cultural significance, galvanising the LGBTQ+
community into action and leading to the clause's eventual repeal
by the Blair government. But it was the establishment of the national curriculum in 1988 that would have the most significant impact
on young millennial minds, creating a prescriptive checklist of what
should be taught and examined. Assessments followed at seven,
eleven and again at fourteen in addition to those already at sixteen
(GCSEs) and eighteen (A-levels). Under New Labour, the Department for Education started to stipulate the amount of homework
each child should be doing.

For the willing players in this 'scholastic arms race', the climax
came when applying to university. As part of this, the UCAS application – a personal statement of 500 words or so – was designed
to outline exactly what we had achieved in our lives up until the
age of seventeen/eighteen. This is where you paraded all your skills,
hobbies and ambitions like a beauty pageant. It's only now, looking

back a quarter of a century later, I realise how bonkers all this was. The pressure up until that point, especially for intelligent kids of a certain class and mental disposition, was to contort everything they did – in and out of the classroom – into a statement that displayed a well-rounded, conscientious (but probably exhausted) high-achiever. We were groomed from a very young age to cultivate a CV. We were told by society, the education system and our parents that this was the pathway to success in 21st-century Britain. And it was, to a point.

It was not just our academic credentials we needed to hone and sell on our UCAS forms. Extra-curricular activities took on am-plified importance. They weren't extra; they seemed pivotal. In my own case, I did what I could and left out key details. And I'm not the only one; according to a recent survey, one in four candidates have lied in their UCAS statement. The soul-crushing fact is that for all the effort we put into writing those applications, and all the years spent building these activities, these personal statements are reportedly only read for two minutes on average.[10]

I signed up for the Duke of Edinburgh Bronze Award, which was supposed to involve twelve weeks of 'service'. I survived two weekends of shovelling horse manure out of stables at a brewery in Wandsworth and managed to bribe my superior to sign off the form. I learned piano for four years, which looked great on paper, but I never managed to muster enough enthusiasm to take grades. No bother, I ticked the all-important 'played a musical instrument' box. I have countless friends who achieved high musical prowess in their adolescence only now for their instrument to gather dust in their parents' attic, with the thought of it stirring memories of draconian teachers and pressured performance. My statement also said that I was in the school swimming team and had represented

London in the county championships. This was not technically a lie, but my career had ended abruptly when I was dropped from the squad at fourteen. Sport during school years meant cut-throat competition rather than what it should have been about: physical well-being.

It is only now as I pass forty and have learned an instrument, exercise regularly and enjoy activities with no intention other than pure fun that I have begun to question the point, price and time of all this at such a young age. If we are the burnout generation, this is why. If we once embraced side-hustle #girlboss culture, this is why. If we are always trying to monetise or professionalise our hobbies, this is why. If the financially privileged amongst us, who have had access to the Bank of Mum and Dad, are denying or obscuring this parental advantage, this is why. We were groomed to work incredibly hard under relentless competitive pressure.

It frightens me to think that I was at secondary school nearly thirty years ago. I wanted to hear from a much younger millennial about their experiences of the secondary education system, because if anything, schooling has only intensified since I went through it.

I speak to Jo, who is in her mid-twenties and was born in Southampton. Her family moved around a lot as her mother was quite high up in local government. Her father had retired early at forty-nine with debilitating ME. The family eventually settled in East Anglia for her secondary school years.

'So, what were those years like for you?' I ask.

'Well, up until that point, my education had been a bit haphazard. Then I went to an intense state academy where it was full on. I was really good at school and enjoyed it. You got to do more GCSEs if you wanted to (I think the average was eleven) and I did fourteen.'

'Fourteen!' I repeat back to her, horrified. 'I did nine and that felt intense enough.'

'Yeah, it was quite rigorous,' Jo explains. 'I did two hours of additional classes after school. It was constant. All my friends did it, so it felt normal. We were in high sets; we were pushing higher and higher.'

Despite getting all A*s in her AS-levels, Jo decided against applying to Oxbridge like most of her friends and ended up choosing a university in Scotland. But things soon started to unravel. 'After all that I'd done to get there, after three months, I knew it wasn't the right place for me,' she confides. 'I basically rang my dad one night and said, "You have to come and get me; I can't stay."'

How did that make you feel, I ask?

'To realise that all of my choices had made me unhappy and especially that I was paying for the privilege made it really difficult to leave. So much of my identity had been about doing well at school and getting good grades. I had blinkers on to get through it,' she admits.

Jo returned home to live with her parents and sought treatment for her anxiety: 'Education had left me burned out at eighteen,' she tells me starkly. Jo also went to work for the first time. 'Up until uni, I had never had a job. My parents were always like, "You must study, we don't want you being distracted by work."' Jo was employed at Blackpool Pleasure Beach, which proved quite a culture shock, and after that worked in a bar. The following year, she reapplied to university, although this time to a less academically rigorous institution and thoroughly enjoyed her time there, despite it coinciding with the Covid lockdown. Jo has been working for a few years and now works for the government: 'It's not paid well and living costs are high,' she tells me.

'So, how do you now look back on your secondary education years?' I ask, sensing the answer.

'Everything was so competitive, even sports at school, you played to win. And if you were good, you played for the school; and if you were really good, you played for the county. I don't have any hobbies I'm shit at; I struggle with that because my identity is so attached to doing things well and being good at that. Everything was about your CV, and then at uni everything was about getting a job. It will be different when I have kids,' she declares.

Interestingly, Jo is not alone in feeling like this. One recent survey found that just 12 per cent of millennials want their children to go to university, which undoubtedly says more about millennials' past experiences of education than their kids' future prospects.

'I look back on my youth and regret that I wasn't in tune with myself enough to realise that I wasn't happy. It was a situation of my own making.' This feels like a harsh judgement, but Jo also admits that pressure to please her parents was a factor too: 'My mum chose her job location for the school, and she thought it would be best for us. She was never there because she was always working. My dad was getting sicker. I felt a pressure to prove to her that it was worth it, and I wanted to prove to her that she had made the right decision. I didn't want her to feel guilty.'

Parenting as an Investment

In the words of author Richard Reeves, parenting in recent years has transformed from a 'noun into a verb. We are not just parents; we parent.'[11] As much as educational attainment was relentless for kids like Jo, it became increasingly time-consuming and expensive for the parents. As families became smaller, more and more emphasis and investment was put on each child's success. One obvious indication of this has been the flow of money within the household. Kids earning pocket money and even their 'keep' used to be normal, but this idea gradually fell out of fashion. In 1997, 42 per cent of students aged sixteen and seventeen were holding down a part-time job as well as studying, but by 2014, this was just 18 per cent.[12] More and more parents prized homework and activities for their kids over early exposure to the working world.

In the private school sector, fees began an unrelenting climb northward – a quadrupling over twenty years – confining a paid education to the elite few. State education, like everything else, became tied to housing, fuelling gentrification and a ballooning market. Middle-class parents went to evermore committed lengths to get their children into decent primary and secondary schools, from temporarily renting a house in the catchment area, crossing counties, even discovering God. This was not just a London phenomenon: by 2017, one in four parents in the UK were reportedly moving to be near a good school.[13] Whereas once families migrated for higher wages, now the main driver was excellent Ofsted results. The more assertive and affluent parents saw state education merely as a starting point, with paid tutoring an essential top-up for their kids. In 2005, 18 per cent of children had a tutor; it is now one in three pupils. In a market now worth £2 billion, this additional support makes a mockery of the idea that state education is a level playing field.[14] All this parental investment was entirely understandable but more to the point increasingly normalised and widespread. It became common to use financial language in respect to parenting, such as 'investing' in one's child. Parents demonstrated ever-greater commitment to ensuring their offspring's success; from taxiing to activities, helping with UCAS forms, attending sports matches, music recitals, PTA meetings and networking on a child's behalf. We usually refer to the Bank of Mum and Dad in regard to property; but as we know, parental financial advantage begins in school, and by the 2000s, this was as evident in the state sector as the private system. Educational prowess became a de facto sign of successful parenting but also evermore competitive and expensive – and therefore increasingly defined by wealth more than strictly merit. And for the baby boomers (as well as the Gen X parents after them), the motivation was often personal. In my father's case, he was especially keen that his daughters succeeded in an educational system that he revered but considered had 'failed' him.

This is not to say that this parental involvement was bad per se – it stems from a natural human instinct to do what is considered best for one's child. But what was driving this overactive parenting culture? It was part aspiration but also in many cases fear, especially amongst the middle classes. A fear of downward mobility. This intensified after the financial crisis, with elevating costs of education, housing and global competition rendering everything much more difficult for millennial and Gen Z kids. Parents felt compelled to do more. At the heart of it was a genuine dilemma: what if my kids in adulthood can't maintain the same lifestyle into which they were born? This was the motivation behind many a pushy parent. First-generation wealth in particular tends to come with a paranoia that more established wealth (be it two generations or two centuries old) does not. If you are self-made, you can personally recall having a lot less; you endured the social climb; you hope you've done enough to ensure your kids don't have to; and you fear the drop that much more. In his book *Dream Hoarders*, Richard Reeves puts the spotlight on established American upper-middle-class parents who, in his words, have 'become more determined to ensure their children stay near the top'. He calls this a 'glass floor' (as opposed to the glass ceiling) built to prevent their children 'from falling down the chutes'. The problem is, as Reeves understands, 'inequality and immobility thus become self-reinforcing'.[15]

During the early 2010s, when I was a university lecturer, I started to notice the increasing presence of mums and dads at prospective undergraduate open days. I remember one occasion when I was asked by my head of department to deliver a lecture on the politics of the 1980s. 'They'll love it,' he said, enthusiastically.

'Will they, really?' I asked, surprised and honoured to be singled out as the department's ambassador. 'But most of them weren't even born by the time Margaret Thatcher had left office,' I said, seeking reassurance.

'Not the students, the parents!' he corrected me. 'They're the ones we need to impress; they're the ones *who are paying*. They lived through Thatcher; they'll love it.'

He was right. Every year I would see families turn up for the open day – parents with their unsure teenagers. It would be the parents who would role-play as enthusiastic students: raising their hands, asking questions and showing a deference to the academics and institution that seemed decidedly lacking in their offspring (who no doubt sensed that the show was not for them).

But isn't this all a rather upper-middle-class and, frankly, white picture so far? Yes. The comedian Nish Kumar has joked about the cultural stereotype of having Indian parents and the pressure of them wanting you to be a doctor, engineer or accountant (and definitely not a stand-up comedian). What is behind this stereotype? The tendency of immigrant communities to view education and the stable professions as attractive routes can stem from a desire to reverse the initial downward mobility that happens with migration but can also be an understandable commitment to betterment and stability for the next generation. There's also a less tangible factor at play: the idea of conforming to the 'good immigrant' stereotype and the 'model minority' myth. As one of my interviewees put it: 'As children of immigrants, there's an undercurrent pressure to "prove" our value to society and being highly educated and in respected professions is a short-cut and sure-fire way of doing that.' But even boxing 'immigrant' communities together is unhelpful. From the data, students of Chinese and Indian heritage outperform those of Caribbean, African, Pakistani or Bangladeshi backgrounds, where a combination of a lack of financial and housing security and some-times language barriers can prove huge obstacles. But the most im-portant factor is economic disadvantage. Around 24 per cent of all pupils are entitled to free school meals, and within that figure there is a disproportionate number of minority ethnic groups. Across the board, of those who received free school meals at age fifteen, just under a third made it to university in 2021–22 and just 5.3 per cent progressed to the top institutions.[16]

Writer Otegha Uwagba has powerfully explored the intersection of race, education, class and finances in her bestselling memoir *We Need to Talk About Money*. Born to Nigerian parents, Otegha grew up on a council estate in south London and won a scholarship to the City of London School for Girls before going on to study at Oxford. I sat down with Otegha over Zoom. I wanted to ask her, as some-one who has written extensively about money and the millennial experience, whether she thought we were living in a meritocratic or inheritocratic society.

Otegha seized on the personal complexities: 'I think people like to think they have achieved certain things without reflecting on how they got there. And certainly, if you are liberal and progressive and you happen to receive an inheritance of support from Mum and Dad, well that kind of subverts a lot of the values you personally stand for.'

This is true; an inheritocracy poses more of a moral quandary for a liberal than a conservative.

I ask Otegha how parental financial privilege has played out amongst her peers. She tells me it feels even more pervasive now she is in her thirties than when she was in her twenties. 'I think the culminative effect of wealth is important here,' she explains. 'Money breeds money. Those of my friends who were able to buy a house in their twenties are now onto the next life stage with multiple kids, whereas others are really struggling to think whether they can afford to have one at all.'

'How do you feel about social mobility and education in respect to your own story?' I ask her. Otegha was unconvinced that her life was simply a tale of social mobility through education, objecting to the simplistic notion of mobility that tends to prevail in the UK and especially our reductive tendencies when it comes to race and class: 'My parents are very culturally middle class, both are educated to degree level, both are professionals. In fact, my situation is more symptomatic of the kind of downward mobility that many immigrants experience when they first move to a new country.' Education was a core part of her upbringing, she tells me: 'Even though there were elements about it that were working class,' in terms of location and money, 'I wouldn't ever describe myself as working class,' she confirms.

One major way our lived experience differs from our parents' is the way that our generation has grown up in a globalised world with the globalisation of wealth. In recent years, UK university campuses have become the new finishing schools for the international super-rich, creating a unique cultural and economic environment. As universities relied evermore on international students for revenue, it became much clearer that British undergraduates were – just like manual workers a generation ago – now competing within a global market. In 2000, 27 per cent of 25–34-year-olds in OECD countries had advanced qualifications; by 2021, it was 48 per cent.[17] I certainly noticed the emergence of this cohort where I taught, with many riding the parental piggy bank by doing a master's in London for a year. I remember one of my more affluent students forgetting their Dior sunglasses in my office on more than one occasion. I was surprised, but she wasn't – she hadn't noticed; she had that many pairs.

As well as the global elite, the consistent winners in this education story have undoubtedly been women. They have long outnumbered men on campuses, but now they are doing so in subjects where they hadn't previously. In law, dentistry, medicine and veterinary medicine, female students are on a ratio of 2:1 to men.[18] In the past five years, the success of girls has started to be framed as a crisis for boys. The former head of UCAS Mary Curnock Cook has predicted that on current trends, 'a girl born today will be 75 per cent more likely to go to university than her male peers', with 'the gap between women and men … larger than the gap between rich and poor.'[19] As we shall see, the gender dimensions of an inheritocracy are as important as the class ones.

The expansion of educational qualifications and tertiary education has not only been necessary for our economy but has also been one of the great social revolutions of our time. It has been of profound benefit, especially for women (and especially for me). The question for our generation has never been whether university is a good idea but rather has a degree lived up to its promise? For Nathalia, it most definitely has, despite the hardship and financial pressures.

Nathalia, twenty-eight, was born on a farm in Ukraine. When she was very young, her father got into debt with the mafia and so went to work in the Czech Republic so that he could send money home to pay them off. Her mother followed him, which meant that for the first five years of her life, Nathalia was raised by her grandmother. Her parents are still in the Czech Republic – her mother works in a bakery and her father is a project manager on a building site. Nathalia had always been a clever child and as a teenager set her sights on studying in England. 'I prefer the educational culture, it is less prescriptive, more democratic,' she enthuses. Nathalia accepted a course at a university in the north-east and was charged £9,000 a year. While still living in the Czech Republic, she saved as much as she could and then once she started university, she worked waitressing in a restaurant in Newcastle and cleaning the student halls.

'I did not go home during holidays, so I was able to keep working and save money,' she tells me. Nathalia's example puts me in the shade. I only worked during the summers in my degree years, and I can't remember ever having to save anything.

One of Nathalia's biggest challenges was finding accommodation and as a foreign student, she faced discrimination when it came to renting without parents in the UK to act as a guarantor.

Like many students, Covid robbed her not just of the university social experience but also of critical learning: 'When Covid came, I was lucky in all sorts of ways. Firstly, the manager of the restaurant gave us all the food in the fridge, so that got us through the initial month, and I was also furloughed. But it was hard, and I eventually went home to the Czech Republic when we were allowed. My university was still charging me fees even though my course was all lab-based and couldn't be taught remotely.' Despite this, Nathalia is adamant that her degree has been worth it.

Nathalia is now living in Reading and working for an IT company. She finally has a bit more leeway in her finances: 'Reading is more expensive than Newcastle, but I am now earning £32k (rather than the £16k I was earning in the restaurant). It is much better. I live in a shared house, but each room has its own bathroom, so it is nice. I'm paying £675 per month, which is so expensive!' Nathalia wants to continue with her education and is currently saving to do a master's in molecular medicine. She also finds herself supporting her family in the Czech Republic and her grandma in Ukraine, who in the war-torn country now requires help with medicine and bills.

'How would you describe your attitude to money?' I ask.

'I would say that money is very important to me. But I know I can always earn money. I've worked in a hotel, cafe, as a secretary, cleaning student accommodation. I guess I'm working class, but I have big ambitions; I want to always grow and build more and more.' But in this, she sometimes clashes with her English boyfriend. He is in his final year of his degree, does not need to work and lives with his stepdad, who supports him at university. 'I'm really careful with money and I have to plan everything. He is not. I think English people are helped too much by their parents. They've had so much more time than me to enjoy their studies, and they take it for granted.'

'Do you resent it?' I ask.

'Well, maybe,' she replies.

A Level Playing Field?

If you are unfamiliar with Durham University, it sits in a medieval city with an imposing Norman cathedral, surrounded by former mining villages. The tension between 'town' and 'gown' is acute. Unlike the bigger university cities of Oxford, Cambridge, Bristol, Manchester or Exeter, where this divide is dispersed, it's hard to do this in a city only approximately one square mile wide. When I was a student there, Saturdays was 'locals' night, with an understanding that undergrads did not go out. When the two groups did collide, it sometimes made for strange encounters. At the local working men's club, I once overheard a young southern male student offering his political assessment of Margaret Thatcher to a former miner: 'She wasn't human, y'know. I wasn't around, but my parents remember. She raped and pillaged the nation. I'll never forgive her, that devil woman.'

The former miner responded patiently and diplomatically to this youthful condemnation of history he had actually lived through. 'Aye, well, she was a divisive figure, and our town is certainly still feeling it. And where's home for you, lad?'

The reply: 'Windsor.'

But the class divide was not just apparent in the city; it was evident in the halls of residence within the student body. Technically, we were all equals, attending on merit. And in the first year, we were randomly all bunched together in a cross-class accommodation grouping. It felt like the first time I had really encountered class, which frankly feels an odd thing to say, coming from London.

Of the most distinct were the 'Rahs', 'rugger buggers' and the 'pashmina girls' hailing from the UK's great public schools. They came in many forms. There were those who were from Scotland but had English public-school accents. Those who arrived in sandy flip-flops and hippy beads straight from their 'gap yah', proudly gushing about how they had spent their time raising £10,000 to fly to the other side of the world to erect a £500 hut for people living on $2 a day. There were also those who would claim to 'shag the compers' (comprehensives) but 'only date the boarders' (private). The local female Durham college was affectionately known as the Virgin Megastore and there were plenty of wannabe Kate Middletons hoping to bag someone with a title. The Rahs had their own sartorial style, stuck to their own bars and restaurants and even their own degree subjects. I doubt very many state school kids studied history of art or classics in 1999. Many arrived already knowing each other from the slopes, sports fixtures or the posh but dingy bars off the King's Road.

Turns out, Durham hasn't changed that much in the twenty years since I was there. In fact, it could be that it has got worse. In 2020, Durham student Lauren White wrote a report outlining its negative class culture. 'At first when they mocked and mimicked my accent, I sort of went along with it, even laughed, but then when I persistently became the butt of jokes about coalmining and started to get called feral because I was local it started to feel malicious,' she said. She wrote an article about discrimination and compiled a report on the 'northern student experience at Durham university'. One contributor talked about the phenomenon of 'rolling in the muck', referring to posh students sleeping with a northern working-class person. The university had to launch an inquiry after wealthy prospective freshers reportedly planned a competition to have sex with the poorest student they could find.[20]

I wanted to check with my contemporaries that I wasn't exaggerating my version of events from twenty years ago. 'Can anyone remember the class dynamics at uni?' I messaged in my university friends' WhatsApp group. 'Yeah, loads of lads acting like their little brothers but dressing like their dads,' Declan messaged, referring to the mass of corduroy and boater shoes then on show. Rebecca, who hails from the north-east, waded in: 'Well, I remember the posh boys took the piss out of my accent.' No change there then, I thought. I hadn't specifically mentioned the Rahs, but that is where my friends immediately went. That in itself was telling: aren't we more likely to look up not down when trying to define our class?

My friend Josh saw it differently. Josh was rare in that he was sort of class fluid, able to inhabit multiple worlds with a social grace I definitely lack. His dad was from Peckham and had made a bit of money and sent his child to public school. Josh immediately highlighted the class diversity at Durham: 'There were the mature students; I remember they worked very hard and had saved to get there. Also, the local students with housing vulnerability and part-time work were so much more isolated.' Josh was right, there was a fair proportion of our year group who operated almost under the radar, were rarely seen in the college bar because they were either working hard or working for money – i.e. without access to the Bank of Mum and Dad. They didn't take university for granted, as we undoubtedly could afford to. Josh added: 'And as for the posh boys, there was a cavalier, callous, risk-taking attitude that comes when you have a safety net. Also, the holidays were telling, too. Us civvies went back home and tried not to act above our station, but the Rahs didn't need to adjust at all.' Rebecca then added an important distinction: 'When you come to think of it, we're all products of first-generation wealth. Those whose parents didn't have much but gave us what they could, so we didn't have to struggle.'

Rebecca was right. We were the inbetweeners, not from generational wealth but reliant on the Bank of Mum and Dad, nonetheless.
Of course, we rarely acknowledged it. We were part of a large form-
less blob in the middle that included kids of builders as well as kids
of teachers and doctors, those from minor independent schools
alongside those from grammars and urban comprehensives. North-
erners with money and big houses, southerners without cash but
property in the south-east. But the point is we never considered
ourselves privileged, especially when we were confronted with the
established upper middle class. Declan elaborated: 'I do think there
was sort of a level playing field at uni. Everyone was intelligent, had
a lot in common in some ways … wanted to do well, but you're just
never quite on the same team. Or if you are, some will always be
picked first. That was the point; when you graduate suddenly the
level playing field becomes a ladder on quicksand.'

That was how class dynamics operated when I was an undergraduate twenty years ago, when fees were a mere £1,000 a year. With
every increase, however, the notion of university as a 'level playing
field' or, in Tony Blair's words, as an 'unleashing of human talent',
has seemed evermore questionable. The introduction of fees and
their incremental increase to the £9,250 threshold was tantamount
to serving the individual with a bill and now a lifelong debt to prepare for the workplace.[21]

But as much as the fees system burdened the student, it was
predicated on most parents stumping up the upfront costs for their
children. The student loan effectively operates as a graduate tax. So,
as students' fees, rents and costs have increased, so parental support
has become an evermore-important factor. One example where
Mummy and Daddy's wealth determined one student's university

experience was Tony Blair's own son Euan. Luckily for him, his parents purchased a quarter-of-a-million-pound property in Bristol as his student accommodation. It caused controversy at the time because of the involvement in the negotiations of a convicted fraudster. Equally contentious were the – hotly denied – press accusations that the Blairs had tried to avoid stamp duty. Looking back now, what is more galling is not only the flat purchase but the fact that they also reportedly bought another property for Euan to rent out. Perhaps ironically, Euan Blair now runs a Google-backed education start-up encouraging people not to go to university but to do apprenticeships, thereby seeking to undo one of the central features of his father's political programme.

But what is the student experience like for someone with minimal support from their parents?

Kayleigh, twenty-six, from Yorkshire is currently mid-way through a PhD in English en route to realising her ambition to become an academic. 'My family is pretty normal,' she begins. 'My dad didn't go to uni. He's always worked in retail or manual labour. My mum came from a very poor background but graduated and became a solicitor.' Kayleigh admits she found her undergraduate years socially difficult and financially testing: 'When I went to uni, I suddenly felt extremely working class. I was surrounded by people whose parents were helping them out, whereas I didn't really have that option.'

Kayleigh was lucky to receive a maintenance loan, but she still had to work throughout uni: 'I really struggled with money and there were times when I was working too much and not studying enough,' she confesses. What made this doubly difficult was that most of her friends didn't have such pressure: 'Both my two flatmates had their rent paid by their parents and that was considered normal. One of them put their student loan into a high-interest account, so they could use it for a house deposit one day. So, even though we would all say we were skint, they had reserves; when I said I was skint, that was it.'

Kayleigh's social dilemma isn't exceptional – 10 per cent of students in the UK have parents who can shoulder the fees and costs of university outright, meaning they will never receive one of those letters from the Student Loans Company. As the co-founder of the Intergenerational Foundation think tank Angus Hanton put it, this 10 per cent 'makes a mockery of claims that the current [fee] system is progressive, since the wealthiest kids are not even in the system'.[22]

Kayleigh was fortunate enough to get a scholarship for her master's in London, but it only covered her fees, so she also took out a government loan. Her master's coincided with the Covid lockdown and she found herself working throughout in a 'dark kitchen' for a food delivery company. Her master's was not quite the intellectual experience she had hoped for: 'I never saw a member of staff in person the entire time; I did it all online. I only went onto campus twice to collect books from the library when it was open.' But Kayleigh is adamant that despite the near £87,000 she has acquired in student debt, it has been worth it. 'I don't consider it a waste of money, as I knew it was en route to a career as an academic … I don't really think about [the debt]. I've never been over the income threshold to pay off my student loans. It is such a ludicrous amount of money; I'm hoping the Labour government will write it off.' While we are on the phone, she pulls out her latest statement from the Student Loans Company, clarifying the figures: 'Well, my undergraduate debt is £74,692, and the interest added has been £500 at 7.8 per cent. I've got another £13,000 for my master's. Like I said, it is just insane amounts of money.'

Buyers' Remorse

If we need any evidence of the pivotal role that parental wealth is now playing in higher education, witness the fact that parents are now protesting on behalf of their student kids. In this era of high living costs, academic strikes and with a continuation of remote teaching after the pandemic, there is serious buyers' remorse – from parents as well as students. During the university exam marking boycott in 2023 (that left many unable to graduate), it was parents who staged a protest. Mother Emma Mahoney told *The Times* that her daughter Millie feared criticising the lecturers who would be marking her degree, so as her mother she had decided to represent her daughter at the protest. As the paying customer, she also felt she had a right to be there: 'We've invested a lot in our children's education and now they're not graduating,' she clarified.[23]

Young people have not been put off from going to university. Far from it. Applications have steadily increased each year since the mid-1990s, although they have dipped in the past two years. This is because a degree has come to be seen as a core requirement for getting any kind of job. But rising costs are changing student behaviour and again access to the Bank of Mum and Dad is playing a pivotal role in shaping these decisions. More and more Gen Z students are rejecting the residential university experience (which is arguably the main reason for going) and are choosing to stay at home while they study. Universities in expensive towns such as Bristol and Exeter, as well as those in London, are becoming exclusively for sons and daughters of rich parents. For those without the parental safety net, student rental costs, dropout rates and even homelessness have become a real problem.

Rising costs are also affecting what subject students choose to pursue. In STEM courses, for example, the graduate premium has been sustained. Not so in the humanities, which is perhaps why the numbers are declining. Those studying English, literature and creative writing, for example, fell by one-fifth between 2012 and 2019.[24]

What has increased are apprenticeship degrees – which come with the benefit of an 'earn-while-you-learn' salary. Even though 64 per cent of secondary school teachers have said they would not recommend degree apprenticeships to high-achieving students, these courses are gaining traction with parents and students alike who are looking for cheaper tertiary education and instant employability. In 2021, they represented 43,000 out of 500,000 university places offered and they are now statistically harder to get into than Oxbridge. Are these new positions a new way of judging Britain's social mobility? If so, the news isn't good. Degree apprenticeships now make up 26 per cent of all courses offered, but the percentage of those from lower economic backgrounds taking up these opportunities has declined.[25] In an odd twist of history, those from poorer backgrounds are now more likely to go through a traditional university degree than to be on these apprenticeships, while middle-class parents, keen to avoid higher education costs, are networking hard, trying to get their offspring on these work–learn schemes.

When I interviewed young millennial graduates for this book, most said that their degree had been worth the money yet also believed they would never pay the loan back. Many are hoping for some kind of debt wipe-out programme from the Labour government. And yet it is in debt repayments where the divide is most acute.

Those who have had to take out a bigger loan will end up paying significantly more for the same degree than those who could minimise it (or have none at all) because of parental support.

It is hard not to overstate how unfair all this is. The interest on student loans is at record levels: swelling from £2.3 billion to £4.8 billion between 2022 and 2023. At the same time, the loan conditions have changed. Under the Plan 5 repayment scheme introduced by Rishi Sunak's government, the payback threshold starts at £25,000 (rather than £27,000) and rises with inflation. The latest loans will not be wiped until forty years after graduation (as opposed to thirty years). As TV's money man Martin Lewis has stated, it is not a debt but a graduate tax, one which has gone up more than any property tax in the past twenty years: 'The majority of graduates will be paying their student loans for most of their working lives.'[26] And because of the long-term interest, women who have children and take time out of the workforce will end up paying more for their education than men. That privileged 10 per cent whose parents have kept them debt free have been given a serious advantage that will play out over a lifetime.

But in all this, we are also in danger of forgetting the roughly 50 per cent who do not go to university and who have been given few solid alternatives. Some, not all, have been able to hitch themselves to a decent employer or learn a trade. Few have received much substantive support from the state, which for twenty years has been so overfocused on getting people to university, it has failed to serve those who do not attend.

While wages have been growing faster in recent years for non-graduates, the real picture is of an education culture not unlike that which existed under the 11-plus: where degrees are prioritised over trades and more practical qualifications. It is also a similar situation in which many have been left behind. Certain jobs only became viable with a degree, and this barrier has blocked many out regardless of whether they were capable. Governments have long talked about apprenticeships, but the lack of tax breaks, investment and status has not made it a viable enough alternative; little wonder that 47 per cent of apprenticeship applicants quit before finishing their course.[27] Successive governments have failed to put money behind alternative routes, which has led to 17 per cent of 22–29-year-old non-graduates being economically inactive.[28] We have yet to see whether the new 'T-levels' (technical) qualifications, which now sit en par with A-levels, will rectify this imbalance. Tellingly, even the term 'non-graduates' defines them by what they do not have.

■ ■ ■

Few would deny that the global expansion of tertiary education is one of the great success stories of the past thirty years – one that our parents, teachers and politicians all bought into. In a knowledge-based economy, we needed knowledge workers. But for the generation who were its guinea pigs, their assessment is somewhat different. They associate educational achievement with increasing pressure, insurmountable upfront and long-term costs, declining rewards and a social and economic divide built on birth rather than ability.

In 2023, it was calculated that graduates were earning £3,000 less in real terms than they had done eight years before, evidence of a shrinking return on all that parental 'investment' and hard work.[29] According to our *Inheritocracy* YouGov survey, 26 per cent of under-45s believe that their university degree was not worth the financial cost. It's not as if a degree isn't important; it remains distinctly important and necessary. But, as Julia explains, her generation are thinking differently about education:

'I can 100 per cent say that I learned more about my current career working in a shop than I did from my degree,' she asserts. Julia is twenty-seven; born in South Africa and raised in west London, she currently works for a global professional services firm. Julia never felt any parental pressure to go to university: 'I think my parents thought that it was a bad idea as they came from countries where only the smartest go to do academic degrees; they didn't think it was worth the money. But I was part of the generation where I had pressure from school.'

Julia received little help from her parents and worked tirelessly, often putting in over thirty-five hours a week working in a shop on top of her lectures and completing her assignments. It was a sacrifice she was prepared to make for her long-term financial health: 'I had less fun, but it also meant that I didn't take a maintenance loan. So, I left with £27k debt, which is a lot less than my peers.'

'Does your degree hold any value for you?' I asked.

'My degree didn't really qualify me to do anything,' she says dismissively. Julia later went on to study for a master's in HR, the area she now works in.

'I log in all the time to see if the debt is coming down. What annoys me is that I only see it going up with interest. Compared to most graduates, I imagine that I earn quite a decent salary, but I'm still only chipping off the interest. I earn £46k a year but am paying £250 per month on my student loan.' Julia is part of that specific younger millennial/older Gen Z cohort, who paid £9,000 a year fees, whose university years were disrupted by Covid and who are now paying it back in a high interest rate environment. She wishes she had done an apprenticeship degree, she tells me, something many of my younger interviewees had mentioned. For geriatric millennials like me, we had a slightly different narrative: university was cheaper, so it was less about debt and more about the challenges of graduating in the aftermath of the 2008 financial crisis and the sense of disillusionment that came with realising that our degrees wouldn't get us where we thought they would. One is disenchanted; the other is questioning the system altogether. Neither are particularly positive.

Julia is now in the next stage of life, a DINK (dual income, no kids) living with her boyfriend in a flat they have bought together in suburban London. Neither received help from their parents, although Julia's did let her move back to save for a deposit. 'I recognise this as a privilege, having spoken to friends who haven't had that opportunity of a roof over their head while they saved. But equally, my parents aren't from wealth so don't understand why they should give us the amount they themselves never received.'

Now Julia is in her late twenties, I was interested to know how the discussions about the Bank of Mum and Dad were evolving amongst her peers: 'It is a point of tension in my friendship group. I think it is partly because British people are just awkward talking about money. If you buy a flat, your friends will just gently probe and say, "So did you get any help?" I think this is because we are all benchmarking ourselves against each other. They want to know that they are not behind or doing something wrong.' Julia, however, considers herself lucky in one regard: 'I am fortunate to not have extremely wealthy friends. My friends are all teachers or work for the NHS. If we had friends who were all parent-bootstrapped, I'd find it annoying.'

Chapter 4

Rise of the Kidults: How Inheritocracy Corrupted Adulthood

I define my twenties by a careful line: I was broke but never poor. It is a conscious distinction. But also, it was a deliberate choice. I was a perpetual student throughout my twenties, first doing a master's then a PhD. I wasn't poor because poverty is chiefly defined by little or no safety net. I never had any money, but due to my parents' support, there was a limit to how far I could fall. I returned to our family home after I graduated. And when I did my master's, I moved into my parents' run-down second home, unfit for the rental market but fine for me. I stayed in this flat first with my mate's band who were trying to make it in London, and then, from the age of twenty-two, with my long-term boyfriend, a DJ turned ticket-tout. We were perpetually broke, often precariously. Regularly, he would go to the pawn shop and flog his speakers or decks, always managing to buy them back within the allotted time before they went on the open market.

I obviously count myself extremely fortunate that I had somewhere in London to stay rent-free, but I wasn't unusual in relying on my parents after graduation. Very few cut the financial umbilical cord completely. Some of my friends were fortunate to have monthly allowances to supplement poor wages in jobs they were 'passionate about'. Others had returned home to live off their parents. Some had fast-tracked into DINKs with their university love but still in significant ways were supported by their parents.

Then there were friends who could afford no such indulgence and had very little help. These were the ones who invariably had lined up proper employment before they graduated. Some didn't move to London, others worked in multiple jobs while we partied. The divide very rarely revealed itself as we all muddled through our twenties pretending to be adults and very often purporting all to be in the same boat. If your twenties are synonymous with anything, it is living payday to payday – drinking before you go out, ducking under the train barriers, having utilities on a meter that regularly runs dry, sleeping in cars – it's a vital part of a carefree youth or mine at least. Two moments, however, stick out for me as illustrative of the endless 'insufficient funds' feeling I had in my twenties. Both, oddly, involve trains.

If you live in the UK, you tend to spend a lot of time on trains. And if you were a student in the 2000s, you will remember how pivotal that discount rail card was, unlocking the whole country with a single piece of plastic. And you'll perhaps also remember the dreaded realisation of having to pay full fares when it eventually expired.

The first train incident came on the way back from a friend's hen party (one who was leaping ahead of me in the adulting stakes). I couldn't afford both the festivities and the train ticket, so I chose to fund the former and hide in the toilet all the way home from York – a trick, I might add, I had often pulled off with success. The trouble was that due to cancellations, the service was so packed that

I was harassed out of the bathroom with people banging on the door desperate for the loo. Fair enough, I thought. But when the ticket inspector approached, there was no defence to be made. I had no money for a ticket, so I was booted off the train at Peterborough and escorted through the barriers. In the station foyer, I took off my red beret, laid it on the floor and, probably still drunk from the hen party, started singing 'Somewhere Over the Rainbow' and performing a click of my heels. If I can't sneak the train ride out in the toilets, I shall sing my way home, I thought. A few sympathetic souls dropped some coins in my hat; many more stopped and laughed. I started to forget the words and lose my nerve, until a gracious and lovely middle-aged woman interrupted me and asked me what I was doing. 'I'm trying to raise money for a ticket home,' I replied. She gestured me over to the ticket machine and bought me a single back to King's Cross, and I rode the train legitimately all the way home, convinced that my impression of Dorothy had 'moved' her somehow.

The second incident occurred while on a research trip to Northampton (yes, that's how I spent my twenties). When I got to Euston to buy a ticket, the dreaded 'transaction declined' message appeared when I tried to pay the full fare. I had a choice: I could either hide in the toilet (again) or tamper with my then expired student railcard and get the cheaper ticket, which I could just about afford. On this occasion, I decided the latter was preferable. Discreetly, or so I thought, I peeled back the plastic cover and changed the expiry year date from 7 to a 9 for 2009. Mid-way through the journey back to London, the ticket inspector entered the carriage and barked 'Tickets please!' I handed over my tickets and student railcard, innocently looking out the window as he checked. 'I'm afraid this is a fraudulent railcard. You've changed the date here. This card is out of date.'

I had been rumbled. 'No, no, I don't think so. Let me see,' I replied, nodding for emphasis and desiring the incriminating evidence back. Everyone in the carriage started looking up.

'No, I need to hang on to this,' said the voice of authority. This
guy seemed particularly officious. He was in full inspector regalia,
complete with a slightly militaristic hat. He asked me for my name
and address. I gave him the name of someone I didn't particularly
like and then a fake address I didn't properly know. He went off to
check and came back. 'I'm afraid you have given a false name and
address, madam.' I had dug a deeper hole. I could tell he was enjoying the prospect of a successful scalp a little too much. He asked me
again for my real name and address. 'If you refuse to comply, I shall
have to call the police.'

I'd seen enough cop shows to know how this worked. 'No comment,' I said, defiantly.

'I'm afraid I'm going to have to arrest you,' he said, and then –
almost certainly overstepping his authority – started reading me my
rights, 'You do not have to say anything... Anything you do say will
be written in evidence.' He was in full flow.

'Is there a lawyer on board?' I jokingly shouted down the carriage.
Now everyone looked away. He proceeded to ask more questions.
'No comment,' I petulantly repeated, folding my arms.

When we reached Paddington, there was a policeman waiting
for me at the carriage door. I was handed over into the custody of
someone clearly at the end of his shift who swiftly decided that my
case wasn't worth the administrative time. 'C'mon love, we all want
to get home, now tell me your real name and address.' I obliged.
Weeks later I got the prosecution letter in the post. If I paid the £180
fine, it wouldn't go to court. I sent off a cheque. But it bounced, as I
knew it would. So, I had to go through the whole rigmarole again,

this time embarrassingly having to ask my parents for the money. Finally, I (they) settled the fine and I was let off.

Just to be clear, I'm aware that these incidents do not paint me in a flattering light. I was a thoughtless, shambolic idiot in my twenties. It is also the kind of petulant behaviour that only a white woman who is not perceived to be a societal risk could have exhibited. Put a young Black man in that fraudulent railcard anecdote and you would have a very different story. I may have had no money in my twenties, but I was precocious with it and ignored the rules in a way you can get away with if you have a guaranteed parental safety net. Let's be clear, this was not Bullingdon Club-level stuff. But the point, as Jonn Elledge in the *New Statesman* explains, is that parental support often means being 'able to take risks many others could not'.[1] That was certainly the case with me. And this was evident not only in my cavalier train ticket behaviour but more profoundly in my choice to do a master's and then a PhD. Like many others supported by the Bank of Mum and Dad, I could afford to luxuriate in yet more study, with no immediate thought of a job, just the love of learning. I worked hard, but I did not need to think in precise terms about the future.

Writing in *The Drift*, US writer Kiara Barrow has unpicked the discrete privilege of those millennials who talk about being broke but have never been poor. The distinction is defined by whether you have access to parental support and the extent to which that tap trickles. This chapter will explore the rise of what, in 2014, was coined BOMAD – the Bank of Mum and Dad – and its evolution as a pivotal safety net for affluent twenty-something millennials and Gen Z trying to navigate early adulthood. We'll also think about what it meant for those who had no such support and the increasing obstacles it posed. As Jonn Elledge reminds us, 'the thing that no one says about the boomers is that they're just so generous' and perhaps, how infantile I, and maybe we, are as a result.

Generational Shaming

Around 2014, we started wondering where all the adults had gone. It coincided with the emergence of the new hashtag #adulting on social media: ironic declarations of mundane achievements that supposedly proved your maturity from paying your car tax on time to maintaining a skincare routine. When millennials were failing to achieve the big adulting things, why not boast these wins however small? The term reached a point of elevation by being added to the Oxford English Dictionary. Older generations regularly scoffed at millennials' deficiency in basic life skills. But didn't our inadequacy only reveal the changing demands of adulthood in the twenty-first century? We might not be able to install a roof aerial, but some of us could create our own digital TV channel. Younger men might struggle to change a car tyre, but a higher percentage than ever before were changing nappies. In an age when houses are not necessarily our own, cars are more like computers and tech itself is designed to never be taken apart, we understandably outsourced domestic chores to TaskRabbit or asked YouTube for once rudimentary knowledge. And yet #adulting was revealing something much deeper within the millennial psyche: our unease at meeting or missing the traditional milestones of adulthood compared to our parents. According to one 2018 survey, nearly 70 per cent of British 18–24-year-olds concurred with the statement 'Technically I'm an adult, but I don't feel like one.'[2]

Another sign was the prominence of the term 'boomerang kids' to describe the rising numbers of us still living with our parents well into our twenties and sometimes thirties. Far from being a UK issue, it was in fact becoming a global trend. In Italy, in the wake of the eurozone crisis where youth unemployment remained stubbornly high, half of all male 18–34-year-olds lived with their parents.[3] They became known as *mammoni* ('mama's boys'), while in South Korea boomerang kids were labelled 'kangaroos', because they were forever in their parents' pouch. Post-2008, with wages stalling and assets rising, economics was increasingly nudging families closer together and forcing young adults to stay at home.

In the 2020s, with rents and housing going up, this trend has only continued. More than one in four London families has at least one adult child at home – a leap of 24.5 per cent between 2011 and 2021 (with 12.2 per cent the national average).[4] What was once seen as exceptional and fair game to mock has become fully normalised and accepted.

In the 2010s, these discussions evolved into an intellectual investigation into the stagnation of adulthood, especially in the US. This went beyond clichéd stereotypes that we were lazy, entitled narcissists and ate too much avocado on toast. Rather, it was a genuine concern about adult development in the twenty-first century. In 2015, Julie Lythcott-Haims, former dean at Stanford University, published *How to Raise an Adult*. She painted an unflattering picture of overbearing parents wielding control over their infantilised children's lives: 'I began to worry that college "kids" were somehow not quite fully formed as humans. They seemed to be scanning the sidelines for Mom or Dad. Under-constructed. Existentially impotent.'[5] Lythcott-Haims was describing a distinctive class of millennials, but her book and viral Ted Talk on the subject clearly touched a wider nerve. Jonathan Haidt and Greg Lukianoff picked up this

theme in *The Coddling of the American Mind*, tracing the burgeon-
ing culture of 'safetyism' and trigger warnings on university campuses. In their view, pervasive over-parenting was a major cause of
an emerging snowflake culture. In 2016 'snowflake' was the word
of the year and rent-a-quote Piers Morgan reliably latched on: 'As a
father of four kids, I think we've just gone ridiculously soft ... The
"snowflake generation", they hate being called snowflakes, of course
they do, they hate everything. And they're frightened by everything,
and they're offended by everything.'[6]

Millennials, unsurprisingly, took a different view. Anne Helen
Petersen captured the generational zeitgeist (and especially a feminised one) in 2019, when she wrote an article for BuzzFeed that
went viral, entitled 'How Millennials Became the Burnout Generation', which later became a book.[7] Petersen began with a simple
dilemma: why did she find it so hard to post a package? I remember
reading the article thinking, 'That is me. Why do I not pick up my
dry cleaning for weeks on end? Why have I not renewed my driving
licence?' Petersen put our 'errand paralysis' down to the 'millennial
condition': the idea that we 'should be working all the time' despite
little economic reward or security. We had been endlessly graded
on the qualification conveyor belt, only to be saddled with debt, a
housing bubble and launched into a post-crash workplace devoid of
job security, proper renumeration and benefits. 'We're not feckless
teens anymore; we're grown-ass adults, and the challenges we face
aren't fleeting, but systemic,' Petersen impassioned.[8]

The 'young people cannot grow up' narrative ran parallel with
the 'our parents have stolen our future' line, articulated most prom-
inently by baby boomer David Willetts amongst others. Laurence
Kotlikoff, professor of economics at Boston MIT, was at the sharp
end of such talk when, linking it with climate change, he exclaimed

that 'intergenerational inequity continues to be the moral issue of our day … The UK, like other developed economies, has engaged in fiscal, educational, health and environmental child abuse.'[9]

Depending on who you believed during the 2010s, we were either victims of an economic deck of cards stacked against us or feckless, weak snowflakes who couldn't survive in the real world. On the one hand, our parents were smothering us, and on the other, they were robbing us. Depending on the circumstances and contexts, all accusations were true.

Think tanks sprung up and the data was crunched, but despite the endless column inches it inspired, shamefully little was done by the Conservative government to address the on-going issues of the young, especially over housing, so hitched electorally were they to asset-heavy older voters. Age did not completely replace class in the way people thought about wealth and opportunity in Britain, but it became a key political indicator. Brexit was the most obvious manifestation, but it also seeped into housing, economic policy and the emerging culture wars. Predictably, there was a tendency to discuss generational unfairness through a middle-class lens by focusing on housing affordability in the south, the decline of decent pensions for knowledge workers and rising tuition fees for graduates: 'How did rich millennials become the voice of generation rent?' *Guardian* journalist Rachel Connolly legitimately asked.[10] Far less prominence was given to the state of apprenticeships, social housing and the living wage. These were boxed too rigidly as 'working-class issues', but they intersected with age in distinct ways.

In truth, all this disguised what was really going on. The generational divide camouflaged the growing class divide. Or more precisely, what started as an age problem gradually morphed into a class problem for one simple reason: the family. Because generations may have been pitted against each other in public, but they were becoming more economically entwined in private. Trickle-down economics may not have been happening in the economy, but it was happening within the family. The intergenerational contract may have been breached within society, but it was stronger than ever around the dinner table. In short, at a time when the market was dysfunctional and the state was being eroded, the broader family, especially Mum and Dad, were stepping up and dishing out. The post-2008 economy with low interest rates, cheap money, stagnant wages and quantitative easing may have favoured Mum and Dad, but many were passing on that advantage, through the gifting of time, money and space, to their kids.

'I describe this process as "good parents, poor citizens". The economist James Sefton was talking to me from his purpose-built lockdown work shed in north London over Zoom, confirming what I was beginning to see was a misguided debate in the 2010s.

'We need to talk less about the intergenerational wealth gap and more about the intragenerational gap, certainly,' he confirmed. Sefton has spent several years trying to figure out the amount of money that moves across generations both within families and in public finances: 'We need to be more precise here because there is intergenerational unfairness. So, if you look within the family, there is a lot of sharing down the generations, yes, but if you look in the public sector, the government has favoured the old, with the triple lock etc., and once you add the debt burden of public sector pensions, you realise how much of the burden the young will carry in the future.'

'So, do you buy the idea that we are living in an inheritocracy?' I asked.

'Well, if you are talking about social mobility – one's opportunity

to make your way up through the social classes – then there is definite evidence that today it depends on the wealth of your parents.
Social mobility is declining as a result, the inheritance economy is
a major driver and this has been the case since the financial crisis.'

I was grateful for the endorsement of my overall thesis. There's
always been inheritance, and parents have always helped their children, but the sums of wealth transferred between parent and child
from the 2010s onwards have been unprecedented and have involved
a wider section of society than before. What we are talking about
here is what is called early inheritance, also known as gifting, which
has been crucial for helping millennials get into the housing market
for example. Sefton, however, provided me with an important
distinction: 'I think we need to recognise that it is social mobility
(movement within the classes) rather than social inequality (gap between the classes) that has been most significantly affected by inheritance. In fact, if you were to ask me whether inheritance increases
inequality, I would say no, as inheritance is crudely speaking a transaction between someone of wealth giving to someone of less wealth,
thereby from an economist's perspective closing the inequality gap.'

I had one final question: 'When we think about inheritance specifically, we tend to associate it with the elite few, but is that right?'

Sefton helpfully clarified: 'We spent a lot of time post-crash talking about the 1 per cent, but this is not a 1 per cent issue: 75 per cent
of the older generation are homeowners, most of them are mortgage free, which means there is inheritance there. This is definitely
more than a 1 per cent issue or a southern problem. It's not just a
property problem either; there is a lot of money tied up in pensions,
too. It could be that the recent shocks of interest rates and rise in
wages may reverse some of that, we don't yet know.'

James Sefton had helpfully set out the economics, but I wanted the personal perspective on what receiving parental gifts throughout your twenties means. I sat down with Steve, a government lawyer who currently lives in Harrogate. At forty-three, he is at the oldest end of the millennial generation, but he recognises now two decades on how pivotal his parents had been in setting him up in his twenties.

'So, was your family wealthy growing up?' I ask.

'Well, it is an odd one. My family's building business has been part of the fabric of the north-east throughout the twentieth century, working on public and commercial buildings in the area. But I wouldn't say we were from generational wealth. The business has gone through busts, and it had needed restarting several times. My mum was also a teacher and subsequently a deputy head. We certainly had money compared to most people in the north-east but probably not compared to anywhere else. Dad built our family home himself, which sits in a national park with two acres of land. But my dad's business went into administration when I was fourteen,' he explains. His father had to cash in his pensions and start over, but they managed to keep Steve in private school.

'When the time came, there was never any question that I wouldn't go to university,' he tells me. 'In fact, I can't think of anyone in our year who didn't go. There were never any alternatives presented.'

Steve's parents paid his fees (then only £1,000) and university costs and although he had a small loan, Steve can't remember ever having to work while he was at university in Sheffield. When Steve graduated, he moved back to the north-east and his parents paid his rent. When Steve's grandfather passed away, his parents let him move into his old house for a year with some friends for minimal rent. When he went to law school, Steve's parents paid his fees – which were around £13,000 – and his rent. While a trainee, his family supplemented his income as well as helped pay for his wedding (along with his in-laws). Then came support for a house purchase. Steve takes up the story: 'We didn't have any savings and it was just after the 2008 recession, and we needed a deposit, so my parents released my grandfather's inheritance of £60k. But then things got really tight with my dad's business when the recession hit. Basically, the help stopped in my late twenties. We had bought a house though; we were set up.' And that is the point: Steve was able to be independent by the time he was in his late twenties and to accumulate his own financial stability and build a family. This is what a parental cushion looks like.

'So what about inheritance, do you expect it, do you think about it?' I wondered.

'If that day comes, great, but our lives are now set up to pay for ourselves. Self-sustaining rather than self-made is what is important to me,' he says.

'Self-sustaining rather than self-made' feels like an apt middle-class millennial mantra.

Who You Calling a Kidult?

Becoming an adult in the twenty-first century is for many a long, winding road with no fixed destination. Millennials have come to solidify a new life phase – kidulthood – stretching from the age of eighteen to our mid-thirties. It used to be that society marked twenty-one as the threshold of maturity; now we celebrate and assume thirty is when we tip over into adulthood proper. There is nothing radical in kidulthood nor should it be considered an insult. Life phases have been constructed differently throughout history. The concept and boundaries of childhood, adulthood and old age, for example, have always been moveable feasts.

The term 'kidults' gained prominence in the 1990s to describe the ageing Generation X who were 'failing to launch'. Stereotypically, it referred to men who were dodging traditional adult responsibilities (and who often had an unhealthy attachment to activities normally associated with youth – think middle-aged men on skateboards).

But millennial kidults are distinct from their Gen X counterparts in some critical ways: kidulthood now cuts across classes, is more protracted, is gender neutral and is intertwined with the inheritance economy.

In the late twentieth century, let's say there were five standard markers of adulthood: finishing education; leaving home; achieving financial independence from your parents; getting married; and having a child. But in each of these, most young people in the twenty-first century have either delayed them, complicated them or completely rejected them.

I could see this occurring in my friendship groups. There were very few who settled down with their university sweethearts; many more couples broke up in their late twenties and moved on to different partners rather than rushing into marriage. There were friends who had quarter-life crises, those who retrained and had dramatic career turns – one from TV to midwifery; another from PR to yoga teacher. Sometimes these came with a break-up or some kind of epiphany or need for purpose. Quite often it meant more education, moving back home and the inevitable reliance on parents. I was fortunate to live my kidult years before the Covid pandemic too, which robbed many younger millennials and Gen Z of these critical years of exploration and experiences.

Why have millennials embraced our kidult years even more than previous generations? Well, firstly, the economy has infantilised us. Just as we entered adulthood, certain things became expensive: the costs of housing (both rental and buying), education and childcare. The big-ticket items in life went up just as wages stalled. So, what became cheap as we entered adulthood? Travel, eating out, technology – three things that unsurprisingly became synonymous with our generation. We know that the 'too much avocado on toast means we can't afford houses' narrative was mostly nonsense. The truth was that we were economically incentivised to eat the 'smashed avo' on sourdough rather than save for a deposit for a house.

We became the experience-junkie generation for a reason: assets were increasingly out of our reach. But there was another factor. We were overworked hustlers, committed to blurring the boundaries between work and rest and hustling to make up for poor income. Many of us became focused on immediate gratification and short-term relief rather than unobtainable long-term goals. Why not spend £500 on an Airbnb for the weekend to unwind, even if we feel burned out the moment we return?

And yet as important as economics are, there is another factor for the rise of kidulthood. The fact is that fewer of us wanted to be weighed down by adult responsibilities in our twenties, especially women. Female millennials have grown up with more freedom, education and financial independence than any other generation before them. This may be an unfinished revolution, but across the globe, women in different cultures and countries, at a different pace but with the same intentions, have been extending their education, delaying marriage and procreation over the past twenty years. Coming of age has never meant so much freedom but also, as we shall see, so much protracted uncertainty, anxiety and insecurity.

The 21st-century road to adulthood is not a shocking plunge into an ice pool of responsibility, as it was for many of our mothers; rather, it is a protracted journey of self-discovery and rediscovery. Say you're a middle-class woman with a degree, a passport and professional parents, you will have fun on the journey to adulthood despite the economic and maybe romantic headwinds. At some point, you will drop your anchor and probably with the aid of your parents catapult into traditional adulthood. The experience is wildly different if, for example, you're a poorly educated man with few qualifications, limited parental support and few skills, you're not even on a ship. You're on a raft with dwindling resources and very few opportunities to find calm waters.

If millennials and Gen Z have delayed adulthood milestones compared to our parents, it is partly because we have had to but also, for many of us, because we wanted to. I spoke to Alina, who is thirty-eight and was born in Mumbai but now lives in London. Alina describes herself as 'upper middle class', which growing up in India meant a certain lifestyle.

'We had the luxury of going to good schools and having help in the house – a driver, cook etc. You grew up expecting it. When I was about fifteen, I started to notice the Indian economy was opening up. Real wealth started to emerge, lots of brands and handbags and all that stuff.'

Alina hated school, which she found extremely traditional: 'If you weren't good at maths and science, you were basically a failure in life. As a woman, you either became a doctor or a housewife. That meant the alternative to maths was cooking and sewing classes.'

Her parents, though, were not very strict: 'I wasn't oppressed, unlike a lot of my friends who ended up getting married at twenty.' After school, Alina's parents paid for her to study animation in New

York for five years: 'I felt free for the first time in my life,' she reminisces. In 2010, Alina met her husband and they dated for two years. They eventually had a traditional Indian wedding. 'My dad had been saving for my education and my wedding since I was three!' she tells me, laughing. The couple eventually moved to the UK where her husband had been educated and where his parents had bought him a flat in Maida Vale.

I asked Alina what she thought was the major cultural difference in attitudes between the two countries.

'In India,' she replied, 'it is naturally assumed that parents help; it is what you do. You make money for your kids to give them a better life and children don't have to be embarrassed asking for help or needing it. It's a big cultural difference to the west. I remember I would hear friends of mine at college in New York who'd say things like, "Oh, my mum loaned me the money and I'll pay her back next month." And I remember thinking, oh, you must pay her back? Wow. In India, we would never do that.'

'But surely there's an expectation that you reciprocate all that support when your parents are elderly and in need of your care?' I enquired.

Alina questioned my framing: 'You don't even feel that there is an obligation because they are your parents; you want to look after them. I feel like modern life is not set up for independence from your parents.'

'Definitely,' I say agreeing, 'but what would you say are the major differences between the UK and India when it comes to wealth?'

Alina responds without pausing. 'The UK is much more humane and fairer than India. There, the wealth is new and if you have it, you go big! There is currently a fashion in Mumbai to build big tower blocks for just one family to live in. It's all about displaying your wealth. But here it is much more subtle. There're no gold Porsches, but then in the UK, people are very embarrassed about talking about money.'

Good Parents, Bad Citizens

In the millennial coming-of-age comedy series *Girls*, the first scene defined what it meant to be a young professional in the early twenty-first century. Lena Dunham's character, the hapless Hannah, is having dinner with her parents who have come to visit her in New York. She is two years out of college, working in an unpaid internship and penning a memoir. It's 2012. She is broke but not poor. Her parents deliver the news that they are stopping her allowance. In disbelief, Hannah spends the dinner trying to convince them to continue to support her. 'I'm busy trying to become who I am,' she pleads. With her allowance dried up, she spends the rest of the episode trying to get a paid job. On the one hand, Hannah's character is perpetuating the entitled young person stereotype whose search for passion and purpose is indulged by her parents. On the other, she is a victim of an economic system where her arts degree doesn't guarantee a job, and she is being exploited for her unpaid labour.[11]

Parents have always helped their children get on in life; it is a natural human instinct. It is also something that the uber-wealthy or aristocracy expect and understand. But in recent years, parental support for twenty-somethings has become much more widespread and increasingly a rigid characteristic of societies with larger wealth gaps.

Historically, parents would have perhaps been expected to help with a wedding, and maybe the cash-rich middle class would have offered support for a marital home. In recent years, however, there's evidence to suggest that parental support for a wedding has actually *declined*. One survey from 2021 found that only 36 per cent of parents contributed to their children's nuptials, even though 42 per cent of parents say they had had financial support for theirs.[12] Of course, increasing numbers of millennials are choosing not to get married at all, but now a third of couples cover the wedding costs on their own. When I got married, I wanted to pay for my own wedding dress on a point of principle, independently of my fiancé and any family (and yes, because I was too embarrassed by the price tag!). The real reason for this decline in support for weddings, though, is that frankly young people would prefer any parental cash injection to be put towards something more substantial and far less obtainable: a deposit for a house.

In the twenty-first century, the Bank of Mum and Dad has wiser investments to make. Parenting has become a thirty-year financial commitment, with the most expensive years after eighteen. This represents a break from how baby boomers, or even Gen X, defined their relationship with their parents. In just a couple of generations, the financial flow within most families has been upended. Gone was the notion that over-sixteens still living at home should pay parents housekeeping money (as was the case for my mother); now, in most (but certainly not all) households, money flows down rather than up the family tree.

The term the 'Bank of Mum and Dad' (BOMAD) emerged around 2014 (not coincidentally, the same year that #adulting did too). Finally, we had the language to describe the new dependency culture in society. In a survey on family finance conducted by Sainsbury's in 2016, it was revealed that on average, parents expected to be financing their children until they reached twenty-nine, whether they could afford to or not. The survey also highlighted that parents were getting into debt to support their adult children and were putting twice as much into their kids' living costs as they were their own future retirement funds.[13] We wrongly assume that all parents can afford to be as generous as they are.[14]

Money within the family doesn't always flow downwards, of course; a large chunk of millennials – 49 per cent according to one calculation – have supported their parents at some point.[15] There is also a noticeable difference in expectations around intergenerational support, care and living across different cultures, as we heard with Alina. The power of the Bank of Mum and Dad lies in access to established wealth over decades, especially property. In this kind of economy, first-generation immigrants are often at a particular disadvantage. For their children, this is in addition to the other challenges they already may face such as language barriers, class and cultural differences. As one of my interviewees put it: 'It's like a double or triple jeopardy for some children of immigrants, especially women of colour, when compared to their peers who can rely on parents.'

In recent years, parental help has been the main way young people have been able to manage the disastrous effects of the pandemic and cost-of-living crisis. Between March 2020 and May 2021, baby boomers and Gen X handed over some £8.2 billion to support family members; 11 per cent of what the government's monumental furlough scheme cost the Treasury.[16] The age bracket that received the most help was 25–34-year-olds. This is maybe because those younger were probably still living at home, and those older than thirty-five see themselves as being the age when you are supposed to stand on your own feet. Overall, what emerged after the 2008 crisis has become normalised in the 2020s, where parents are now expected to absorb the financial shocks of their adult children.

But for the affluent, the Bank of Mum and Dad is not an emergency ATM; it's more like a lifelong investment account. They are the recipients of what some economists call a 'living inheritance'. Under current UK inheritance law, the most effective way of passing on wealth is to do it while you are alive and well. And this is increasingly what families have been doing. Somewhere between £14 billion and £17 billion is gifted or loaned informally each year between parents and kids, with 30 per cent of young adults in the UK being in receipt of a lump sum over any eight-year period.[17] To be clear, in our inheritocracy, the really privileged are those who receive part of their inheritance while their parents are still alive (and therefore earlier in their own life). This is the critical distinction that divides friendship groups and society at large. Those who get that lump sum are able to get on the housing ladder, build their wealth and create financial security much earlier than those who stand to inherit later or not at all. This launch pad for the affluent becomes reinforcing, enabling them eventually to upgrade their home, combine inheritances, build more wealth, amass a pension and very often not have to worry about the financial costs of having children. This is frequently the difference between those who have a smooth pathway into adulthood and those who remain forever on the threshold. Becky O'Connor, director of public affairs at PensionBee, has put it most succinctly: 'Parents have become the gatekeepers to their children's adulthood; the wealth level of the previous generation [is] ultimately determining which milestones are achievable and which are not.'[18]

There's an important regional story here, too. Parents in the south-west and the south-east are twice as likely to offer an early inheritance as those in Scotland, the north-west or the north-east. And your parents' status is a worthy predictor of how much you are likely to receive: those whose parents are renters are unlikely to receive a transfer of over £5,000 when they buy a home; those whose parents were degree-educated homeowners receive an average of £26,000.[19]

I was reminded of what David Willetts had said to me in our interview:

> If you see any figures on gifting, my advice would be to multiply it by ten; it is so hard to quantify this stuff. It's huge sums. As well as financial, there are also lots of other ways that parents help ... We tend to think it is money, but sometimes the gift is time or just shelter; a roof over your head while you build a deposit; help with childcare, saving you from nursery [costs]; or an indirect payment of private school fees.

In other words, money is not the only advantage; nor is a house deposit. If you have a mother who lives nearby and can do three days of childcare a week, or parents in London who let you live in their home rent-free while you build a savings pot, that is as valuable as any gift.

But there is an obvious problem here. All of the above presumes a traditional family set-up, which is not the reality for an increasing number of families. Divorce rates reached their peak in the baby boomer generation and blended families are now the fastest-growing household type – there's been a rise of 66 per cent in the past decade.[20] Tellingly, most of the data on BOMAD assumes both parents are around and that they are still together. It does not reflect the evolving family unit. This is a problem because blended families, however harmonious, bring a level of complication and sometimes economic disadvantage to the inheritance/gifting dynamic. This is especially true if there is a second marriage with much younger children, which can result in competing priorities between siblings and stepsiblings who are at different life stages. In other words, if your parents have stayed together and you receive a minimal pot from BOMAD, you are potentially better supported and have a better guarantee of an inheritance than those who are from wealthier backgrounds but whose parents have divorced and remarried.

I spoke to Greg, thirty-one, from Surrey, who grew up in a single-parent family without access to the Bank of Mum and Dad. I wanted to know how, if at all, this economic disadvantage had conditioned his attitude towards money. Yes, it absolutely had, and in ways that surprised me.

'I grew up in Surrey, and my schooling was at a bad state school. While I was there, it failed its Ofsted and the whole leadership was fired. There were a couple of murders. It was tough, I would say the worst end of the state education system,' he tells me. When Greg was fifteen, his mum sat him down and warned him that there were limits to how much support she could give him.

'She said that if I wanted financial freedom, I was going to have to work for it. So, I started work at sixteen. I became a sales assistant. And I've basically been working since then. I've normally had one or two jobs each year, in parallel, too.'

Greg won a place at a prestigious university in London, the first in his family to get a degree. One that he is highly proud of and grateful for. 'I managed to juggle it by working every Saturday, earning £380 per month, which combined with my means-tested grant and loan meant I could survive. I moved back in with my mum for the third year, and although she didn't help me with finances, she did provide a roof over my head and some food. I had £28,000 debt when I graduated and had repaid it by the time I was twenty-six.'

Greg entered work on a graduate scheme and started

supplementing his income by being a private tutor for rich kids, paid for by their parents. 'Did you resent them?' I wondered.

He laughs. 'I actually went to counselling to get over my anger at other people's wealth and family support. I'm not joking … I was tutoring all these wealthy kids who literally had everything on a plate and very stable environments. You know, I remember this one person: he lived in a beautiful house and used to have a maid that served us Russian tea and biscuits, and he would have six other tutors that day. All these hard-up millennials coming in selling this guy their knowledge. I found it quite depressing, as here I was scrimping for like £100. I felt like the underclass. I was trying to survive on London wages, which was impossible, so I was propping up my wages with tutoring. I didn't know how to handle it … The therapist went really deep into my family and my relationship with money. She told me I needed to come to terms with that. I couldn't help but see the irony that my student would pay me £100 for tutoring and I passed that straight on to the therapist to help me cope with it!'

No longer tutoring, Greg is now in a lucrative job earning £160,000, but he finds that money is affecting his ability to find a partner. He chooses not to disclose his earnings when dating.

'My last relationship ended in 2022 because of financial reasons. The guy did not have a job and I was supporting him a bit too much.'

'You've spent your life seeking financial autonomy, you don't want to be dating someone who is dependent on you. I get it,' I say.

'Ummm, well there was this rather funny encounter I had in my twenties,' he confides. 'There was a particular guy that was a top executive and worth millions. We got to know each other and then he flew me out to San Francisco and proposed to me. He actually said, "I'll probably die in twenty years and then you can inherit everything." He also said, "Just quit your job and I'll look after you. I can give you $5 million tomorrow and that is you and your mum taken care of." I mean, it was full on. I thought about it and said no. In all seriousness, though, it felt like the true test of my grit and it only made me more determined to gain financial freedom for myself.'

If Greg has a financial plan, it is earning enough money to support his mother in her old age, but they are also collectively thinking about how she can help him right now buy a house: 'I think when I hit £200k, I'll be giving Mum a couple of grand a month. She's leaving her house to me, which is worth £320k, just under the inheritance tax bracket. Yes, we've checked. We were looking into her doing equity release to give me a deposit, but her house is a leasehold not freehold, so we won't be able to do that. I saw my grandparents in social care homes, and I would never do that to my mum. I'll be responsible for her as she gets older. That's also the reason I want to work hard and earn a lot of money because I want to be able to afford in-house care for my mother. If I can't afford it, I shall have to move in. My hope is that is at least ten years away, but you never know.'

Have You Ever Been Clubbing with Your Mum?

According to one survey from 2015, one in four millennial women have shared the dance floor with their mother. The trend has only continued with Gen Z, where 'going clubbing with your mum' has had over 5.7 million views on TikTok. Commenting on the results of the survey in 2015, social psychologist Dr Terri Apter observed: 'Mothers today feel they have much more in common with their daughters than they had with their mothers.'[21]

What do intergenerational clubbing habits have to do with inheritocracy? It's a small indication of how families have changed this century. As we saw in Chapter 2, children aren't rebelling against their parents today like many baby boomers and Gen X did; in fact, they are socialising and cohabitating more. For all the talk of a generational culture war, the truth is that most of us have a greater affinity with our parents than previous generations did. And that's on everything from relationships to tech, from TV programmes to, yes, nightlife. The relaxation of social mores has also made it possible for parents and offspring to hang out. In most family households, sex is allowed before marriage, which has arguably taken away the main incentive for flying the nest.

You may not have been clubbing with your mum, but maybe you've been on a multigenerational holiday with your parents. If so, you are in line with most Britons. In 2019, one survey found seven in ten families had taken a multigenerational break. Virgin Holidays, which ran the poll, commented that 'multigenerational travel is on the rise, with time-poor families looking to maximise the experiences they have together'.[22] This figure, I suspect, will continue to rise especially with millennial parents seeing the benefit of childcare support while on a break. This all sounds lovely and harmonious, but it's also true that (usually) the baby boomers are paying. What the rise of multigenerational holidays, dining and leisurely time together indicates is the fact that families are closer than ever. From multigenerational hen parties to 'twinning' outfits, our lives are increasingly organised around parental dependency and multigenerational inclusion. Culture has merely imitated what is going on around our family dinner table, with celebrities, TV formats and podcasts now in the form of dynasties – the Beckhams, Kardashians, Knowles, Olivers, Osbornes, Wares, the list could go on. Every family on *Gogglebox* and every TikTok intergenerational skit collectively reinforces the idea that we all get on. Underlying all of this, though, is the economic imbalance: it often isn't a good idea to upset the bank manager. Parental dependency is the theme in many families and the issue we aren't prepared to admit is whether we are in danger of infantilising younger generations with all this support.

Back in 2007, the University of Michigan surveyed American employers to ask what contact, if any, they had had with the parents of their graduate recruits: 25 per cent of employers had received communication from parents over initial application enquiries; 41 per cent of businesses said parents had requested further particulars on their kids' behalf; while 4 per cent of businesses had had parents attend job interviews. In extreme cases, the researchers found that Mum and Dad had been helping with work assignments and involved in contract negotiations and disciplinary procedures.[23] If you are surprised by these results, you probably shouldn't be. Former Pepsi CEO Indra Nooyi is one boss who actually welcomed this parental involvement in the workplace. During her time at Pepsi, she wrote letters to the parents of her staff thanking them for the 'gift' of their children. She once even phoned the mother of a potential candidate to encourage her son to take a job. He did.[24] This may seem excessive, but Nooyi's policy makes solid business sense. It used to be that the company had to make sure the wife was on side; now it makes sense to win the parents over, especially as many employees are still living with Mum and Dad. If today's employers or managers complain about flakiness or lack of loyalty from their Gen Z or millennial recruits, consider the fact that in an era when wages have not increased to the same degree as the cost of education, housing or childcare, the stark reality is that in the 2020s affluent parents offer more certainty and a better springboard than any employer. When a gift is more likely to guarantee you a house deposit than wage savings, it is no wonder that employers are struggling to recruit, motivate and retain their young staff.

But how open are we about this culture of parental reliance? It seems that there is some discrepancy depending on who you ask: parents or offspring. Data from the US found that in 2019, 45 per cent of young adults said they had received a lot or some financial help in the past twelve months; but 60 per cent of parents said they had gifted money.[25] How many people who have received support from their parents expect it, take it for granted and maybe don't even consider it help? Who would want to publicly proclaim to their friends (or maybe themselves) precisely how much they've been aided? Who would openly wish to admit that the only reason they've been able to afford to do the big things in life – be it graduate, pursue a certain career, get on the housing ladder, fund a career switch or raise two children – is because of withdrawals from the Bank of Mum and Dad (or, even more difficult, the Bank of In-Laws). Parental support can cause resentment amongst friends, can be the source of great tension within relationships and can infantilise the beneficiary. Not to mention the fact that in some cases, there are often unspoken conditions attached.

The national conversation around the Bank of Mum and Dad tends to treat the UK as a special case, but evidence suggests this is a global phenomenon. A survey by the Royal Bank of Canada found that 96 per cent of Canadian parents were subsidising 'children' aged eighteen to thirty-five, while a further 48 per cent were still helping offspring aged thirty to thirty-five.[26] In 2019, a US study by Merrill Lynch calculated that 70 per cent of young adults aged eighteen to thirty-four had received financial support from their parents in the past year.[27] What is clear, though, is there is a tension in how this dependency is viewed across society. White parents in the US, for example, were more likely than African American or Hispanic adults to think that parents help their kids too much, even though they were the ones who helped their offspring more. So, while white US parents think that, as a society, we over-parent, they are unwilling to admit that they themselves are guilty here, with 63 per cent saying they do the right amount for their children.[28] There is an important distinction here too: for African American and Hispanic communities, economic interdependence within the family can often be about economic survival as much as social elevation. There is nothing inherently wrong with parents helping their kids, but when it becomes the main and only advantage, parental generosity becomes an economic and social problem.

'Homeownership Is Now a Hereditary Privilege'

That was the damning conclusion by *Financial Times* journalist and data supremo John Burn-Murdoch in 2023. This was the year when millennials finally reached an important milestone; finally, more were homeowners than were renting or living with their parents.[29]

The housing story is a messy one, but if you aren't aware just how messy it is, here are a few facts that spell it out. In 2016, it was calculated that by the time millennials are thirty, they will have paid £44,000 more in rent than baby boomers.[30] In 2020, Legal & General found that 65 per cent of people who bought a property said they would have been unlikely to have purchased it without parental support.[31] According to our *Inheritocracy* YouGov polling, 69 per cent of Britons are in agreement that we are too reliant on the Bank of Mum and Dad for getting people on the housing ladder – tellingly, there was little discernible difference across the generations or regions in the UK. Whichever way you look at it, a whole generation of buyers have grown up with a warped housing market and viewing ownership as only possible for those with rich parents. Coming of age in the aftermath of the 2008 financial crisis, which saw a doubling of wealth to income, meant that making your way independently through wages alone, although not impossible, became a lot harder. For a generation that had been nurtured in a culture that prized homeownership, millennial disillusionment was inevitable. We were simply born at the wrong time. This is the view of Lisa Adkins, Melinda Cooper and Martijn Konings, authors of *The Asset Economy*, who claim that millennials were the 'first since the post-war boom to really experience the impossibility of building up wealth and securing access to a middle-class lifestyle on the basis of wage-labour alone'.[32]

This was not something I was conscious of as I moved into my late twenties. I was still living in the area where I grew up in south London, still studying, still reliant on my parents for a crash pad, but the area was morphing into something else, reflecting the changing economic landscape. Tooting had been home to one of the earliest council housing estates built in London in 1900, but it was unique in that it also had rows and rows of private terraced houses, rather than post-war tower blocks. It also had a direct Tube line to central London and a bustling shopping centre and market. Its attractiveness for families and young professionals meant that throughout the 2010s, it became an increasingly expensive location to live. The place I called home was acquiring all the trappings of cosmopolitan living: destination points for food tourism and decent nightlife that people would travel down the Northern Line for. First came the hipsters, then the families (or the hipsters had families), then came the yuppies from Clapham rejoicing at the extra square footage. Out went the white working-class families, the high-occupancy buildings, the Irish- and Afro-Caribbean-owned businesses. Tooting High Street remained as important as Brick Lane or Birmingham's curry mile for south Asian culture and food, but behind the main street, subtle changes were afoot. Lace curtains were replaced with white shutters; front houses had planters instead of piles of rubbish. Cycle lanes emerged, as did the idea of 'Tooting Village', defining an emerging middle-class enclave. The local schools improved, largely because the economic status of the pupils did as catchment areas began to determine local house prices. Tooting has never become as gentrified as east London. It remains, even in 2024, a class and racial melting pot, but from the point of view of someone who has lived her entire life there, it feels like a different world.

We know that in the 2020s, the housing market in London and the south-east is fast becoming a first-time buyers' market only for those with inherited wealth. And because we are such a centralised country, this is creating a class and geographical barrier for those who wish to build a career in our national cultural institutions, media and government – not to mention for hospitality, public sector and blue-collar workers, who are vital in making our capital work. I remember one CEO of a marketing business who is Glaswegian telling me how shocked she was to find that, of her young recruits from the past five years, no one was from outside the M25 and they were all significantly supported by their parents. Her employees were diverse in terms of race, economic and educational status but not regionally. Unless you have connections or wealth, London is a no-go for a new graduate in a low- to medium-paid job. The ripples of our inheritocracy are affecting our economy in different ways.

We've been hearing for a long time that the Bank of Mum and Dad is one of the UK's top ten mortgage lenders. We therefore tend to think only in terms of a deposit, but that is only a fragment of the influence that parents have on the housing market. The BOMAD has many products on offer: from rent guarantors to rent payers, as landlords to mortgage repayors. In some instances, this has meant parents enduring considerable hardship or sacrificing their own financial security to guarantee loans, take on debt or release equity for their children. According to Legal & General, if you are not living at home, your parents are probably helping to pay your rent. Back in 2017, BOMAD was reportedly funding £2.3 billion of payments on nearly 460,000 properties in the UK.[33]

One of the main but often uncited reasons as to why the buy-to-let market boomed in the 2010s was the number of parents who bought rental properties for their offspring. In 2016, the Post Office calculated that some 730,000 parents were renting out second properties to their children. Only 5 per cent charged their kids the market rate, while 30 per cent of parents allowed their offspring to pay what they could afford. Many have since sold the property, having made a tidy sum in the process, and handed over the profit to their children for a deposit.[34]

Darius, thirty-five, from Wolverhampton is one millennial who had help from BOMAD to get on the property ladder, although in his case, his father took a rather unconventional approach. 'My upbringing was completely crazy,' he begins. 'My parents were animal trainers who worked in the film industry, so it was chaotic. Schooling was a mess, though. I didn't really settle and ran away to London when I was fifteen.' Darius ended up getting involved in drugs and living on the streets. But when he was eighteen, his mum got ill. 'I said to myself, "You know what, you can't behave like this," so I went home.' Darius lived with his parents, got clean and started his own business. He finally left home when he was thirty-one, but his father was adamant that he didn't rent.

'My dad is a very good businessman; he is very savvy. He is from Saudi, so he never spends money. We bought a place in Oxford that I lived in and then we bought a flat in north London. I put in everything I had and paid £150k of the price and then my dad lent me £160k to pay the rest, but like a bank, he has charged me interest on what is a loan. I am still paying off this mortgage six years later. My father did the legal contract, deeds, rights, everything.'

'OK, wow, so the Bank of Mum and Dad, in your case, is acting like an actual bank?' I ask, bemused.

Darius laughs and agrees. 'The point is I can't mess up. I feel so obliged. The number of times I've sat there and thought, shit, I can't afford my mortgage. With a bank, you can default, but you can't do that with your parents. I've still got to sit down for dinner with them on a Sunday, so I can't mess up … Even now, I put everything through my dad, and he manages every penny of my money. If I do that, it means I'm not being bollocked by him for spending it. My dad didn't just hand me the money; it was a business transaction.'

I was impressed with Darius and his father's disciplined generosity and boundaries. I took a mental note of how I wanted to approach money with my own kids. Over the course of these interviews with affluent millennials, I had been surprised by how many had said that parental reliance had made them bad with money, so I asked Darius, 'Do you think you are more respectful of money and parental support than your friends because your father had such strict conditions around it?'

Darius agreed. 'I've got friends who are completely reliant on the Bank of Mum and Dad. My best friend, in his thirties, has got his parents on tap; if he is out on a night out, they will still put money into his account and keep his slippers warm for him when he comes home! With my dad, nothing happens without a week's worth of negotiation and terms and conditions. But it keeps me on the straight and narrow … When my best mate gets his inheritance, it will be more like *Saltburn*: "Go and do what you want with it." Mine will come with strict T&Cs.'

We tend to assume that the housing issue and parental support is a purely London or recent phenomenon, but it isn't. In 2016, 30 per cent of first-time buyers in Wales and the north-west stated they would need parental help to get on the housing ladder. It was only in Scotland where the proportion of buyers who expected help was lower than those who did not.[35] Moreover, BOMAD support does not necessarily correlate to house prices. For example, in 2017, while the average London buyer was in receipt of £29,400 from their parents, those in the north-east (the region which has some of the cheapest housing in the UK) were given £24,200. That amount then made up a 20 per cent deposit in the north-east but only a 6 per cent deposit in London.[36] Londoners continue to be the most desperate for the support, and yet across the UK, the mortgage facility of Mum and Dad is not only expected but required.

It has been estimated that those who have had money from their parents are able to buy a property on average 2.6 years earlier than those who do not (the difference is 4.6 years for London buyers).[37] And timing, as we know, is everything when it comes to money and investments. Of those who had parental support, 39.9 per cent were in a couple, while 25 per cent were single. The inheritance divide isn't just between those who have parental support and those who don't – but between those who get support earlier and those who must wait.

Before we blame everything on a long period of Tory government, we should probably recognise the fact that this is a global story rather than a UK peculiarity. In the US, BOMAD is a top ten mortgage lender, with 43 per cent of homebuyers under thirty-five in receipt of help.[38] In Australia, 40 per cent of 25–34-year-olds expect to call on the Bank of Mum and Dad to achieve homeownership.[39] In China, an impressive 70 per cent of millennials own a home, but at least 40 per cent have achieved this only through money from their families.[40] Parental expectations may have peaked there, though; there is now a law that protects ageing parents from children demanding support.

But the data across countries perhaps isn't as revealing as the comparisons between genders. There is an indication that when it comes to the precise amounts given by the Bank of Mum and Dad, sons tend to get more than daughters.[41] Even when it comes to parental support, there's a gender pay gap, it seems, with a larger proportion of men living at home than women. In an inheritocracy, if families are relying on ageing parents more, we are also relying on the male breadwinner less. The interlink between men, meritocracy and class is the subject to which we now turn.

Chapter 5

Soft Boys, Henrys and Deanos: Why Class Sits Differently for Millennial Men

I was forty-two years young when I first discovered the term 'soft boy'. But I immediately realised that it perfectly described the type of men who dominated my dating life throughout my twenties and thirties. In fact, I don't know many millennial women in my admittedly small social circle who *haven't* dated a soft boy.

One was a guy I met smoking outside a random bar in Angel, north London, back in the days when people smoked and met in bars. He described himself as a 'filmmaker' working on 'something big' while jobbing at an arthouse cinema to 'tide himself over'. Let's call him Renoir Ryan. Even though he was always on his laptop, he never appeared to shoot a scene. Ryan and I met smoking and smoking turned out to be a major part of our relationship. He smoked rollies, naturally, folding them with a concentration and intensity that I found deeply alluring. He would seal the cigarette with a delicate lick of his tongue along the adhesive paper with the meticulous precision of a skilled artisan. As he inhaled, he liked to turn his head to the side in pensive gaze, chin to the heavens, and then exhale stiffly out of one side of his mouth. I'd often ask him what he was thinking: 'Nothing' would be the intriguing reply.

We spent most of our time in arthouse cinemas. I'd always hated foreign-language films, preferring irreverent screwball comedies and musicals to the macabre of black and white high-brow stuff. And yet in the way women often contort themselves in relationships, his passions became mine. As an aspirational film director who wanted to, in his words, 'document pain', Ryan spent a lot of time watching sad movies with a reverence that ultimately crippled his own artistic output. We made it through a complete Akira Kurosawa retrospective, an Iranian cinema season and saw enough French movies for me to retake my GCSE. I was in my hedonistic twenties, and this is how I chose to spend them; seduced and titillated as I was by this tortured artist and, especially, his apparent fascination with me. We would deliberately walk through London in the rain, fall asleep in royal parks, get drunk and paint; he once painted me entirely head to toe using my body as the canvas. But for all his supposed desire for me, the fact was that Renoir Ryan was a profoundly frustrated person and an emotionally stunted boyfriend. He barely called or returned my messages and often did not bother turning up to dates. He was crushed by his ambition and others' success, to the extent that I naturally concealed my own. For six months, we were caught in what would now be described as a toxic relationship. My day of reckoning came one night when he was so drunk, he rose from his bed, half asleep, lifted open his laptop imagining it was a toilet lid and peed all over his magnum opus. I left and never went back.

Never went back to *him*, I mean. Because there was also the struggling actor whom I dated for three years. Let's call him Sam. Everyone loves a successful actor; everyone mocks an unsuccessful one. For a long while, certainly for longer than was necessary in my early thirties, I was the supportive girlfriend of soft-boy Sam. He would deliver monologues, he would love-bomb me with endless texts and books of poetry. On our first Christmas together, he gifted me a framed portrait of his latest headshot.

His passion for his craft knew no bounds; he would spend dinners in 'method' and would weep through the 'In Memoriam' bit of the Oscars, explaining, 'It's times like these I realise the fallibility of my profession.' He would say, 'I didn't chose acting, acting chose me.' Which was, in a sense, a problem. Acting involves a huge amount of rejection and Sam was the least equipped of anyone I knew to deal with it. At least, I felt, Sam had not sold out like most of my corporate friends; his passion and thwarted ambition were part of his charm, even if they did take the odd turn. On the opening night of one production, he asked me to pretend to be his friend rather than girlfriend; the producer was gay and as Sam explained it, 'sexually ambiguous men are more likely to get parts'. Remarkably, I obliged.

Much like a doting mother, I sat through everything he appeared in. The Iraq invasion interpreted through dance (think the toppling of Saddam Hussein's statue in leotards with balletic pulling movements), the murder mystery farce in the middle of nowhere starring a long-forgotten '80s pin-up, and a wailing and blood-soaked production of Joan of Arc whose lead had only bagged the main role because she had secured the theatre at a cheap rate. But the most puzzling was a historical piece in which Sam played a cockney mercenary in a play about the American–Mexican war (no, I didn't get it either). The performance only livened up when the main prop – a cannon – broke and rolled off stage. I erupted into the kind of hysterical laughter where your whole body rhythmically shakes like a chugging train. I would have got away with it had I not been one of only three people in the audience. I sunk further into my seat, but it was no good. I'd been laughing so aggressively that by the interval, Sam texted me to say that I should leave by the back entrance as the cast were livid at the 'rude woman laughing so loudly' in the audience.

In truth, Sam's performances on stage were nothing compared to those off it. My friends nicknamed him Epic Sam because of the demonstrative ways in which he would exhibit his love, which was crude compensation for his multiple infidelities (or 'artistic connections', as he liked to frame them). When we broke up one Christmas, he sent me a letter with a Megabus coach ticket to his seaside hometown inside with the words: 'If you love me, meet me at the pier on New Year's Day, I shall be waiting.' I didn't go, in part because he hadn't bought me a ticket for the entire journey – the pier was twenty miles from the bus station.

The final climax, though, came in New York, where he had a part in an off-Broadway production; a moment of success that, unsurprisingly, had gone to his head (or, more accurately, his pants). I confronted him, but even in the heat of an argument, his world was a stage. We fought; we kissed. He imagined himself Burton to my Taylor in *Who's Afraid of Virginia Woolf?* But we were probably more like Kat and Alfie out of *EastEnders*. Me with mascara-blotched eyes, he on the floor, head in hands. I screamed; we slumped over each other like exhausted toddlers. I screamed again, 'I want to slap you.'

'Do, *do*, I want you to...' he pleaded. Then he raised a protective arm, 'But not the face, anywhere but the face.'

My anger immediately subsided, and I physically folded into laughter. The thing is, Epic Sam still had two performances as the gay communist intellectual in small-town America, and the part just wouldn't have worked with a black eye.

'You're not only a bad liar, Sam, but you're also a bad actor.' I left New York soon after.

But for those readers unsure or unfamiliar with soft boys, it may be worth detailing what one is. He is a self-defined intellectual who intellectualises, probably over-intellectualises, everything from social media (too intelligent and able to dismiss it) to your psyche (he will love you unlike anyone else can, apparently). He probably has rejected the corporate hamster wheel. He is often overeducated and underemployed; free from traditional constraints, often pursuing something he deems much more worthy. He is not as savvy as a tech bro, and less trendy than a hipster. His uniform is chinos and a scarf, low-soled scruffy trainers, never without a spine-creased Penguin classic in his pocket. He loves French existentialism but prefers Simone de Beauvoir over her partner, Jean-Paul Sartre. This is key. He's a self-proclaimed feminist and ally with supposedly the emotional intelligence to match his academic intelligence. He may lecture you about the patriarchy.

If anything, soft boys are even more pronounced today in the 2020s than they were when I was susceptible to their charms in the 2010s. I asked author Ela Lee, who at twenty-eight is fourteen years younger than me and at the youthful end of the millennial demographic, for an answer. Her novel *Jaded* features a soft boy as the white male protagonist who in one memorable scene delivers a lecture to his girlfriend's Korean parents on the history of the Korean War. 'How would you define soft boys?' I text her.

'He's into bands you've *supposedly never heard of* ... which end up being Joy Division or New Order,' she immediately texts back. 'And he excels in virtue-signalling. Today it's all about him acknowledging his privilege as a cisgender male.' Still in her twenties, Ela has dated in a very different climate to mine: the MeToo movement, the unpicking of privilege and the culture wars.

It seems women younger and wiser than me are on to soft boys or at least equipped with a greater awareness than I had at their age. There is even an Instagram account 'Beam Me Up Softboi' that allows women to upload recent incoming messages from any soft boys they've encountered. One reads: 'Currently writing an essay on Camus and absurdism, drinking lemon San Pellegrino with ice out of a mason jar, all whilst listening [to] Tame Impala, I hate the life I choose to lead.' And here's another:

> Just picture, for a moment, the feeling of being in a high-rise in Central London. Can you feel the cool breeze brushing against your skin from the open window? The vibrant city lights, dancing below, reflecting in your eyes. Can you hear Drake's smooth beats creating a rhythmic pulse in the background? It's an experience to cherish, isn't it?

And just one more, I promise:

> Like you know that movie pulp fiction. Idk if you've seen it, you should. But that movie is a masterpiece. But it's so unethical in the sense that it's so different. And that's not a bad thing, like it's different and it works so well. It stands out, doesn't blend in, a masterpiece … which I guess is what I think of you.[1]

I've definitely fallen for this kind of thing. If my experience was exceptional in any sense, it was probably because of what I was prepared to put up with – certainly if I compare myself to my friends. Let me stress, when it came to Renoir Ryan and Epic Sam, I was no innocent victim. I played my part in the ridiculousness of these encounters and relationships that in the end provided great anecdotes for my parents, much laughter for my friends and a necessary antidote to the hours I spent slavishly immersed in academic study. If I'm perfectly honest, I craved the drama and often engineered it.

Epic Sam and Renoir Ryan were very different people. But they shared something in common, and it wasn't just a comic level of bullshit; it was legitimate aspiration combined with severe frustration. Both were working-class artists, both from the fringes of the UK, down and out in London – an aspiring actor and film director – struggling in arenas where it was increasingly only possible for rich kids to keep going, let alone succeed. The pipeline of privilege that defines these professions making them almost impossible to muscle your way into.

My dad had been an aspiring film director in London in the '60s, and we grew up in a home where there was a carousel of artists and musicians coming through the house, all in London trying to make it. But for Sam and Ryan in the 2010s, there was a different level of pressure. It was a combination of false expectation, thwarted ambition and carrying the weight of living in one of the most expensive cities in the world. Their frustration was inextricably tied to the economics of early adulthood in the twenty-first century.

This chapter explores the impact of inheritocracy on men, especially those who had been led to believe that they were living in a meritocracy. As family wealth rather than earning or learning power became a definer of opportunity, so we have come to redefine class, occupation and success in the twenty-first century.

Soft Boys, Elite Overproduction and a Whole Lotta Frustration

There have always been soft boys. Search back into the not too distant past and you could argue that every wannabe writer, actor, musician and painter has been a soft boy – Picasso, Hemingway, Bowie. But as millennials came of age in the 2000s, a particularly prominent and specific breed of 'soft boy' emerged. Firstly, there were more of them, undoubtedly a product of more of us going to university and, in particular, the elevation of the humanities. Perhaps another key reason was the gradual erosion of traditional structures and ideas of masculinity – notably the male breadwinner. Graduate millennial women (even more than their Gen X and baby boomer counterparts) were encouraged to think beyond economic stability and status in a male partner. We had every right to expect a 'deeper connection'; that's what culture told us, anyway. A (seeming) union of equals. Forget the traditional polarisation on show in *Bridget Jones* with the gentleman Mark Darcy and the cad Daniel Cleaver. Millennials grew up with the sensitive intellectual: the verbosity of James Van Der Beek in *Dawson's Creek*, Heath Ledger's Patrick, the anti-jock character in *10 Things I Hate About You*, and stunted Ross in *Friends*. And most recently, of course, Connell in Sally Rooney's *Normal People*. These were prominent and attractive creative types, who appeared to appreciate women as individuals and for their minds. It was a vision of manhood that I, for one, found incredibly intoxicating. But how then are soft boys, who are admittedly a small subcategory in society, a product of our inheritocracy?

Professor Peter Turchin, I suspect, has the answer. Turchin is associated with the theory of cliodynamics (using data science methods and applying them to spot recurring patterns throughout history). When analysing contemporary trends, Turchin discovered that when wealth flows into the 1 per cent, as we have seen over the past decades, it narrows opportunities for others. It creates too many 'elite aspirants' competing for a fixed number of jobs, positions or status. Turchin has christened this process 'elite overproduction', a process that 'develops when the demand for power positions by elite aspirants massively exceeds their supply'.[2] He entreats us to think of it like a game of musical chairs, where, over time, the number of seats decreases, forcing greater competition and greater resentment. According to Turchin, elite overproduction was not so much a problem for the baby boomer generation in the west because the minority who were fortunate enough to get a degree had an almost cast-iron guarantee that it would provide a pathway to greater opportunity. As we know, this turned out not to be the case for many millennials. Having a degree became a necessity for a job rather than necessarily a realisation of our individual ambitions. In this way, Epic Sam and Renoir Ryan, and other 21st-century soft boys, are products of elite overproduction.

Let me clarify, I'm not suggesting that Ryan and Sam's behaviour was purely down to their economic circumstance, but it certainly helped reveal it and perhaps makes it more understandable. Soft boys, in many instances, are part of what Turchin calls the 'frustrated elite aspirant class'. And in the UK, they are predominantly graduates, white and overwhelmingly residing in the south-east, with pockets of concentration in the university towns: Bristol, Oxford, Cambridge, Manchester.

If I could identify characteristics that Renoir Ryan and Epic Sam shared, they were disillusionment and frustration. These were the clever boys in school who could write an essay, pass exams and did everything that was required. They slotted into the image of what society (and they) had always perceived to be intelligent and successful: white, male, well-spoken and highly educated. They read books; they got to university. More to the point, they grew up believing in a meritocracy and equality, the idea that with enough hard work, passion and creativity, their human skill could be converted into capital gains. But the highly educated, under-paid man has understandably become one of the most frustrated in an inheritocracy. And all this frustration turns into an understandably toxic dynamic when it's pitted against a seemingly successful, self-sufficient or privileged woman like me with a parental crash pad. Elite over-production and frustration exist for millennial women, too, as we shall see in the next chapter, but it plays out differently: milestone pressure, bewilderment at a limited dating pool and burnout.

At least Sam and Ryan knew they were in precarious sectors; they weren't deluded enough to assume they would be the next Martin Scorsese or Laurence Olivier. In the twenty-first century, frustrated soft boys became especially prominent in certain sectors – the arts, journalism, media, advertising, publishing and academia – arguably, the once-deemed 'cool' jobs. Their professional discontent was also partly down to the fact that these industries underwent transformation just as they entered them. The US commentator Noah Smith has explained that in the 2010s, there was a bulge of humanities graduates who had been fed two expectations of the labour market:

Everyone has told you that you can (and should!) find a career doing something you love, something that helps the world, and something that uses the education you paid so much to get. Then you graduate and … magazines are dying, newsrooms are dying, universities aren't hiring, and your best bet is either to roll the dice again with years of grad school or to claw your way into some corporate drone job.[3]

The savviest realised this shift early on and moved careers. Some forged their own path, although that came with the inevitable uncertainty of being a freelancer and a lot of necessary 'brand-building'.

Arguably, it panned out differently for STEM students who probably have good reason to still believe in the rewards of a degree, with greater career opportunities and decent pay much more forthcoming.[4] For STEM dudes, it wasn't even dependent on formal education or exams. All that time spent during their teenage years gaming or coding in their bedrooms often paid off for these folks. Those STEM workers who now live outside the capital but can command London salaries have been the real winners.

Gen Z are clearly seeking to learn from millennials' experience when it comes to course choices and career stakes. In the US, the number of computer science majors now equals the entire student body of humanities subjects.[5] In the UK, there has been a 50 per cent rise in computer science applicants and a 400 per cent rise in acceptance on AI courses. It could be, however, that these individuals will soon be vulnerable to the same dynamic of oversupply; in the age of generative AI, we may once again need poets rather than coders.

According to Noah Smith, 'for elites, especially those on the humanities track, the years after the Great Recession were a particularly brutal slap in the face'. During my twenties and thirties, I could see the level of resentment amongst hard-working young academics employed on short-term teaching contracts with no long-term stability. Many needed multiple jobs just to make ends meet, with little time for the research upon which career progress depended. Many did not 'qualify' until their thirties and even then, they faced a couple of years of campus gigging before tenure. A similar but slightly different trend emerged in advertising and marketing, although with skewed economics. Despite a 42 per cent increase in annual advertising spend since 2011, salaries for junior and mid-level roles have declined by 4 per cent, further exacerbating the gap between industry growth and wages.[6]

In most creative sectors such as advertising, publishing and journalism, the millennial generation were the digital guinea pigs. In my case, I went from being paid £800 for a commission print piece in a newspaper to £100 for an online submission in just a matter of years. Within journalism, those now graduating are entering a profession where the regional talent pipeline, especially for working-class journalists, has gone; local newspapers have seen a loss of nearly 300 titles since 2005.[7] A recent report by the National Council for the Training of Journalists found that 80 per cent now come from professional and upper-class backgrounds, code for bankrolled by Mum and Dad.[8] Those who have stuck it out in this profession may be aware of how fortunate they are, but that often provides little comfort. A friend of mine, a millennial father of two who is at the top of his journalistic career, will often bemoan the fact that he is only able to afford a medium-sized flat in leafy south London. It's all relative, of course. He's not comparing his fate to those on a living wage who clean his desk each morning but the more senior figure in the opposite booth, maybe only a dozen years older than him, potentially from humbler beginnings, but who has had, simply by year of birth, a well-oiled career in which his salary has got him more: including a London house, kids in private school and financial security. The point is that the professions that once guaranteed status, stability and high reward, and that were publicly exalted when we were growing up (i.e. often those involving the written word), no longer confer financial gains. You could call it the downward mobility of entire professions. It is no wonder then that some 'soft boys' cling to their metropolitan sophistication, anti-corporate credentials and Penguin classics.

Back in 2010, Peter Turchin predicted that the next decade would see growing political instability precisely because of this overproduction of young graduates and their tussle with the elites.[9] As we know, this decade was politically unstable for many reasons, but Turchin had correctly judged a generationally specific moment: the rise of millennial socialism. In the US, this centred around such figures as Alexandria Ocasio-Cortez and Bernie Sanders. Here in the UK, it was, of course, Jeremy Corbyn's Labour Party, which amassed the largest party-political membership in Europe.

Corbynism, despite its baby boomer leader, had a young slant and attracted precisely the frustrated, metropolitan graduate elite – the soft boys, if you will. Millennial socialism, however, was misnamed: it was always a response to the failure of capitalism. Without access to capital, or at least the benefits of capital, why would they have a stake in capitalism? Dubbed by left-wing writer Keir Milburn 'Generation Left', they had, in his words, been 'deprived of much of the material security that their older counterparts have enjoyed – like secure housing, or secure work'.[10] Did Corbyn supporters believe the remedy was traditional state socialism or trade unionism? Well, not really, but they did invest heavily in his pledge to reverse tuition fees. Corbyn, though, had tapped into the mood music of a generation who had a legitimate sense of individual frustration and saw solidarity in collective victimhood. Noah Smith later wrote: 'When socialists with college degrees talked to me about the "working class", it became clear to me that the class they were describing was *themselves*.'[11] In the 2019 election, Corbyn's Labour won big in graduate-heavy metropolitan centres but saw a collapse in Labour's traditional working-class base. What has happened to Corbyn's millennial support base? Well, they got older. And all indications are that Gen Z young men are more right-wing than left, growing up influenced by a misogynistic online culture that purports to be about reclaiming traditional masculinity. But millennial socialism in the UK hasn't completely dissipated.

In the 2020s, as millennials enter mid-life, we are bucking the trend that says that people tend to become more right-wing with age. That's what happened to our parents. Not so millennials – as the 2024 election demonstrated, all signs are that we are maturing into more pragmatic left-wingers.[12] Some radicals, however, shifted from Corbynism into eco-activism, interlinking the causes of climate change with anti-capitalism. Eco-activism comes with a degree of individual puritanism that may also offer some personal comfort. If you are someone who consciously opts out of mass consumption, car-buying, foreign holidays, even children on behalf of the planet, then you are also reframing your situation as a path you have chosen for a higher cause, rather than cards you have been dealt with by the economy. And yet eco-activism is also a community where the tension between millennial family privilege and the class divide plays out.

Because when we talk about soft boys, there are really two types here. There are, firstly, the aforementioned Epic Sams and Renoir Ryans – by-products of elite overproduction, those without much parental support and whose brains and creative talent maybe haven't got them where they legitimately thought such skills would. But they are being trumped by another, who we may call the 'signet-ring soft boys'. They are the ones who will insist on not being a corporate sell-out but are often bankrolled by a corporate sell-out dad. That is to say, their anti-capitalism and eco-warriorism often come with Freudian complexities. Signet-ring soft boys can reliably tap into the parental ATM, which is why they are increasingly to be found in those professions that are now incredibly hard to make a decent living from, especially in London.

Political rhetoric in the 2010s rightly fed on critiquing the global 1 per cent, but this perhaps obscured an equally important tension closer to home: those who had the comfort of Mum and Dad, were raised by wealth rather than wage and were capitalising on assets in addition to any brain power.

I was intrigued as to how commentators on both the left and the right were viewing our generational story. I decided to speak to Alex Smith. Starting his political life in 2010 as a left-wing blogger, Alex went to work for Ed Miliband before founding an intergenerational community charity – the Cares Family – which brought old and young together in cities across the UK. He now works for the Barack Obama Foundation. Alex is a rare breed in that he is a Londoner, like me, who still lives near where he grew up. Also like me, he has only been able to achieve this due to help from his mum and dad. His parents rode out the boom and bust in the 1980s and now own a million-pound five-bedroom house in Holloway. 'My dad grew up in a council house in the austere 1950s, so he likes to see those seven figures on a piece of paper; it means something to him about how far he's come,' Alex tells me.

I wanted to know where Alex thought it had all gone wrong for our generation. 'Well, our parents were told, "Buy a house, earn a living and you can create a decent life." People had a stake in society and felt society had a stake in them. But for the younger generation, the more common narrative appears to be "You won't have a house, climate change is looming and everything is precarious."'

Alex was right. Instability and uncertainty are two key threads for sure. 'But who can we blame for that?' I asked him, somewhat basically.

'Well, obviously we didn't replace the housing stock when council houses were sold off. That inflated house prices, leaving one generation better off than the next, but also New Labour putting so much emphasis on higher education as the key opportunity to progress was a mistake.' Alex's answer surprised me, but he was also making a broader point: 'We needed to invest in working-class jobs, vocational training and in valuing the dignity in the working-class experience. We needed to broaden opportunity across the class divide rather than expect everyone to follow the same path into the professions.'

Alex was obviously right about university as the only route to social mobility, but he also seemed to be putting a question mark over the entire concept itself. The expansion in education has been a net benefit for most graduates. But what Alex was saying chimed with what I heard from many interviewees. They were not 'edusceptics' ranting about 'Mickey Mouse' degrees, just frustrated young people who were unconvinced that education was the springboard they were told it would be. I wonder: was our generation in danger of blaming higher education rather than the failures of capitalism for our stunted trajectory?

We grew up thinking that working your way up was possible. We have since been told that the wealth gap has widened, and we are the first generation that will be worse off than our parents. In 2023, the Institute for Fiscal Studies concluded that social mobility was at its worst in fifty years, especially for those born into low-income households, living outside of London or from ethnic minority backgrounds, with inheritance proving to be more and more of a condition for success.[13]

This is perhaps not something our parents truly understand. As political scientist Ben Ansell has succinctly put it: 'The old think they did it on their own (or at least that others should). The young think success is outside their control … To the degree there is a "British dream", the mostly retired think it exists and those entering the workforce think it's a sham.'[14]

I decided to speak to Paul Johnson, head of the Institute for Fiscal Studies, to see whether he thought the influence of the inheritance economy could be countered: 'Well, if you believe in any type of equality of opportunity, then you would hope that inheritance would matter less. Whereas we know that it matters more than it has in generations … A lot of this is the accidental by-product of other things: the growing rise of assets, lack of interest rates, destroyed occupational pension, stagnation in earnings. We never intended any of that. It has become more important over time, but it is still less important for people's lifetime income earnings, and what they gain from going to university, because inheritance comes later in life.'

I liked the idea of 'inheritance mattering less', but Johnson seemed to refer to actual inheritance rather than arguably the bigger problem: the constant tap of parental support throughout life. Nor did his comments feel *that* reassuring. His statement 'We never intended any of that' almost felt like an apology. It was as if he was saying that the rise of our inheritocracy was somehow an unintentional by-product of a set of economic circumstances that few in power imagined or had any control over.

So, how do millennial Conservatives, born under Thatcher and who reached adulthood under Tory rule, view recent history? I spoke to Sebastian Payne, former journalist and now head of centre-right think tank Onward. Payne was fully aware of the problem: 'Well, I can barely think of anyone my age who has bought a house without the help of Mum and Dad.' In his own case, it was only through an inheritance from his grandmother, who had purchased her council house under Thatcher, that he was able to buy his flat in London. Here the benefit of one generation was directly passed onto another. Rather than condemn the 1980s as a generational zero-sum game, Payne believes that 'Right to Buy' simply needs replicating for the next generation: 'You have a lot of young people who are culturally middle class who don't own homes, who are frustrated and don't have a stake in society. And this is obviously something the Conservatives, who believe in a homeowning democracy, must admit.'

Sebastian Payne had correctly diagnosed the issue, but given the Tories had been in power for fourteen years, why hadn't they addressed it? 'We have this generational disparity in politics and aspiration which is greater than it has ever been,' he agreed. 'But also, the geography of this is as important as the economics. Life looks very different outside London,' he reminds me. In 2021, Payne published *Broken Heartlands*, a tour of the so-called red wall areas that voted for the Conservative Party at the 2019 election.[15] Outlining what he called 'Barratt Home Britain', he explained a key element of his book: 'There are a fair chunk of millennials in traditional areas in the Midlands and the north who are homeowners, often in new builds, doing very well for themselves and living the homeowning dream.'

Payne was right, but these opportunities did not generate long-term political loyalty to the Conservatives. The 2024 election saw this demographic, battered by rising interest rates and Tory fatigue, swing back to Labour.

Both my conversations with Alex Smith and Sebastian Payne had come back to one critical thing. 'Essentially, it's about class,' Alex tells me. 'And contrary to belief, class has never been off the agenda.'

In his own words, Alex grew up 'sandwiched between the upper middle class and working class of Camden' and so always considered himself working class. 'I no longer do,' he told me.

'Why?' I asked, relating to his predicament.

'My parents are working class; I grew up in a working-class household. But I've got my own property with help from Mum and Dad. I'm mortgaged up to the hilt, but I can't seriously call myself working class any more.'

What Class Are You?

Millennials entered adulthood just when class labels seemed to be becoming irrelevant. 'We are all middle class now,' John Prescott famously claimed, which coming from Tony Blair's northern Deputy Prime Minister seemed to carry serious weight. More and more of us were second-generation graduates and had grown up in properties our parents owned. But this was a false reading of British society. Class remained critically important, especially where it intersected with race. Britain's multi-ethnic population was becoming less homogenised, more diverse but also more multi-class in its make-up.

For a brief period in the mid-'90s, class centred on popular culture. We indulged in tit-for-tat territorial wars between middle-class Blur and working-class Oasis, but it was Pulp with their satirical anthem 'Common People' that really signposted the direction of travel. By the time that Owen Jones's seminal book *Chavs: The Demonization of the Working Class* came out in 2011, the writing was on the wall. The white working class, culturally and politically dismissed, was a point of both ridicule and fascination for the chattering classes.[16]

The conversation around class started to change, though, as the financial crisis began to bite. The ensuing years of austerity sparked a new conversation about social inequality, one that led to two prominent academics, Mike Savage from the LSE and Fiona Devine of the University of Manchester, together with the BBC, to launch the biggest class research project in Britain's history.

Up to that point, class definitions had focused on an individual's job or income. The BBC survey, however, aimed at a much broader definition, asking people a series of detailed questions about their income, housing, wealth, social network and cultural tastes. The class calculator, in turn, told participants which class they belonged to.

If the UK was in any doubt that it was confused but consumed by class, consider that 9 million people – then more than one in five of the British adult population – clicked on the BBC's class calculator when it was launched. It became one of the most important and talked-about data sets of all time. There's even evidence that it triggered changes in behaviour. Demand for theatre tickets in London, for example, increased by 191 per cent in the week after the survey launched, presumably because theatregoing was deemed a critical indicator of middle-class status by the class calculator.

'This survey has really allowed us to drill down and get a much more complete picture of class in modern Britain,' announced Professor Savage.[17] Rather than the traditional three social classes, the survey revealed that there were in fact *seven* different classes in Britain. See if you can find yourself amongst them: firstly, there were the 'elites', deemed the wealthiest and most privileged group in the UK. They held the most in terms of social, cultural and economic wealth and power, attending the top private schools and best universities, and representing 6 per cent of the population. The second group were the 'established middle class', representing 25 per cent of the population. They worked in management or traditional professions, hailed from middle-class backgrounds and experienced a diverse range of cultural activities. These were followed by the 'technical middle class', which represented 6 per cent of Britons, again predominantly middle class in origin but worked in science or tech and preferred non-traditional culture. Then there were the 'new affluent workers', which represented 15 per cent of the population. They were economically secure without being well off. They engaged in emerging culture, emanated from working-class backgrounds and lived in old manufacturing centres in the Midlands and north-west. Then there was the 'traditional working class', which made up 14 per cent of the population. They scored low for economic, social and cultural status, but many did have financial security, owning their own home. Then there were the 'emergent service workers', which made up approximately 19 per cent of the population, who were financially insecure with low savings and living in rental accommodation. They were engaged in emerging culture and congregating in inexpensive large cities. Then, finally, was the 'precariat', which made up 15 per cent of the population and represented the poorest and most deprived group with more than 80 per cent in the rental sector.

I went back to the BBC online survey (which can still be found on the website) and answered the questions as my thirty-year-old self in 2011.[18] Did I own a property? Nope, I was still living in my parents' second home. I had zero savings and minimal fixed income as an academic amounting to around £10,000 a year. I also did some training on the side, which was bringing in about £4,000, and I had recently taken on a weekly cleaning job, which was generating £60 per week in cash. The survey asked me whether I knew: an electrician, yes. Artist, yes. Cleaner, yes. CEO, no. Next were my cultural pursuits; did I go to stately homes or the opera, listen to jazz? Yes-ish. I didn't play video games or do arts or crafts or watch dance or ballet, but I did listen to hip hop and rap and used Facebook and Twitter.

Confusingly, I came out as traditional working class, yet the category I most closely matched at that point in my life was probably the 'emergent service worker'. I was in a middle-class profession but on a very low wage. The survey had assumed that I was economically independent of my parents, which, of course, I wasn't. And yet it was this safety net that was then the most important indication of my economic status. I decided to email Professor Savage asking whether he felt the survey had perhaps underestimated the importance of parental dependency and wealth in determining one's class in the twenty-first century.

'Yes, I fully agree,' he replied. 'We asked about savings, house price and income, which was useful, though also pretty crude. We didn't ask about inheritance directly, though our overall arguments about the growing significance of economic capital certainly suggested that inheritance was of growing significance. Thomas Piketty has this concept of the "patrimonial middle class", i.e. a substantial number of people in the rich nations who can expect to inherit significant sums during their lifetime. I think this captures an important phenomenon.'

As Mike Savage later explained in his book on the subject, class cannot be separated from age any more because the under-45s are operating in a different economic context to their parents, one defined by asset inflation, parental aid and wage suppression.[19] If you perhaps think that Britain feels more middle class now than when you were younger, that might be because as a society we are better educated. But also possibly because the middle classes are more siloed and sheltered than ever before. In many respects, the arguments around meritocracy versus inheritocracy are a middle-class preoccupation – which is why so much of this book focuses on the middle class. But while the divisions within the middle class have widened, middle-class knowledge, interaction and empathy with the working class has also diminished.

The 2011 class survey had defined culture as a key class indicator. As we saw in Chapter 2, this was true for our parents who grew up with a clear distinction between high and low culture that ran along class lines. If you listen to Radio 4, frequent art galleries and read the classics, you are middle class, but if you listen to LBC, watch *Coronation Street* and read *TV Quick*, you are working class. Millennials, on the other hand, were nurtured in an environment where the digital world democratised and flattened knowledge and, in turn, also diminished cultural snobbery. When he launched the iPod, Steve Jobs famously claimed it was '1,000 songs in your pocket'. Soon access was endless, and the age of the cultural omnivore was born. We could embrace both high and low culture, listen to Beethoven as well as Beyoncé and see them both as having equal value. Cultural kudos for our generation, therefore, is in our breadth not our narrowness. High and low culture are all up for critique and consumption, be it corset classics or reality TV. One of the most successful early millennial podcasts was the *High Low* with Pandora Sykes and Dolly Alderton, which aimed to see the rich tapestry of life in 'high low journalism', a phrase originated by baby boomer Tina Brown but only realised by her millennial intellectual offspring. Indeed, now millennials are assuming charge of cultural institutions and output, one of our key motivations is developing this cultural breadth and diversity.

Class identity is a complex myriad of things from consumption to education, but, in an echo of former times, it once again centres on your parents and your access to their wealth.

The Class Mash-Up in an Inheritocracy

The term 'self-made' is one of the founding motivations and characteristics of a capitalist economy. The thing that unites the mythical heroes and villains of modern entrepreneurial culture. Or does it? Because the uber-wealthy today are not made up of the self-made but increasingly of heirs. A report by Swiss private bank UBS found that for the first time since data had been collated, the richest 0.00004 per cent of society derive most of their wealth from inheritance rather than through their own hard work or entrepreneurship. 'This is a theme we expect to see more of over the next twenty to thirty years, as more than 1,000 billionaires pass an estimated $5.2 trillion to their children,' a spokesperson for UBS confirmed.[20] Not many are thinking like American financier Warren Buffett, whose stated aim is to give away 99 per cent of his wealth, so that his heirs have 'enough to do anything but not enough to do nothing'.[21] The point is that inheritance rather than wealth accumulation is the main force driving the global elite in the twenty-first century.

When conducting interviews for this book, I found that the demographic least willing to talk to me were professional men in high-income brackets who had received help from their parents. It seems that men are less comfortable talking about the Bank of Mum and Dad than women, particularly those men who earn a lot and have been in receipt of a gift or inheritance. Why is that? Possibly because we like to retain the myth of the self-made man.

It is this demographic that the wealth management industry likes to call Henrys (high earners, not rich yet). The emphasis is on 'yet' because, yes, there's a guarantee that some inheritance is coming. If we were to flesh out this stereotype, we could probably assume that Henrys have been supported by the parental ATM throughout their early adulthood and probably still very much rely on it. Because of their lubricated path, most command high salaries, or some Henrys (those signet-ring soft boys) thanks to their parents have the luxury of working in industries where pay is less. Henrys may have had their tuition fees paid, maybe graduated without any debt or their parents might have bought them a first flat or helped with a deposit. Henrys' parents may not be graduates, but they are asset rich and possibly from multigenerational wealth. This demographic probably underestimates the role their parents have played in their success, and prefer to reference how hard they have worked for it. Many of them legitimately complain about the cost of housing, childcare and school fees because the price of these things and tax on higher wages now mean that it is considerably harder to sustain the lifestyle they had growing up without their parents' support.

Crucially, Henrys are likely to receive an inheritance when their parents pass, which they probably don't talk about and probably don't bank on, but the promise is there in the distant future, offering security. Henrys tend to be the only demographic apart from the uber-wealthy who can afford to comfortably live in London or exist on one salary alone. Henrys very often have the triple privilege of a high salary, parental gifting and combined wealth through marriage.

I spoke to Tom, thirty-four, from Guildford. Tom fits this stereotype but also challenges it in important ways.

Tom grew up in Surrey and by his own description had an 'idyllic childhood with lots of animals in a big old house in the south of England'. His parents were both lawyers, he had a nanny and his schooling was all private. 'My mum was usually home by 6 p.m. while my dad was in the peak of his career, so very busy. I remember staying awake, knowing his train would get in around 7.30 p.m. and [calculating] he would be home within fifteen mins and come in to whisper goodnight.'

From an early age, Tom was conscious of his advantage and people's reaction to it. 'You were made very aware at prep school that you were in a privileged position, but when I went to public school at thirteen, it was different. There was one moment when the school was placed into shutdown because there were raids from comprehensive school kids inciting violence against us. It was the first time I became aware that there are [those] who resented people like me.'

Just like his father, uncle and brother, Tom went to Oxford. 'If I hadn't got in, I doubt I would have ever got over it,' he says, only half joking. He paid £3,000 a year fees: 'It was all taken care of by my parents, of course.' But at Oxford, Tom encountered a class rage he found confusing. He was dismissed as 'posh' by the lower-middle-class kids and bunched together with those he considered 'really posh', all the aristocrats and global elites. 'Up until the point I got there, I'd never thought of myself as posh, which sounds ridiculous,' he tells me. 'I know I present as posh, but I don't self-identify as posh. You only need to go back three generations, and you will find working-class grandparents. My life is a product of upward social mobility after the Second World War.'

When he left university, Tom pursued his dream career of becoming an actor, which his parents had been happy to fund, as Tom is willing to admit. 'I moved into my mother's central London flat that she got free with her job. I was being completely financed by my parents, either directly by paying fees or indirectly through free accommodation. I was expected to earn money, but it was about earning enough to maintain a bit of respect, nothing substantial.' But after seven years of trying to carve out a career as an actor, Tom decided to pack it in. Knowing something of the lifestyle and challenges of that profession, I asked Tom how he now looks back on those years.

He doesn't hold back: 'I was just so fucking lazy. I justified it at the time, but now I think I should have been doing more. I wish someone had said to me, "You should be earning more money; you have a lot of advantages." There were lots of contemporaries of mine who were having to earn money to live and I wasn't. I didn't have that problem and yet I didn't take advantage of that properly. I count that as a personal failure.'

When Tom met his future wife, it forced him to assess his financial priorities and privilege. 'She is the complete opposite to me when it comes to money. Savvy as hell,' he tells me, beaming with pride. 'She once showed me this flow chart of her fifteen current accounts with standing orders, which she'd arranged for interest. She didn't get an ounce of help from her mum and dad at all and managed to save £40k. I really bucked my ideas up when I met her. I married someone from a different class and with a different attitude towards money and it saved me,' he admits.

When it came to buying a house, Tom's parents gifted him a lump sum for a deposit, but it turned out not to be enough. 'My father had set aside £50k for my brother and I for a house, which when he set on that figure was a substantial fee, but when I came to use it, it wasn't enough to buy in London. We have managed to buy a house, but that is largely down to my wife's frugality more than anything.'

Now in his mid-thirties and a father of one, Tom struggles with the fact that he will not be able to replicate the upbringing his parents gave him. It's a situation that he blames himself for: 'I feel guilty. It bothers me that I won't be able to give my son the same educational advantage that I had. I can put that down to the fact that I decided to spend my youth trying to become an actor rather than doing something that actually made money.' But Tom also recognises that the economic circumstances today are also very different from when his parents made those choices: 'Private school fees have gone through the roof. I'd need to earn more than six figures and that is not happening anytime soon. And oddly that is a comfort. I am now earning well beyond the national standards, but I feel like there is no point trying to compare my life with my parents any more. I cannot recreate that life, not even a small portion of it. Having a kid at thirty-four is telling in itself. We delayed it because we couldn't afford it.'

Finally, I ask him whether he thinks about any inheritance that may come in later years. Tom speaks tentatively: 'There are quiet moments when we have very delicate conversations about how much money we expect to get … And that leads to the question of social care and whether you can rely on inheritance at all. And we do not rely on it. We allow it to be part of our conversations, but we do not plan around it.'

Tom's cushioned experience obviously contrasts with those middle-class kids who did not enjoy quite the same leg up from their parents: the soft boys. I feel compelled to add here that not all soft boys are crap boyfriends; many soft boys have become devoted partners and fathers. In fact, in an era of dual-income households and rising numbers of women outearning their partners, many millennial men are reframing their masculine identity away from being breadwinners to their role as fathers. I realised that my experience of soft boys was somewhat prejudiced by my dating history, so I spoke to Rich, forty-three, from Birmingham, someone whose educational aspirations led to frustration but who has found meaning in fatherhood.

Rich is the son of two teachers and was raised in a household where education was prized above all. He passed the 11-plus and attended the local grammar school, which, in his view, came with pressure and a promise: 'At the time, it was in the top ten state schools in the country. It was all about elevation. The message was "Let's pluck you out and through education put you into a different class."'

For Rich, the university path was inevitable and so was Oxbridge. Or so he thought. He applied, received an offer but did not end up getting the required grades. He went on to study English literature at Swansea.

'I found it crushing. All my friends went to Oxford, almost a third of my year group. I was really unhappy at university. I found it hard to find people who were academic. It was full of clubbers wanting to go to Ibiza, which wasn't really me.'

After graduation, Rich decided to pursue a master's in print journalism, which his parents paid for while he had to fund his own living expenses. But it soon dawned on him that he'd made a mistake. 'During the master's, I could sense [print journalism] was a dying industry. It was 2003 – online was just starting, local news was declining, and I couldn't afford to live in London. So, I started exploring PR but that didn't work out either. I felt at a dead end at twenty-three,' he says, laughing in exasperation.

It was then that Rich decided to follow in the family profession and sign up for teacher training college, which was then subsidised by the government. But it wasn't easy. He experienced discrimination as a man wanting to teach reception-level kids. He also gradually became disillusioned with the education system altogether: 'Teaching was too rules based and mechanical. It wasn't for me.' After twenty years of searching for career fulfilment, Rich assures me he has now reached his destination point: 'I have finally found my thing in online tutoring … I teach students across the country, in my own way, and at all different levels. I love it.'

I ask him how he now looks back on his career.

'To be honest, I'm quite resentful of it all,' he says, reflecting. 'I've tried to make the best of the situation I've got. The route I took was full of mistakes. I was told that aspiration was in these boxes, and they weren't.'

Rich's wife is a headmistress and the breadwinner within the family that includes two daughters. But Rich has struggled with his identity in all this. 'Sometimes I feel emasculated. I am gender fluid, but I don't think society is.' He found it particularly challenging when the girls were young. 'When we had kids, we decided that it made sense for me to do the bulk of the childcare. I thought of myself as John Lennon looking after Julian Lennon in the 1970s, but society dealt with me differently; there was a lot of hostility from the mums especially.'

'I just have one final question,' I tell him. 'How do you think your experience has affected how you see your own children's education and future?'

'Well, I'm sending my girls to private school because state education is such a hothouse geared towards exams. I know, I've taught it; there's no time for creativity and nurturing of skills. I want my kids to work hard but also want them to be savvier than I was. I also want them to be happy and confident in who they are and that the skills they've got are worth nurturing and not dependent on exam results.'

Rich's and Tom's stories, though, should not be seen as the archetypal millennial path. There are many who have risen socially and whose professional career has provided them with the financial security they lacked in childhood. Let's call these men the 'meritocratic millennials'. More often than not, they work in traditional professions or emerging fields: accountancy, law or tech or as solopreneurs. They have built their wealth and stability through wages alone. In these families, the money tends to trickle the other way; meritocratic millennials are quite often financially supporting their parents.

Sean was more than happy to talk to me in between Zoom meetings in his professional role working for one of the Big Four accountancy firms. 'Social mobility is a subject that is close to my heart,' he tells me. Sean, thirty, was born and raised on a council estate in Newcastle. His dad had worked on the rigs. When he was three, Sean was assessed as having a severe learning and language disorder and was placed in a specialist school. It was only when he returned to mainstream education in his late teenage years that he felt able to thrive.

Sean went to university, paid £9,000 a year in fees and then proceeded to do a master's by taking out another loan. 'Looking back now, if [degree] apprenticeships had been more visible, I would have definitely done that,' he tells me, reflecting on the £60,000 debt he is now paying off.

I asked what kind of experience he had had at university. 'Did you get a sense of how much your peers were being supported by their parents?' I asked.

'I saw a lot of kids with parental support,' he replied. 'It plays out in different ways: parents getting their kids work experience, rent being paid etc.'

Sean continued to live with his parents during his studies and financially supported them when he could: 'While I was a student, my head space was … "What can I do to help out at home?" rather than a more selfish attitude like "How can my parents help me?" I feel like I've been financially independent since I was seventeen years old – that is how long I've worked. During my undergraduate degree, I was working part-time, in my master's I had two jobs, working in Argos and delivery driving.'

Sean speaks with warmth and pride about his family, who he still lives with. He feels obliged but not burdened to provide them with greater financial stability. 'I'm really close to my parents and I will be near them, helping them while they are healthy and alive. I also want to be helping my nephew out too; I've already bought a textbook to help him with his GCSE maths. I might emigrate later in life, but what is really important to me now is that we are all around if things get tough. Some people just relocate their lives, and I couldn't do that. I don't want to be living in London, paying £2,500 for a poky flat on my own. I want to be successful, but in my own way, which means having my family around me and doing right by them.'

Sean's life, however, is about to change. After years of saving and sacrifice, he has managed to amass a deposit to purchase a home: 'I feel proud that I've done it on my own.'

He immediately contrasts his hard work with those who have had it gifted to them. 'The people who are getting help aren't really talking about it because they probably feel like they've cheated the system or something. If they've had a leg up, then that's great. But when I think about my deposit, I think that has been me, only me, and I've had to do it the hard way.'

Sean is aware that in becoming a homeowner, his life is about to be very different. I was curious to know if he had considered what this might mean for any future children he may have and how he plans to raise them. 'I definitely want to have kids. In some ways, I want them to have the upbringing I've had. But I know they will probably grow up in a better area than I did. But I want them to understand that they have to work hard for something, and that it doesn't happen overnight.'

Before signing off, Sean interrupts me with one final thought. His comment, coming from someone who has 'made it' in modern Britain, feels more than a little demoralising: 'I've been really disheartened about my age and the gap in opportunity. I honestly don't know, for example, if I was living twenty years ago and working in my local supermarket and worked up, would I have been better off than in my current situation given how house prices have gone up? I guess I've just gotta accept it. I call myself middle class, but I feel working class, especially at work where I can honestly say I've only encountered one other working-class person there. I am an upper-middle-class earner now, but it doesn't feel like that. I feel like in the UK, it's not wage but the assets you have which determine your wealth long term. I don't have assets; I don't have that kind of wealth. I just see that as a block from birth.'

In his book *Broken Heartlands*, Sebastian Payne referred to what he described as 'Barratt Home Britain'. More recently, commentators have given this millennial demographic of homeowners another label: 'Deanos' (both labels feel patronising). If the 1980s had Essex Man, then Deanos is the label given to the aspirational class of the millennial generation. Deanos don't follow traditional blue-collar or even white-collar distinctions but are defined by the fact that they live outside the south-east. The critical thing is that they have managed to build a salary and buy a house without help from Mum and Dad. I spoke to Cole, thirty-two, from Hartlepool. 'I am 100 per cent working class,' Cole insists. 'Honestly, up until three years ago, we had nothing. I drove a car that I didn't know if it would get me to work. When I was a welder, I used to think, is this it? Now I'm earning money I didn't think I'd ever earn.'

Although growing up Cole's family owned their own home, money was always tight: 'We never went on holiday, never anything fancy. My dad was a bricklayer.' Cole counts himself extremely fortunate to have gone straight from school to a four-year apprenticeship in welding: 'They were a great company; I don't think I will work for a company as good as them ever again. I got really lucky: they paid for me to do a degree as well and so I don't have any debt. After nine years, I was earning £44k.'

When he decided to buy a house aged twenty-six, Cole did not receive help from his parents, rather from his employer. 'My old company did a share scheme, which meant that for every £1 you put in, they put 50p in. When I was an apprentice, the share price was quite low, then by the time I came to buy a house, it had increased by about six times in price, so it was a nice pot of money. It was a savings account that I never really touched.'

'Wow,' I say, impressed. 'Why aren't more companies doing that?'

But after nine years with the same employer, there was little room for promotion, so Cole decided to apply for a leadership position at a plant in the south-west of England. In his new role, Cole has doubled his salary to £100,000 a year and commutes down south on a weekly basis. 'We have a nice four-bed detached house which we can live in comfortably ... We have plenty of holidays, two cars and the kids are very fortunate, but I still don't have savings. We go away four times a year. We just enjoy the money because it might not last.'

Cole is insistent that he's been lucky in life, although I can tell by his telephone demeanour that he is someone who can probably command the attention and respect of both his seniors and his juniors with ease. I ask him what he worries about. After a long pause, comes a long list: 'I worry about my health. I work in an office and then sit in a car. I work ridiculous hours, fourteen hours a day. Although I earn more money now than I could ever imagine earning, I worry about money. I worry what happens if this job finishes and I can't get another job as good. I also worry about being away from the kids and my wife. We've been together since we were sixteen; but working away is hard.'

If the stories of these four millennial men – Tom, Rich, Sean and Cole – reveal one thing, it is that old class distinctions around education, wage, profession, homeownership and opportunity are being remade in 21st-century Britain. I sat down with Alan Milburn, one-time minister for health under New Labour and up until 2017, chair of the Social Mobility Commission, to discuss how the Bank of Mum and Dad was flattening opportunity in Britain. Setting out what I thought was the complexity of the problem, he stopped me mid-flow: 'If I can interrupt you there. Social mobility is, of course, stalling, but it is a multi-sided problem. On the one hand, there is inheritance, and that is confusing middle-class boundaries, but that's not where the real crisis is.'

Milburn was right – inheritance was confusing the middle class. He was also challenging me for highlighting those groups that tend to get heard the most in the media and politics: i.e. the middle class. He offered a corrective: 'The real crisis is much bigger: a transformation of the labour market, which is no longer a ladder of opportunity. If you are a cleaner today, there is less chance of you making your way through the labour market than there was fifty years ago.'

Author Guy Standing was the first to properly analyse this recent phenomenon, in his book *The Precariat: The New Dangerous Class*, describing this growing class with no assets, no inheritance, navigating an unstable labour market in 21st-century Britain.[22] He argued that globalisation and the gig economy had caused the emergence of a new underclass: those living and working in short-term jobs, without decent wages or social protection. Under this label, it includes migrants but also the traditional working class; gig economy workers but also those with fixed roles. One way of determining the size of the millennial precariat within the UK is the number of children who today receive free school meals: 2 million, that is one in five pupils and therefore millions of parents.[23] They are just as likely to live in rural areas as urban enclaves. They have little or no ability to get on the housing ladder and while they have seen an increase in their wages recently, this has proved inadequate compensation in a cost-of-living crisis. What is more, collectivism no longer offers adequate protection. Unionism has become a support system that works most effectively for the public sector, rather than something that the working-class precariat can rely on to deliver changes in their material conditions.

'The fact is the rungs of the ladder have got wider and there are many trapped at the bottom,' confirmed Milburn. He was pointing to the fact that the working poor – those on endemic low pay – are unable to shift upwards, which was partly down to higher education qualifications creating a barrier to entry.

Milburn explained: 'In my lifetime, it has become necessary to have a degree to become a nurse. Soon it will become necessary to have a degree to work in childcare. Education has provided a route for some, but that system has closed it for others. I'm actually of the view that we need *more* graduates *not less* to get everyone moving up the ladder.'

I was sceptical that more degrees were the answer in their cur-rent form, given student debt levels and the state of our universities' finances. But also, by focusing on universities, weren't we allow-ing companies to get off scot-free when it came to training their workforce? In the age of AI, automation and a fluid labour market, workers of all descriptions and all ages are going to have to con-stantly be upskilling to keep pace with technological change. This is why it seems bonkers saddling young people with debt for a degree that is unlikely to equip them with the skills needed for a working life that could end in their mid-seventies.

As a baby boomer, Milburn was prepared to admit that per-haps his generation had fed their millennial children a false ex-pectation of the future: 'I was born in 1958. Opportunities were there for me in a way they wouldn't have been for my parents or grandparents. Our generation believed, and perhaps so did our kids, that transformational mobility was always going to be replicated.'

Implicit in his statement was that millennials (and their parents) needed to get comfortable with the idea of downward mobility – an idea that frankly doesn't fly when you are trying to win votes.

In an inheritocracy, your view of class, wealth and financial priv-ilege is very much defined by where you were seeing things from. Inheritance, even as a concept or a conversation, is one predomi-nantly being had within the upper echelons of British society, and an economic tension most pronounced between the upper and lower middle class. But it is also an economic driver that ricochets across all income divides.

Still, you may have noticed a glaring omission from all these class cut-outs in this chapter. That's because inheritocracy is playing out in a very specific and different way for women.

Chapter 6

Milestones, Marriage and Mating: Why Inheritocracy Is a Feminist Issue

There's nothing like being on bended knees scrubbing hardened encrusted poop out of someone else's toilet pan forty-eight hours after your PhD graduation service to make you question where your life is going. This was me at thirty-one. Scan my CV and it all seemed like it was going according to plan. I was a Doctor of Philosophy, teaching at one of London's leading universities and writing a book. But this concealed a much more urgent truth: my academic job paid £10,000 a year, I was reliant on my parents for a roof over my head and I had a £60 a week cleaning job.

My kidult years were continuing well beyond most of my friends'. I stretched the 'education' section of life to the age of thirty. My PhD had not led to a stable career but short-term teaching contracts. A sharp divide had started to emerge in our friendship group between those who were nailing adulthood and those who were not, those who were homeowners and those who were not, and the real break, of course, especially amongst my female friends, between those who were having children and those who were not. It obviously went unsaid that those who were achieving these markers were often being launched into adulthood by their parents. Friends were understandably reluctant to promote their privilege, hiding behind groans about house prices and 'the market'.

By my mid-thirties, rejection of milestone culture became my key identifier. While my friends were getting fitted for wedding dresses, I was waking up in clothes from the night before. While they were at Bump & Baby groups, I was climbing the Great Wall of China. I was the one who still turned up to family gatherings half-cut with someone inappropriate and ten years younger on my arm. Relegated to the kids' tables at weddings, I embraced the role of wayward auntie to my sister's children, holding my newborn nephews like delicate vases, stiff and at a distance. I was frequently told by others that I was 'not the mothering kind'. These statements, originated from a binary and bonkers view, are still very pervasive in our culture: one that characterises childfree women as liberated but lonely figures and mothers as overwhelmed but loved.

I would often compare my timeline to my mother's. She was married at twenty-eight and had her first child at thirty, which, in her words, was 'embarrassingly late in those days'. I stayed in education fourteen years longer than my mother and was financially dependent on my parents for fifteen more years than my mother had been on hers. For comfort, I preferred to compare myself to my father, who had lived in the same house his entire life, had never had a consistent job and courted my mother for eight years before marrying her. But even my father sat me down the night before I turned thirty-four and advised me to start thinking about my future. Coming from life's bohemian, it was a humbling experience. Like most women of my generation, I had spent my twenties and early thirties enjoying my freedom and, of course, working on my career, but in truth, I had very little to show for it, except *a lot* of degrees and dependency. As traditional expectations took hold, the pressures began to feel like an alarm going off, quietly at first, but getting gradually louder. By the time I reached my mid-thirties, the ringing in my ears was at a high volume.

The Tyranny of Time

Millennial women did not invent milestone expectations and pressure; the negative projection of the spinster has a long history, for example. But we have perhaps internalised it more than any other generation. It was not that we believed that we would have it all, but we were given more agency than any other generation of women before us. We have had greater freedom and therefore higher expectations, but paradoxically or perhaps inevitably, it has also triggered a greater level of anxiety, frustration and disappointment amongst our generation.

This is partly down to the fact that growing up in the 1990s and 2000s, we were fed a confusing set of narratives around life and how it should pan out. On the one hand, we were the educational and career pioneers with a growing, albeit far from equal, stake and say in the world. In our lifetime, female aspiration, ambition and achievement knew no bounds. My father liked to say to me that I could become the first female Archbishop of Canterbury. This was not an ambition I held (unlike becoming a jazz singer), nor was the position of first primate then even open to women (still waiting), but the fact that I never challenged his premise says a lot about being a girl in this era. And it probably says quite a lot about my father, too. Despite the chronic misogyny that prevailed in culture and society in the 1990s, meritocracy and social mobility took on a distinctly feminised flavour when we were young. And it came with a historical impetus, as if our mothers and grandmothers were whispering in our ears: 'Do what we couldn't.'

While popular culture liked to tell us that the two genders were distinct inhabitants of different planets, the real story was of a growing convergence between men and women. Lads had their female counterpoint in ladettes in the 1990s. These were labels that were always more manufactured than real, of course, but did symbolise a closer alignment not just in drinking habits but in adulting journeys, too. Men and women both enjoyed their carefree twenties, and for millennials, it has drifted well into our thirties. But if anything, millennial women are aware that 'settling down', after an extended period of freedom, involves even more complex compromises than it did for our mothers, and certainly for our male peers. Millennial women also inherited an idea, promoted by the baby boomer generation, that having children was potentially the end of freedom, expression and fun – something I've realised is palpably untrue since becoming a mother.

Millennials grew up in the era when female autonomy was being commercialised and increasingly depicted, rather than considered deviant and revolutionary. But this ran parallel with 'body-clock' narratives in the 1990s and 2000s that collectively made for some mixed messaging. Some positive, some less so. It was the era of Bridget Jones on the one hand, Samantha Jones on the other. This was the time when the *Daily Mail* wrote about women as SINBADs (single income, no boyfriend, absolutely desperate) and PEGIs (perpetual girlfriends but never wives). In one *Friends* episode from 2001, Rachel turns thirty and is depressed at ageing, upset that she has not achieved what she wanted to by this milestone birthday. Rachel does the backwards maths, declaring that she wants three children, the first one before she is thirty-five. However, her calculations show that she must already be with the man she wants to marry. The episode concludes with all the main characters admitting they struggled when they passed thirty. In other words, it is depicted as a gender-neutral experience not an exclusively female one.[1]

Sex and the City too aired at an impressionable time for millennials. I watched it again recently and realised it was not only the sexual liberation of the four female protagonists that was revolutionary – but their age. Sure, their masculine approach to sex was then deemed fresh and modern, but more significant was the fact that these women weren't in their twenties but their thirties, when the adulting script says you should be having babies. Even the conservative counterpoint within the friendship group, Charlotte York, may have had traditional expectations and fixated on her age, but her incessant planning is curve-balled by a failed marriage. Besides, her traditional outlook doesn't stop her from enjoying sexual liberation as much as her friends.

Having said that, it is Charlotte's struggles with her fertility that shone a light on how the sexes sharply divide in their thirties. In 2003, Sylvia Ann Hewlett published *Baby Hunger*, a somewhat sledgehammer analysis of the dualism between motherhood and career and that pervasive but fearful idea of 'leaving it too late'.[2] Its publication made the cover of *Time* magazine and was dissected by Oprah. If Hewlett was advocating anything, it was that women could have it all, they just needed to *plan for it*. As a result of this conditioning, millennials embraced a different mindset to our predecessors as we entered adulthood: it was less 'having it all' and more 'being it all'; a subtle difference in framing, but one decidedly less passive and more individualistic. The onus and responsibility belonged to us through continual self-development and incessant planning.

Not only were we fed this idealised vision of female independence but also a conflicting script about model companionship. Unlike many of our mothers, most of us have been saved from the religious and societal expectations of a young marriage or any marriage at all. Instead, we have been raised on the idea that once we have found ourselves, we need (ideally soonish) to find someone else – possibly through visualisations, manifestation boards and the whisper method. Ideally, this significant other needed to appear just after the right amount of messy romantic encounters; ones that didn't leave you too bitter or jaded but knowledgeable enough, so you recognised the right person when they came along.

Although the ideal of sexual and emotional companionship came about in the 1960s, it was only fully realised in the 1990s as women gained more autonomy over their bodies and finances. This was not the Disney fairy tale but frankly something even more fantastical: the heteronormative ideal in which a man embodied the best bits of traditional masculinity (stable and secure) and modern manhood (a sensitive, progressive type with a growth mindset, who wanted kids). We too needed to live up to the idealised vision of 21st-century womanhood – that was just the right balance of feminist assertiveness and attractiveness.

In the stereotypical millennial script, companionship is a union of two individuals in which you are both supposed to reach your potential while remaining equal and raising well-adjusted kids. Spot the inherent contradictions there. And we needed to do this while navigating spiralling house prices, mounting childcare costs, income pressures and economic fluctuations (and global pandemics). I don't need to tell you how unobtainable all this is. On the one hand, millennial women have a greater sense of self, while on the other, have raised expectations of coupledom – and all this in a society where just under half of marriages end in divorce, dual incomes are the norm and the traditional foundations of masculinity have been upended.

There is an additional pressure here too: we must achieve all this on a *schedule*. Most millennial women are terrorised by time. Not just daily, with an iCalendar dictator, but by the timing of the really big things in life. It comes from being overeducated and groomed in the cult of perfectionism. We were the generation that were told don't get pregnant too early. But we were also told don't leave it too late. We were warned don't get married too young but also don't get left on the shelf. We were encouraged to travel the world before being weighed down by responsibilities but also to prepare for those responsibilities all the same. We were advised to have fun and not to take life too seriously in our twenties but also to invest in our careers and save for a house. We were told to live in the city for just long enough to savour it but to leave before our kids are corrupted by it. The fear of leaving life too late, or running out of time, mirrors the relentless torture of a dripping tap.

But is our generation's 'shoulds' and 'shouldn'ts' a cage of our own making? It's certainly a pressure our mothers find difficult to comprehend, but then baby boomer women lived their lives to a different rhythm. They front-loaded adulthood and told us to do the exact opposite. Research by UK *Stylist* magazine found that 87 per cent of young women feel an overwhelming pressure to achieve everything they want in life. Labelling young women as 'Generation Tick Tock', it surmised: 'Essentially, we feel like we're in a battle against time, and we always seem to be losing.'[3] And this stress, according to polls, isn't coming from our families or society but from ourselves. The fact that this pressure is self-imposed tells you the degree to which we have ingested a version of lean-in feminism. We tend to place the burden of change on us rather than addressing the broader systemic inequalities and narratives.

And while it is hard to deny that women in the twenty-first century have enjoyed more freedom, this milestone timetable has led us to exercise a worrying level of control freakery – over our lives, careers, workloads and, of course, our bodies – all in an effort to squeeze the big life stuff into a couple of years. We are so obsessed by time that many of us suffer from pre-emptive anxiety – worrying about things that are probably years away from being worth considering.

But time is inextricably linked to womanhood in the way that it is not to manhood for two obvious reasons: firstly, patriarchal; secondly, biological. Donald Trump famously said in 2016 on the Howard Stern Show that thirty-five was 'checkout time' for women. I remember it because I was thirty-five at the time, single and child-free. It cut deep. Why did a flippant comment from an overweight sexist septuagenarian nutjob matter? Because it takes an extremely thick skin not to ingest the patriarchal discourse of women being 'on the shelf', 'past their sell by date'. A notion that is also closely associated with fading beauty – women's historical currency and one we need to admit still lingers. But a women's 'best-before' date has shifted in time and varies across cultures. In China, the number of unmarried twenty-somethings, particularly women, has long been a matter of concern. In 2007, the Chinese Ministry of Education publicly shamed women who were twenty-seven years or older as 'leftover women', urging them to adjust their 'unrealistic' standards for marriage. For my mother's generation, on the shelf was judged to be thirty. For a woman of my class, culture and generation, there's all sorts of unnecessary pressures that hit in your mid-thirties. I remember one of my male friends admitting that when he reached thirty-five, he decided to 'drop a decade' and only date women who were in their early twenties, as only then could he be sure their body clock wouldn't dominate their outlook. Don't worry, I took him to task, and yet his defence was also a legitimate one. He did not yet want kids, nor did he wish to lead a woman in her thirties on. If only all men were that honest.

Timing, in a biological sense, as Rachel from *Friends* calculates, has come to traditionally mean meeting the right person at the right time, ensuring you have a few years together to nurture the relationship before it's ultimately put to the test with children. And all this before you are labelled a 'geriatric pregnancy' by medical professionals (thirty-five, by the way, although many now use the equally insulting term 'advanced maternal age'). And that's assuming everything goes biologically according to plan, which, of course, there's no guarantee. For some women in certain professions, this also means ensuring that your career ladder is in sync with your fertile years. Since the 1990s, we have allowed a corporate culture to develop where women are almost encouraged to think that they need to get to a certain point in their career before they can have children. This is madness and fuels a culture where egg freezing is sold as a job perk. While for others, the obvious pressure is financial, when is it viable to have a child? How financially secure do you need to be? This speaks to the legacy we will pass on: low birth rates in an age when it is evermore expensive to procreate.

One person who has written about this life stage in detail is Nell Frizzell, author of *The Panic Years*.[4] 'I wanted to write about that period between mid-twenties and early forties where decisions are made about jobs, homes, savings, friendships, partners – all of which are impacted by a woman's biological deadline,' she tells me over Zoom.

'Yes, that was very much me!' I said, punching my chest in solidarity. 'But what about the unmentionable… money? What role does that play in the panic years?' I ask.

'Women experience these years in a way that men seem to avoid,' Frizzell says, becoming increasingly animated the more feminist her statements. 'I mean, it's primarily biological but economic too because women have to plan to have a child in a way that men don't… especially these days. It is so gendered that men and women are really having two different conversations.'

Finances permeate every element of a woman's decision to get pregnant, she says, 'Not just the cost of having a child but potentially fertility treatment, career breaks, even pensions.' It divides mothers when they go back to work, too. She recalls: 'After I had just given birth, I remember looking on in wonder at several of my peers doing all these wonderfully productive things just after they had had a baby, and I was like, how are you doing that? Some were honest enough to admit they had the money to hire a nanny, others not so much. But then I had the help of my mother and mother-in-law, which many don't.'

Frizzell rightly highlights the importance of being open about the amount of help and support you have, to yourself as well as others. As we shall see, those nailing the panic years (conventionally defined) have a lot of help, very often being launched or kept afloat by parents. The ability of women to work post-motherhood is increasingly tied not just to their partner's support but the availability of Grandma to help with childcare.

Such honesty about the support of Mum and Dad is often missing from social media posts. Millennial women entered adulthood in the era of mega*phones*, where life became about curating timelines on social media. Seeing someone else's life unfolding, daily, only intensifies any existing vulnerabilities. Algorithms are designed to generate that unnerving feeling on which consumer capitalism feeds: the idea that there is something lacking, and you want what others have.

That is especially true around milestone culture. We are each lined up on our feeds, as if in a race, peering into each other's lanes. Who's ahead, who's behind, who's pulled a metaphorical ligament, who's dropped out completely. And in this race, it is not just our friends but everyone we love, like, hate, secretly envy, once befriended in a club toilet when drunk – i.e. anyone under that flabby modern term, 'our social network'.

Frizzell admits that she finds herself frequently admiring women who have taken a different path. 'I recently became obsessed with trad wives on Instagram, especially the Ballerina Farm account. I do sometimes fantasise about being one; staying at home married to someone rich.' Frizzell chucks me a cheeky grin when she says this, but then she ponders seriously on the role that money and work have played in her life: 'I actually think about this often. I remember meeting those people who had got on the career ladder quite early on and thinking they were strange. I sort of had this idea that doing something creative and interesting was important, if not more im-portant, than making money. I also married someone who thought the same, which is frankly really annoying now because I wish we had more money! I wanted the '90s dream of novel writing with a side job in advertising. Well, that is no longer the reality.'

Frizzell was right to point to the 'trad wife' phenomenon because it is raising feelings of both fascination and fury amongst young women. Is it any surprise that in an era when couples are both slogging away with little let up, we find ourselves fantasising, albeit momentarily, about a life dominated by female domesticity and financial dependency on men? Our feminist liberation sometimes feels like a false one. A recent *Sunday Times* profile uncovered the reality behind the idyllic portrayal of Ballerina Farm, revealing the complexities of Hannah Neeleman's life.[5] We knew it, readers cried! Behind the filter appeared to be an overbearing husband controlling her life and restricting her freedom – or was he? Judging by Neeleman's swift denial and the discussion on social media, it is all up for debate. Whether we paint her in the guise of a frustrated, passive 1950s housewife or a privileged white woman exercising her autonomy, both depictions reveal how we are using trad wives as a mirror to question our own freedom.

Nor is it any coincidence that in an era when economic forces feel beyond our control, we tend to focus inward. Self-help in the millennial era has been about contorting ourselves into these conflicting and impossible frameworks, keeping ourselves in check and on time: hacks, tricks, podcasts, apps, memoirs and manifestos to help us realise who we are, how to meet our significant other, how to nail that promotion, how to navigate our twenties, how to achieve the perfect body, how to self-regulate everything – our REM sleep, steps, calories, hormonal cycle, social media consumption. Everything. We are so immersed in this culture of control that, as Anne Helen Petersen correctly surmises, it is little wonder we became the burnout generation.[6] Self-help culture, though, pulls the metaphorical silk sleep mask over our eyes, obscuring the actual economic obstacles, realities and constructs that really shape us. And yet a feeling of individual autonomy, awareness and savviness is also necessary. Self-knowledge is power; so is understanding or rejecting the narratives our generation were told.

So, if you are reading this thinking, 'I rebel against all this! I don't fit this mould!' You are right to. And you are also increasingly becoming the rule not the exception. There has been a conscious undoing of this prescriptive, conventional path into mid-life and motherhood for a very obvious reason: few can afford to do it. We are not the first generation to break the status quo; but more and more of us are rejecting the rigid rule book. Contemporary feminism has been about lifting this curtain, exposing these constraints and pressures. We are having non-linear careers. We are procreating in our forties. We are having babies without men. We are rejecting the term 'childless' and embracing the notion of being 'childfree'. We are cohabitating, not as a precursor to marriage, but with successive partners and *instead* of marriage. We are returning to education again and again. No one can make assumptions about when or what any more, especially when it comes to women. This, however, has come about not only because of economic obstacles but also because of greater freedom and social acceptance. And, I should add, a global pandemic, which paused or restricted relationships, fertility treatments, qualifications, the lot.

If millennial women are feeling anger or rejection at this notion of a fixed point of adulthood, it is entirely justifiable. The idea not only feels parochial; it's also pointless. We should embrace ripping up the life script. Millennials, like their Gen X and baby boomer counterparts, are currently reconstructing the three-stage life model of education, work and retirement that dominated the late twentieth century, and reshaping it into one that is more complex, individualised and better aligned to economic and gender relations in the twenty-first century.

Early evidence suggests that our Gen Z sisters are experimenting to an even greater degree in terms of gender roles and identity, pushing the boundaries of conventions and expectations. They are not only questioning the idea of reaching these milestones but also questioning the milestones themselves. Whether we are talking about the pernicious influence of Andrew Tate or the birth strike movement, all are reactions against the broken pathways into adulthood for young people.

But there are more positive sides, too. Gen Z are already talking about their fertility in a more knowledgeable way than I did in my twenties. Because of this, Frizzell doubts whether her book *The Panic Years* speaks to Gen Z women today: 'My version of meeting a man, getting pregnant is probably less relatable because of the different conversations young people are having about sexuality, gender and fertility. It's also so affected by race and class that it is so difficult to say what culture these young women are being influenced by. You can no longer just say *Friends* as a cultural touchpoint, because those type of shows watched by millions no longer exist. Identities have shifted into silos.'

And here Frizzell gets to the nub of the issue. As much as I may have spent the past few pages describing the millennial female position and referencing *Friends*... there's a problem. It is an overwhelmingly urban middle-class professional portrait. It doesn't mean it's not true, but let's not pretend it's universal. Even the notion of adulthood as a meandering journey with a specific (albeit thwarted) plan is one that feels like a distinctly middle-class paranoia. It is very hard to plan anything if your only certainty is economic precarity. The tyranny of time is a distinctly middle-class obsession, so is planning your children around your career. It is also an overwhelmingly heterosexual view. The average age of gay and lesbian couples getting married falls out of Frizzell's panic years, for example, with women in same-sex unions marrying at forty-two and gay men at forty-six.[7] It is also distinctly lacking in cultural nuance.

South Asian journalist Kim Bansi has written in *Stylist* about what it is like for millennial women of her heritage to break cultural conventions by moving out of the family home and to live their lives according to their own rules. In defying the model that sees marriage as the ultimate end goal, she describes how this often leads to challenging relations with parents and the broader community. Mal, for example, was raised in a supportive Pakistani family, but when she chose to leave home, she felt an air of disapproval as time went on. It was as though she could break the rules but only for a fixed period:

> I compared it to when my brother got married and moved into a new home; my parents were doing his shopping for him and going to IKEA, but I had to manage things myself ... I felt like I was only going to get that love and support from my parents if I got married.[8]

And yet even the assumption that millennial women of colour are living in natural defiance of their more traditionalist elders is far too simplistic a picture. My friend whose mother had an arranged marriage and did not have a career encouraged her daughter to live the complete opposite and also provided her with the financial means to do so. It's a pressure to pursue a feminist path that my friend has sometimes felt a little too much. The gap in the experience between mother and daughter may be wide, yet the mutual empathy is overwhelming. As the millennial lives in this book attest, the transference of a set ideals of womanhood from mother to daughter are conditioned as much by individual family history as they are by economic, cultural and social macrotrends.

Writer Rebecca Liu has rightly shone a light on our tendency to view the concerns, fears and narratives of white, middle-class female millennials as somehow universal truths, while boxing other stories, struggles and constraints as 'other'. Grouping Lena Dunham's *Girls*, Sally Rooney's *Normal People* and Phoebe Waller-Bridge's *Fleabag*, Liu unpicks the way we laud certain cultural output as generational poster girls, revealing how this illustrates our elevation of 'upper-middle-class white voices to the level of unearned universalism'. These archetypes, of the millennial 'hot mess', according to Liu, share common characteristics. They are always 'pretty, white, cisgender and tortured enough to be interesting but not enough to be repulsive. Often described as "relatable", she is, in actuality, not.' Liu continues:

> She's often wealthy but doesn't think too much about it. Her life is fraught with so much drama, self-loathing and downwardly mobile financial precarity, that she forgets about it, just as we are meant to. Her friends, if she has any, are incorrigible narcissists, and the men in her life are disappointing and terrible. Try as she might, her protest against the world always re-routes into a melancholic self-destruction.[9]

Liu may well have just been describing the autobiographical elements of this book! This, of course, is the probing point. White, middle-class, urban millennial women have so much validation in mainstream culture of our struggles, priorities and neuroses that we are in danger of not seeing beyond them. Liu reminds us that 'the world-weary malaise of the privileged has always had a sort of narcissism to it': 'The many socioeconomic divisions that mark our generation are flattened beneath the vague language of collective burnout and mutual suffering that comes with living under the boot of capital.'[10]

You don't need to be a radical Marxist to sympathise with Liu's argument that our generational motifs, heroines and even concepts such as 'burnout' may preclude middle-class millennial women from seeing beyond what is right in front of us.

When it comes to our financial privilege, it's a particular challenge because our broad-brush generational narrative is one of economic victimhood. One that those in the middle- to upper-income brackets retell more than any other. In this era of individualised Instagram comparison culture but shamelessly little face-to-face interclass interactions, we can't help but juxtapose ourselves against those with more and bemoan that we have less. How often do we think about our circumstances and how they are inextricably linked to those who have far less?

I met Candice a couple of years ago at a corporate event I was speaking at, where she rightly challenged me on my generational stereotyping. Her story as a Black British woman from south London didn't fit my neat analysis, she told me. Candice, thirty-eight, grew up in Brixton: 'When my birth mum left, it was just my dad and me. He was working as a trader in the City, having done a degree in economics, but he left that to become a manual labourer as it worked around childcare better.' Her father met her stepmum when Candice was seven and they set up an estate agents' business. 'We had a nice car, house. We were "well-to-do" in our school.'

Candice's family moved out of Brixton when she was seventeen. Her childhood area is now unrecognisable, she tells me: 'I didn't really realise how much it had changed until I went back. I mean the first sign was the Starbucks, but then I was hearing things about Brixton Market – that was where my stepmum used to drag me to buy fish and meat and it used to smell. But then I was hearing that people were going out for glitzy drinks and dinner there, which seemed crazy to me.'

Going to university was a culture shock, she says. In London, Candice had attended a school where 95 per cent of the students were Black, but university was the complete opposite: 'I remember looking at the table of everyone's lunch cards on the first day and not seeing any Black faces. Also, the white faces were different from where I was from. I remember saying to someone, "I love your scarf," and she corrected me and said, "It's a pashmina, darling." I had friends who were middle class, but some were from a different world; one of them was related to the author of *Winnie-the-Pooh*. But also, I noticed how old their parents were; my parents were in their thirties and forties, but most of their parents were retired in their sixties.'

I ask Candice how she sees her parents' experience compared to her own. 'I think my parents' generation had it easier when it came to buying property, but they faced greater discrimination. I remember my stepmum, who is from Jamaica, having to fight for the right to remain in the UK. Both me and my father were the only Black faces at uni. I don't think that would happen today. I remember there was an Afro-Caribbean society … but most of the people there were from Nigeria. That felt odd. The only connection we had was skin tone, and most of them were wealthy, so we had even less of a connection. But I do think to incorporate and navigate spaces as a Black woman, it is easier for me and my stepsiblings than it was for my parents. I am a second-generation Black British woman.

Most of my friends are first generation, whose parents did not go to uni, whereas both my parents went, so that gives you a different confidence. I'm not going into spaces thinking, "I'm the one that made it."'

Candice finished university and completed a master's before hitting the corporate workplace just after the financial crisis, which inevitably proved a challenge. After a couple of years living with friends, she decided to move back to her parents' home to build a deposit for a flat. She saved all she could and with the Help to Buy part-ownership scheme bought a two-bed flat 'in a place in south-east London I'd never even heard of before I moved!' she jokes. Candice rented out her room and eventually bought the rest of her property.

'You've been savvy,' I tell her. 'So do you feel the social divide of the Bank of Mum and Dad amongst your friends and colleagues?' I ask.

'Well, none of my London friends are supported by the Bank of Mum and Dad – they either are in council houses, renting or living at home. Some from uni are though.' As a homeowner who has made it on her own, Candice doesn't feel resentment for those who have had help. If anything, she realises how lucky she is. 'I don't feel that parents' divide thing because I got on and bought my flat. I am now earning a decent salary. I know whole families live on my salary, so I know how privileged I am. But I do feel trapped.'

'Why?' I ask, intrigued.

'When we were kids, me and my friend used to walk around Clapham and say, "We're gonna live here when we're older." That's obviously a joke now! But I would like to move closer to where I'm from; I just can't afford to. In the future, I want to keep my flat and have it as passive income, but in the past few months, my mortgage has gone from £900 to £1,400 alone. Plus, I might have cladding on my building, which is a whole different story.' Candice is an independent, ambitious woman who has done all the right things, but cladding, the mortgage crisis and navigating the London property market means she is struggling to move up.

But there's also another issue, she tells me: 'I'm single. I'm aware that if I was in a couple, it would be easier: two incomes, two deposits, shared savings. However, I'm stuck.'

'How do you feel about our generation of men?' I ask her.

'The men I've dated, well, how can I put this? It's not about money or having a house; its mindset. They've all been on a different plane to me when it comes to life and money. One guy I was dating last year, he'd been in the same role for sixteen years and he was hitting forty. I was like, why? If you are just there because you are scared of a challenge, then that's not the right attitude. It's a problem.'

Partnering Up

Aged thirty-six, after a slow, meandering and cushioned entry into adulthood, life came at me fast. When my husband and I got together, everything happened very quickly and probably because it needed to. Within six months of dating, we moved in together. Within seven months, we were engaged. Within eight months, I was pregnant. Within twelve months, my father was diagnosed with cancer. In 2018, everything came to a climax. I found myself organising my one-year-old son's christening, my father's funeral and our wedding (in that order), all taking place within four months, which was a juddering bolt into adulthood if ever there was one. I still wonder why or how I thought combining those things would be a good idea. The algorithms on my phone mirrored my internal chaos: my feed a mix of advertisements for honeymoon destinations, Co-op Funeralcare and personalised baby rattles.

Back when I was six months pregnant, my in-laws mooted the idea that we should go and see a financial advisor. I was an adult, and this is what adults did apparently. Plus, I was so ignorant and infantilised when it came to money, it seemed like a good thing to do. Two months later, we ventured to the City and sat down in a big office, with a massive oval-shaped mahogany table and leather chairs on wheels. On the table was a wooden box with a quality selection of teas and sparkling and still water. Two men came in, sat down, one in his sixties, the other in his thirties. They both shook my husband's hand and then the elder addressed me, or rather my protruding stomach: 'Congratulations. When are you due?'

'We have two,' the younger one butted in before I could reply. 'We're through the nappy stage thankfully!' rolling his eyes in mocking relief.

Prior to the meeting, we had been asked to list our assets, outgoings and incomings. It was a quick exercise, especially for me, then a freelancer in the latter stages of pregnancy. We were London renters, living in Borough, Zone 1, paying an extortionate sum to landlords just ten years older than us who had picked up the house cheap when the area wasn't as nice. Our rental payments were now enabling them to live somewhere bigger and even nicer. We spent far too much of our income on holidays, eating out, and not enough building pensions, savings and assets. If ever there was a millennial embodiment of 'too much avocado on toast is preventing you from buying a house', we were it.

We had too little money for them to be interested in us as clients. Instead, over the course of an hour, we were subjected to an infantilising lecture on sound financial behaviours for would-be parents from a rather smug baby boomer and his subservient millennial mini-me sidekick. It was reminiscent of that scene out of *Mary Poppins* when the children, Jane and Michael, visit their father's bank. Michael is told he must invest his tuppence by the bank's elders, but all he wants to do is to give it to the old lady selling breadcrumbs outside St Paul's to feed the birds. 'Birds', in our case, being the slightly less altruistic 'brunch'.

Why should such an inconsequential meeting stick in my head nearly seven years later? Well, because throughout the entire meeting, the two men never looked at, nor addressed, me once (bar pregnancy pleasantries). Their entire financial sermon was directed at my husband. I probably shouldn't have been surprised, but I left that meeting pissed off that I had been ignored but also confident of their short-sightedness. Within two years, I was earning the same amount as my husband, within three I would inherit money after my father's passing and within four years, I became the sole earner while my husband stayed at home to look after our second child. They imagined us to be the archetypal twentieth-century couple. We weren't. We were a 21st-century one, where the economics of marriage and cohabitation have been shaken up, and inheritance and the parental ATM is playing a key part.

In 2005, the Centre for Economics and Business Research produced a report that collated all the figures on women's financial positions in the UK: their past, present and predicted future. Whichever way you looked at it, this report confirmed that women were rising in the financial stakes compared to men. There were more female millionaires aged between eighteen and forty-four than male ones. In 2005, 70 per cent of women were in work compared to 56 per cent in 1971, while the rate of men in employment had dropped from 92 per cent in 1971 to 80 per cent in 2004. It reflected also on the rising numbers of female graduates and predicted that although the gender pay gap would persist, it would continue to narrow. In 1970, women received 37 per cent less gross hourly earnings than men; in 2005, the gap was 17 per cent. It predicted that by 2025, the gender pay gap would be 10 per cent. In 2005, 48 per cent of personal assets were already in female hands; it predicted that by 2025, 60 per cent of the nation's private wealth would be owned by women. Daughters were showing greater independence from their parents, with two-thirds of young women living outside the familial home compared to under half of men.[11] The report concluded that rising female financial empowerment was also combined with the advantage of longer life expectancy, which often made women first inheritors of male wealth. But this was combined with a discernible rise in women becoming independently wealthy, due to higher rates of education, entrepreneurship, improving wages and pensions. Finally, and perhaps most significantly for millennials, daughters in the twenty-first century were being granted the same economic opportunities, investments and gifts as sons.

So, how does the data stack up today? The female employment rate has continued to increase, albeit nominally to 72.1 per cent (it declined slightly after Covid), while the male rate has continued to fall, albeit by just 2 per cent to 78.1 per cent.[12] Women now outnumber men at university but by a significant amount: 28 per cent.[13] The gender pay gap is, of course, stubbornly persistent but below 10 per cent – 7.7 per cent for full-time workers.[14] Meanwhile, male adults living at home still outnumber women at a ratio of three to two.[15]

And yet there is one area where there has been barely a nudge: young single female homeownership. In 2004, there was talk of the new generation of financially independent and single women, the

'Bridget Jones generation', being responsible for almost a quarter of new mortgages, an increase of 10 per cent since the 1980s.[16] And yet over the past decade, the number of female mortgaged owner-occupiers has barely changed, rising just 2.7 per cent between 2011 and 2021.[17] So, despite increasing female financial independence, paradoxically, this has not manifested in greater levels of asset wealth. In the US, it is a different story: single female homeowners now outstrip single men.[18] Why the difference? Critically, the cost of a property in the UK. Despite our economic advances, women are delaying buying a home until they are in a couple because of the cost. But crucially, women are bringing to a relationship a level of financial independence, earning power, personal savings and inheritance that is equal to or sometimes surpasses their male counterparts. This has completely upended the economic dynamics between male and female relationships.

If our generation's love story has a predominant narrative, we would probably assume it was algorithmic. Online dating has been around now for a quarter of a century, first via websites such as Match.com and eHarmony in the early 2000s, then onto apps from Grindr to Tinder, bringing a culture of unending choice and unromantic gamification to the process. But there's evidence that millennial relationships are increasingly determined by wealth as much as algorithmic fate.

'It is a truth universally acknowledged, that a single man in possession of a large fortune must be in want of a wife.' *Pride and Prejudice* is a Regency tale where inheritance, fortune and wealth are the key determinants of a 'successful' marriage. Could it be that in the twenty-first century we are returning to Jane Austen's world? Probably because these are crude subjects and British people hate talking about them, money, marriage and class garner very little attention in our contemporary discussions about partnering up. In Olivia Petter's comprehensive dissection of the dating habits of our generation, *Millennial Love*, she does not address the role of wealth and money.[19] And yet economist Thomas Piketty in his seminal work, *Capital in the Twenty-First Century*, does. In his analysis of modern capitalism, Piketty goes back to the novels of Austen, amongst others. His goal being to show that when wealth is primarily inherited rather than made, marriage is a critical way to preserve or improve your status. In other words, in a 21st-century inheritocracy, there are heirs and heiresses, and it is mutually reinforcing if they marry each other. But what Austen never imagined, nor Piketty fully considered, was that the financial empowerment of women shakes this dynamic to the core.

It was once thought that opposites attract. In the 1970s, evolutionary biologist Robert Trivers expounded what he called 'parental investment theory'.[20] In his view, because the evolutionary goal is reproduction, and given men and women play different roles in that process, the genders (albeit in heteronormative relationships) tended to look for different characteristics in a mate. While women would veer towards security and protection, men would seek out the caring gene in women. Trivers was writing more than half a century ago. Since then, a new theory of attraction has come to supersede it.

As women have gained a stronger educational and economic foothold in society, it has upended how and what we look for in a partner. Rather than seek out opposite qualities in our partners, evidence now suggests we are attracted to similar characteristics. In short, women in modern societies with high numbers of female graduates have increasingly sought partners who match their values, education and even looks. This process, called 'assortative mating', is common in nature; birds with the same bright markings tend to mate with those with similar bright markings. Human beings, however, have different status indicators. As the number of graduates rose, so graduates increasingly tended to marry graduates.[21]

In 2023, the journal *Nature Human Behaviour* analysed data from more than 8 million couples – those that were married, engaged, co-parents and cohabitating partners across the US and the EU. They found a surprising degree of correlation between partners, not just on religious and political values but even physical traits such as height and body mass index. But there was a particular link with education – i.e. people with similar qualifications tended to be in relationships with each other.[22] Given that graduates often migrate to the same cities, work in the same professions, frequent the same places and operate within the same social networks, this isn't that surprising. Baby boomer unions were not defined by this educational matching but Gen X, who entered the marriage market with increasing numbers of female graduates, definitely were. Assessing the research, Peter Coy in the *New York Times* put it succinctly: 'Women have become better educated and prosperous, on average, and they would rather marry someone who is their socioeconomic equal.'[23]

The problem comes when there are significantly more female graduates than male graduates. This is something that David Willetts mentioned when I spoke to him. 'It's such delicate territory,' he said, prefacing his statement with an important caveat: 'When you have many more female graduates than male graduates and have assortative mating, there will inevitably be a group of female graduates who cannot find someone to partner with.'

Most of the data on assortative mating tends to concern heterosexual couples. The limited evidence on same-sex relationships, however, suggests there is not the same level of similarities in couples but much greater social diversity and income disparity. In the US, gay couples are less likely to have a partner with similar characteristics (e.g. of the same race, similar age or income). But lesbian couples are more likely to demonstrate commonalities, especially in education and income, which reinforces the idea that assortative mating is female-driven.

As a society, we are more gender and sexually fluid than ever before. There are also more interracial households than ever; just over a tenth of the population now live with someone of a different ethnicity – an increase of 8.7 per cent since 2011.[24] And yet when it comes to partnering up, there are signs that we've become evermore rigid in terms of class and educational status. In one UK survey, 40 per cent of upper-class participants said they would not even consider entering a long-term relationship with someone from a different social class.[25] And in our YouGov survey, 54 per cent of under-45s thought financial compatibility was important for the success of relationships.

Often, the blame for assortative mating is put on women for 'being too picky'. Feminist radical Germaine Greer, in typical blunt form, has suggested that intelligent women need to lower their expectations and 'marry truck drivers'. Speaking on Louis Theroux's podcast in 2024, Greer voiced her scepticism of what she called a 'balanced marriage':

We always think that we need that status in our husband. He doesn't think he needs that status in us. So, there's an imbalance at the very beginning … I mean [look at] Ted Hughes. Now, what do we think? Ted Hughes is a great poet and Sylvia [Plath] is a woman poet, a female poet and a martyr … The notion that you should be in competition with your husband is a bad notion.[26]

The Hughes/Plath example is one often cited, a tragic tale of women's submersion in marriage. And yet Greer misses the point here. The economics of marriage have been completely upended since she was rallying against it in the 1970s. Today, it is not that women are callously looking for 'status' in a husband. It is much more logical than that: a recognition that if a woman wants children (or frankly even if she doesn't), in an era where dual incomes are the norm, house buying is a challenge and childcare costs you more than your rent or mortgage, today's partnerships (in any form) come with greater financial and domestic expectations than ever.

So, what does assortative mating have to do with the inheritance economy? It's key because when people of a similar education, class and wealth marry, social inequality widens. A boss marrying his secretary technically helps reduce inequality, but when a lawyer marries a lawyer, it is a case of two members of the professional class combining forces. One of the unintended consequences of more women going to university and marrying male graduates is that joint brain power tends to mean joint wealth. Marrying within your class has always been the way for the aristocracy to preserve and protect their assets. Are these practices now being aped lower down the social scale?

A report from the think tank the Resolution Foundation concluded that 'people tend to couple up with those who have similar inheritance expectations to their own' and that 'assortative mating is likely to amplify these absolute gaps in individuals' future wealth transfers at the household level'.[27] In other words, we are potentially seeing a triple privilege solidifying in society, whereby monied, educated, high-earning millennials are coupling up with other monied, educated, high-earning millennials, reinforcing this privilege and merging two Banks of Mum and Dad.

It is these couples who can afford to buy in London, it is these couples who can comfortably afford to start building a family, it is these couples who are more likely to marry rather than just cohabitate. Perhaps it doesn't need saying, but this is all decidedly unromantic, goes against most of the dating advice and narratives we were told growing up and something we are rarely open about as societies, couples or families. I do remember a particular conversation with one ex-boyfriend of mine who told me that he couldn't afford to subsidise the life he would want for us. At the time, it felt like an odd thing to say – especially as we had only been dating a few months. It wasn't like I was some wannabe housewife of Cheshire demanding a mansion or, frankly, at that stage of our relationship, even dinner. We were woefully incompatible in more important ways too, but that conversation stuck in my head as being both honest and a mercenary approach to life. Tellingly, he subsequently went on to marry someone extremely wealthy. In fact, he is the one who has become the Cheshire housewife.

In the eighteenth century, it was common for the bride's family to pay the groom a dowry – a sum of cash upon marriage. Today, we are seeing an updated version emerging in the privileged class, whereby women are bringing to marriage personal wealth but also a parental gift or a promise of a later inheritance. This is why parents and in-laws are more involved in supporting couples than ever before, in the form of housing and, increasingly, financial investment for the grandchildren. If ever there was an appropriate time to call marriage a marriage market, it is today.

Who Is Getting Married These Days?

The institution of marriage has been out of vogue for a long time. It was our parents' generation who started to reject 'till death do us part', with marriage rates steadily declining since the 1970s. Cohabitation has been rising since then, but millennials are doing it differently from previous generations. We are more likely to cohabitate with successive partners rather than just one. I lived with two men before moving in with the one who became my husband. Those previous relationships involved blissful years nesting like DINKs with trips to IKEA, housewarming parties and shared bookshelves. Both ended with removal vans, Big Yellow Box storage rentals and redirected post. Most of my friends' experience was the same: in long-term relationships with those you lived with but not necessarily for ever. Our parents didn't do this to the same degree, with living together often working as a trial marriage. But we millennials are unlikely to marry our first cohabitating partner nor be with them indefinitely. The rise of the Gen Z DINKs (logical in a cost-of-living crisis) also suggests that this trend is continuing in the next generation, too. Cohabitation with multiple partners is evident across all classes. When it comes to marriage, however, it is a different story.

Marriage may be in decline overall, but the middle classes are still getting hitched. In the UK, the number of lone-parent families has remained consistent over the past decade at 15 per cent, while cohabitation – nearly 20 per cent of couples – has been the fastest-growing family type.[28] But today, unions are sharply divided by class, in a way that they were not in the 1970s and 1980s when our parents were getting married. And it is not cultural; it is not that the middle classes 'value' marriage or family life more. The fact is, for the middle class, when you have asset wealth, it makes more sense to get married – and to stay married.

US academic Melissa S. Kearney, author of *The Two-Parent Privilege*, is very clear on the reason for the decline in working-class marriages: the collapse of job security and wages for working-class men, especially since the 1990s.[29] To be blunt, the loss of status, good jobs and decent pay, along with affordable housing, has made working-class men supposedly less appealing in the marriage stakes. But as much as this is a difficult story about men, it is also an empowering story of the rising economic independence of working-class women. According to Richard Reeves, in the US, men's wages peaked in the 1970s and have declined ever since. While professional men at the top have surged ahead, working-class millennial men will earn about 10 per cent less in real terms than baby boomer men. Women's wages, on the other hand, have risen across the board.[30]

The Pew Research Center in the US has gone so far as to say that there has been a 'gender role reversal in the gains from marriage … In the past, when relatively few wives worked, marriage enhanced the economic status of women more than that of men. In recent decades, however, the economic gains associated with marriage have been greater for men than for women.'[31]

I spoke to Sarah, thirty-one, from Newcastle, about the challenges she has faced as a millennial lone parent with two kids. She has relied on her parents to help her where they can and received support from the council for her housing, but fundamentally, her story is one of independence from men and an impressive tale of female fulfilment.

'My parents divorced when I was very young, but they've remained close, like best friends,' she tells me. Sarah's father is still working in a factory, while her mother has done multiple jobs 'although less so now because of her health – she struggles to stand up all day', Sarah clarifies. Her mother rents a council property and is in the process of buying it, while her father has always owned his own house.

Due to her dyslexia, Sarah always struggled in school, but it was a traumatic incident when she was in her early teens that derailed her school years: 'I had no memory of it, and I didn't talk about it as I didn't understand it, but I guess now when I think about it, it is why I was probably so distracted in school. I stopped going to class altogether. Obviously in the long run it wasn't great. My brothers both went to uni, whereas I didn't.' Sarah got pregnant at sixteen and continued to live at home. 'I was focused on being a mother … I was kind of lost, though. I didn't really know what I wanted to do.' She started going to college, doing hairdressing and getting creative online with make-up, but she struggled to get a job or stick to one. She moved into her own council house when she was eighteen.

'That was when I met my son's dad. We had [a] child, but he was a bit of a player and slept with someone else. So, I broke it off. I struggled a lot with my mental health. I was on antidepressants.' Sarah tells me her biggest challenge, though, was when her first partner took her to court for custody of her daughter. Her mum paid for a solicitor for the initial court hearing, but after that Sarah had to defend herself. 'It was honestly the most terrifying thing I've ever done,' she tells me.

As part of the court settlement, Sarah was given access to a therapist, which 'changed her life'. She was able to address her childhood trauma and has been able to get her life back on track. Sarah elaborates: '[the therapist] helped me understand things in my life, how my mind works and how certain things happen. That was the point I started finding myself and I started getting on top of things.' Sarah came off antidepressants and started getting physically fit. 'I no longer struggle with my mental health. I also got a job I was able to stick at.' Sarah also informs me that she has started her own business. 'You're gonna think I'm mad, but I'm selling therapeutic crystals. It's my absolute passion. My absolute dream is to have a shop one day.' Sarah speaks with an energy and lightness that suggests that after all her challenges, she has found focus. She is full of plans for the future. 'I would also eventually like to get my own house. I want to show my kids that it doesn't matter if you haven't done well in school, it's all about finding something you are passionate about and working hard on. I often think about when I'm old what will I have to give my kids? Not much, but I can give them desire, dreams and passion.'

'You're giving them an example,' I say, 'which is the best inheritance there is.'

Our conversation had swerved around the main themes of the book, and I wanted to bring it back to the central premise. What did she think about family privilege in the UK? Surprisingly, and perhaps wisely, she brings it down to a difference in mental health and resilience.

'I believe that families in harder positions struggle more with their mental health. I'm not saying those who have opportunities don't struggle, but they have more in place to thrive from. Our dreams and goals aren't as easily achieved; we have to grow on our own without the world already having our backs.'

Joint Earners, Separate Accounts

Dual-income households are now the norm in the UK. It depends, of course, how many children you have as to whether the mother works part- or full-time, but the proportion of mothers in any type of employment is now 73 per cent.[32] Overall, 58 per cent of families with children have both parents working full-time. It is a fact rarely commented on that our parents lived in predominantly male-breadwinner households; whereas we are living in predominantly dual-income households – that are effectively working twice as hard but are half as rich!

But dual-income households pose a distinct question for men. If women have increased their economic contribution to the household, for this to be fair, equal and even practical, men *have* to increase their domestic contribution to the household. Most millennials can't afford to do what previous generations of middle-class women have done, which is outsource this labour (be it cleaning or childcare) to working-class women or migrant labour. There's positive evidence that millennial fathers are stepping up more than their predecessors, but we're far from parity. In a sign of the times, we have a new term for the domesticated millennial male: the 'doesband'. That is those who are relieving their female partner of a fair chunk of unpaid labour at home. A doesband, amongst other things, knows where the Calpol is, contributes to the parent WhatsApp groups and does just as many school drop-offs as Mum.[33]

Millennial partnerships may be edging towards greater equality in the domestic realm, but this is a slow, unfinished revolution that raises a new set of complicated questions: whose career is more important? How do we divvy up the unpaid domestic labour? How do we manage childcare? Can women let go of the domestic load and allow it to be done even if it is not completed to their standards? These kinds of questions and tensions were brought into clear focus during the 2020 Covid lockdowns, with many working mothers forced into fighting for the time and space to work while home-schooling. Nor has there been any let up since, with the subsequent economic squeeze, which has prompted many mothers to step out of the workplace altogether. This shake-up of gender roles requires more than ever subtle negotiation, balance and compromise. There are no easy answers. But one factor is taking on increasing importance, potentially alleviating or aggravating these tensions: parents and in-laws. Maybe they part-paid for the house, maybe they regularly help with childcare, maybe they are paying for the child's school fees or university fees, maybe they are funding two weeks in the sun. Maybe one set of parents stumps up more than the other. The point is that millennial marriages are now not only about navigating the new gender rule book with your spouse but also navigating the new parent/in-law dynamic in an inheritocracy.

Another indicator of this shake-up of money within marriage has been the decline of the joint bank account. A survey from 2019 found that just 32 per cent of couples aged between twenty-five to thirty-four had a joint account compared with 59 per cent of baby boomers.[34] It was something that I personally resisted for a long time, especially when my husband was earning more than me. I only succumbed to the idea when I was on maternity leave. The tipping point came when I called him at work in a panic asking him to transfer some cash into my account so that I could buy some nappies for our son. It is some bizarre logic that I was perfectly happy to rely on my parents throughout my twenties and early thirties yet felt deeply unnerved by even the thought of being financially reliant on my husband while I was caring for *our* child. In the end, we opened a joint account, but I kept my own.

I did a straw poll of my friends and only one said she had a joint account. But again, like me, she likes to keep her own money for security. This protective and independent streak amongst millennial women is backed up by the data.[35] When asked about separate finances, couples say their main reason for doing so is wanting to retain control of their own money. Some worried about the relationship breaking up, while some said they didn't want to explain their purchase decisions to their partner. One-third of women said they would never consider opening a joint account, while one-fifth who set up a combined account for things like bills and joint expenses admitted that they had a separate account for their own spending. Sure, instant banking and money apps may have negated the need for a joint bank account. But the broader rationale is that we are entering partnerships later, after years of being financially independent, and also live in a world where divorce is common. Millennial women have been conditioned to think that being financially self-sufficient or financially reliant on your parents is safer, more secure and possibly more enabling than being financially reliant on a man. Tellingly, women are more likely than men (24 per cent versus 16 per cent) to see their inheritance as theirs rather than something to be shared with a partner or spouse, according to the *Inheritocracy* YouGov survey.

Lucy, forty-two, lives in Scotland and embodies this attitude of female financial independence. Lucy grew up in a middle-class but not especially wealthy family in south-east London. Her parents divorced during her A-levels and they sold the family home, which meant unlike most of her friends, Lucy did not have a base to come home to during the university holidays.

Lucy tells me that she has always been good with money. By the time she was twenty-five, she had a deposit for a flat – a combination of her grandmother's inheritance, her own money and additional help from her mother.

'I'll admit I couldn't have done it without my mum,' she explains, 'but equally I look at all my friends at that time and they were all spending their money going out. They used to get so annoyed with me for being so boring. But then they also all had a home to go back to, which I didn't. I wanted somewhere that was mine.'

After renting out the spare room to friends, Lucy moved her then boyfriend in, and they have been together ever since. 'When it comes to your partner and yourself, how do you view your money and assets?' I ask.

'Well, it's always been my flat; not ours. We don't have a joint account, and we are not married, on the basis that should our relationship ever break down, I don't want him to get half of anything that is mine. It sounds really harsh, and I love him very much, but I've also seen how people who love each other can go awry. When it comes to our relationship, his money is his money and mine is mine. I've always earned more than him; and even when he was unemployed, I let him know that I wouldn't support him for long. I know that's unromantic!'

'Far from it, it sounds sensible,' I reply.

Lucy's mum is now living in her flat while she has moved to Scotland. 'I don't charge her rent, but she pays bills. She's been very savvy with money too, especially when it comes to property – she has a couple of flats across London that she rents out. In fact, me, my mum and sister have a joint account to run these properties. She didn't have a big enough income to get a mortgage, so she used me and my sister as the second buyer. I'm named on the two flats she bought.'

'So, you have a joint account with your mother and sister but not your male partner?' I say, surprised and fascinated in equal measure.

'I guess so,' she laughs.

I wondered how often Lucy sees her father and what, if any,

support he gives her now or she expects in the future. 'My dad is very quiet about [money] and tight; he will moan about parking fees. He has lent me money in the past but made it very clear that it was a loan. Part of me thinks he paid for my sister's wedding, and I've never got married so I think I was sort of owed that money. It is so different from my mum who actively always wants to help.'

'How often do you see him?' I ask, realising I may be stepping on sensitive terrain.

'I see him maybe three times a year. He has remarried and has three stepchildren who have all been given money. Sometimes it feels like it is my inheritance that is being spent on them. I'm a bit resentful of that. It has never been discussed; I've never met them. I sound like a terrible person, but it is weird it is not said.' Lucy's honesty revealed the complications that divorce and remarriage bring to the inheritance equation, while the financial solidarity between her, her mother and her sister showed an impressive all-female alternative.

I decided to speak to Professor Helen McCarthy, historian of modern Britain and author of *Double Lives: A History of Working Motherhood*, about female dependency on the Bank of Mum and Dad and a declining reliance on men. I presented her with my theory on the economic status of millennial women.

'Well,' she said, 'the picture you describe in the twenty-first century sort of feels like a very weird throwback to the independent women of the nineteenth century.'

'Were they financially reliant on family money then?' I asked.

'Yes, just look at someone like Beatrice Webb,' McCarthy replied. Webb was a leading sociologist, Fabian, feminist and social reformer in the late nineteenth century. With her husband Sidney Webb, Beatrice founded the London School of Economics and the *New Statesman*. 'She was given a private income from her family, the

Potters, who were Liverpudlian merchants, and when her father died, she was given an endowment for life,' McCarthy tells me.

Beatrice was in a relationship with radical politician Joseph Chamberlain for several years, but she broke it off when he refused to accept her need for independence. She later married Sidney Webb, and it was her private income that enabled him to give up his job and for them to both concentrate on their social causes.

McCarthy offers an important caveat to this historical comparison, though: 'Beatrice Webb was very much the exception. Few women had this familial independence. The idea of marriage as offering security to women was very much the nineteenth-century ideal but so was the idea of a spinster, an unmarried childless woman, as an object of pity.'

I liked this idea of 'familial independence' and recognised it in myself; the idea that for some, the Bank of Mum and Dad has paradoxically afforded women greater independence from men but also comes with greater dependency on parents.

Breadwinning and Breeding

My family was unique in one critical way in the 1980s: I was raised by a stay-at-home father while my mother was the full-time breadwinner. She worked for the John Lewis Partnership, which from a child's perspective, seemed a generous environment for a working mother. I remember regularly hanging out at her office after school. She always made parents' evenings, shows and was usually home by 7 p.m. Yet from her perspective, there were subtle and some not-so-subtle difficulties in being a working mother back then. The questions asked about the length of her maternity leave, the almost public denial she had to exhibit about wanting children before she had them, the assumptions made about her husband's job and salary. Today's female breadwinners face far less stigma and fewer questions.

In the UK, one poll from 2018 found that one in four women make more money than their partners.[36] Rather depressingly, there is also evidence that female-breadwinner marriages are more likely to result in male infidelity and divorce.[37] Managing male emasculation in this scenario is a challenge that is frankly not talked about enough. Nor does it naturally follow that in female-breadwinner households, men take on more of the domestic load. Researchers at University College London found that 45 per cent of female breadwinners still do most of the household chores despite earning the most.[38] Even in households where there is wage parity, 93 per cent of women do the majority of unpaid domestic labour. Raina Brands, who led the research at UCL, suggested that this isn't always because men are not doing enough or won't step up; rather, it's women's compulsion 'to compensate for violating traditional gender roles' and therefore 'redoubling their contributions at home'.[39] I must remember that when the guilt and victimhood takes hold.

Women are marrying later, marrying those of similar economic status and bringing more to the marriage in terms of wealth and earnings. But what happens when things go wrong? When couples get divorced, UK law stipulates that there is an equal split of wealth, including pensions and any gifts or inheritance. The law was constructed chiefly to prevent husbands from leaving wives and children destitute, but in an age when many women are bringing wealth and wages to a marriage and set to lose a lot if it goes wrong, is the current framework still workable? In Switzerland, they have legislated against the notion of continual financial dependency after a separation, although early assessments of the new law suggest that women remain at a financial disadvantage, particularly if the woman in question has taken time out of the workplace or not developed her financial earning power while married.

One critical sign of the importance of inheritance and wealth in marriage has been the rise of prenuptial agreements. Long associated with celebrities and the uber-rich, they are now gaining popularity amongst the wealthy middle class.[40] If marriage is not just the uniting of two separate assets but the uniting of two separate inheritances, it makes sense to safeguard it. It is no surprise that much of the impetus for a prenup has come not from the couple but from the parents anxious to protect their assets. Kate Daly, co-founder of the Amicable divorce service and host of *The Divorce Podcast*, explains this rising trend: 'We are now in the situation where baby boomers are passing down their wealth, and because people are marrying later, they have a higher chance of acquiring assets today in business and property prior to coupling up.'[41] Prenups for cohabitees are also an evolving trend. One CEO told me that he instructed his lawyers to generate a contract for his daughter's boyfriend when he bought his daughter a flat, so that the boyfriend couldn't claim any of it if they broke up.

Prenups are not legally binding, but they have become increasingly legitimate thanks to one case. In 2010, in a landmark ruling, the UK Supreme Court judged for the first time that a prenup could be considered in the case of Katrin Radmacher. Overturning centuries of legal history, such agreements were previously not seen as resolute because women had never been able to sit at the bargaining table on equal terms.

Heiress to a large fortune, Radmacher met her future husband Nicolas Granatino, a French banker, in a Mayfair nightclub in 1997. Though they both came from well-to-do families, she was significantly wealthier than Granatino, who at the time was on a £120,000 salary as a banker at JP Morgan. On her father's insistence, a prenup was signed before the wedding, which stated that neither would benefit from the wealth, inheritance or property of the other if they divorced. At the time, Radmacher saw it as the necessary proof for her father that the pair were marrying for love, not money.

Eight years later, the prenup was put to the test. Granatino had by then left his job at JP Morgan and was now an academic in bio-tech at Oxford University, earning significantly less, at £30,000. During the initial divorce proceedings, Granatino argued that the prenup was not legally binding as the family had hidden the extent of their wealth when he signed it. He was originally awarded a total of £5,560,000 to cover two properties, shared parenting costs for their two children and an annual income for life. That is, until Rad-macher successfully appealed the decision. Her defence was that the prenup had agreed that his long-term needs should not be funded by her family inheritance. On winning the case, Radmacher's lawyer summed up the significance of the Supreme Court ruling uphold-ing prenups: 'Couples can now decide in the best of times what the outcome will be in the worst of times.'[42]

And it is to the worst of times that we now turn.

Chapter 7

Will Millennials *Really* Be the Richest Generation in History?

On his deathbed, my father had one request: he wanted to be buried in the garden of the home in Tooting where he had lived his entire life, and which had been in our family since the 1940s. Not knowing what this would entail, but desperate to say yes, my two sisters and I tentatively agreed.

In the days after my father's death, I got my teeth into this bureaucratic challenge, which was a worthy distraction tactic to soothe my aching grief. While it may take months of submitting plans and navigating laws to build a side extension on your house, it turns out it is comparatively easy to get permission to dig a grave and bury the dead on your property. Our vicar friend was happy to administer the necessary spiritual process of consecrating the land. All we needed was special dispensation from the council. This was swiftly given the green light, although the official on the phone felt compelled to warn us: 'You might want to consider how a burial site on your property has the potential to devalue the house by some £50,000.'

'Oh, that's not a concern for us', I immediately replied, knowing that it was not my mother's plan to sell. Just as well, since graves are understandably not one of the chief characteristics house-seekers are looking for when they log on to Rightmove. Aristocrats are often buried on their vast estates for the very reason that the land is expected to remain in family hands. A burial in a semi-detached house in Tooting? Not so much. But my dad's request felt like the ultimate example of baby boomer 'man and his castle' behaviour. No doubt he would be happy that we could only sell our ancestral home semi-literally 'over his dead body'.

I should explain that my father's grave sits in a ninety-foot garden of lush green lawn and flowers, rather than the concrete patio that makes for most London outdoor spaces. He was laid to rest under the apple tree where he and my mother had spent the night of their first anniversary as a couple half a century before in 1967. The coffin had been lowered, as per my father's request, to the sixteenth-century King James Bible burial rites followed by the Sex Pistols' riotous anthem 'Anarchy in the UK'. We stood solemnly in silence at the foot of the grave as the priest read 'ashes to ashes; dust to dust', then the thumping drumbeat kicked in, followed by the rooster-like sound of Johnny Rotten's voice screaming about being the anti-Christ and anarchist. As the pall-bearers judderingly lowered my father's coffin, our sadness switched to smirks and, for some, an urge to pogo.

Up until now, we have focused on what an inheritocracy looks like while our parents are alive. But what happens when they die? We have never known life without the baby boomers, but we're about to find out what that means. I write about my own father's passing because in a book about inheritocracy, it is too easy to think in crude terms of monetary gain or cold data. But in the immediate term, it is the emotional, logistical and bureaucratic burdens that prevail. Dying, death itself, funerals, wills, financial advice, probate all take an emotional toll but also involve complexity and time. When it comes to inheritance, it may take up endless *years*, cause a family dispute and result in no inheritance at all. Still, it is only in that transfer of wealth down the family tree over the next twenty years that Britain's inheritocracy will be realised.

This chapter will explore how that will happen, and what it means.

How the Baby Boomers Will Go

Sex Pistols and the King James Bible – a mixture of anarchy and tradition – my father's funeral was very, well, *my father*. It was as ambitious as any state funeral. After the church service, his wicker coffin was placed on a grocer's cart, pulled into the middle of the road, down Tooting High Street, led by a tartan-clad bagpiper playing 'Going Home' (and no, we're not Scottish). The 100-odd congregation walked the half-mile route five generations of my family have trodden since the mid-nineteenth century. We held up traffic through this major south London street; many people stopped, a few respectfully doffed baseball caps. We passed the grand cinema, once host to film premieres, latterly a decaying bingo hall.

I envisaged it back in its glamour days: the place where my grandfather, a professional gambler, had first met my grandmother, a young milk delivery driver with a horse and cart, asking her for a light on *those* cinema steps in wartime England.

The wake was held in our garden. My young father's art studio was reconstructed as if he had just downed his tools for tea, the toy soldiers and circus he had built us as children laid out like it was Christmas morning. His life in photographs scaled the length of the ninety-foot garden fence. The singers and musicians who had come through our house over the years were reunited for one final gig and played once more as we danced and sang round his grave till midnight. To make the day as 'dad' as it could be was not just the best way of honouring him; it was in truth a selfish act on our part, then the only way our grief could morph into action.

'There wasn't anyone there who actually knew him,' lamented my dad's best friend as he was leaving. He was right; he had known my father since their early teens, but he was the only one there that day who had. In part, this was because my father had outlived most of his hedonistic friends; an uncommon number had reached tragic ends early in their lives. But it was also right that most of the congregation were my age. It may take a Doodle and about 100 WhatsApp exchanges these days to get my friends and I together around a dinner table, but in this instance, they dropped everything when I needed them. They were there not just for me but because my father was as much a part of their upbringing as their own. Friends' parents are the additional authority figures in your formative years, always more benign than your own and you are always more grateful for their hosting, cooking and taxiing services than you are your own. And even as you hit midlife, they are amongst the few people in your life who still think of you in freeze-frame, as the awkward but aspirational pre-adult you once were. But all this is coupled with a morbid realisation that when your parents' friends die, a generation is gradually fading away, marking the inexorable passage of time and the inevitable changes that accompany it.

Everyone commented what a remarkable day my father's funeral was, but even in this, he may be typical of his generation. Not that more people are getting buried in their gardens – I doubt he has established a trend there. But in unique funerals that celebrate life, which is something that baby boomers, as they die out, are revolutionising.

Over the past fifty years, as other Christian ceremonies – marriages, baptisms and holy communion – declined, funeral rituals for a long time were the one sacrament that held firm. No longer it seems. Today, just one in ten people say they want a traditional religious funeral.[1] There's still some desire for the familiarity and gravitas that Christianity brings to the messy, humbling end to life, but there's now a tendency to cherry-pick and mash it up with what we want. As a society, we've airbrushed out the bits of Christianity – hell, sin and humility – that jar with modern sensibilities. These days funerals tend to focus not on death as a reunion with God but rather the remembrance of a life lived.

How we think about death tells us so much about how we view life. As we saw in Chapter 2, baby boomers were the first generation of individualists, baptised as the 'Me' generation, a culture of individualism that has only intensified since. In 1952, participants in the US were asked, 'Do you think you are an important person?' Only 12 per cent of people thought they were. When the question was repeated in 1990, 80 per cent of people said yes.[2] There is no greater statistic to explain the past seventy years of social change. And when we consider ourselves as incredibly important, commemorating death tends not to imply that the best is yet to come.

One study in the US found that baby boomers see their funeral to be 'their crowning performance. They want to be the writer, the director AND the star.' This has been coupled with the rise of location funerals, which, according to one survey, now include zoos, golf courses, even a McDonald's drive-thru as modern sites of solemnity.[3] Likewise, personal memorabilia, from racquets to guitars to teddy bears, have replaced rosary beads as the 21st-century burial items of choice.

Tech will only make this more possible and more naff. How long before holograms of the deceased are giving their own eulogies? I'm only half joking. Baby boomers are the oldest generation en masse to have handed over their personal data to tech companies. When they die, these digital vaults will, very soon, become big business. Want to remember your mum's apple crumble recipe? No fear, Grim Reaper Zuckerberg will be on hand to generate an AI deepfake of your mother to guide you through it. Want your children to meet their grandfather who'll read them *The Gruffalo* as a bedtime story? No problem, just ask ChatGPT to clone his voice and deliver it along with the entire Julia Donaldson back catalogue. If this sounds extreme, note that there is already a website where you can scan your old family photos in and make them come 'alive' via AI-generated videos. If the dead have the potential to live, digitally, for ever, surely that will change not only how we commemorate them but potentially how we feel about inheritance.

All this is probably not what someone in the prime of life wants to read, but we need to recognise that, just as an ageing society and a low birth rate is our future, so, as morbid as it sounds, we need to prepare for one that is dominated by our parents' generation passing. In death, as in life, baby boomers will continue to control the conversation. We are set for a future where assisted dying becomes increasingly common, social care abuses will take on ever-greater salience and inheritance disputes will be a regular feature for many families. As more people die, with more inheritable fortunes, this issue will go mainstream, dominating the political agenda as much as pension promises or house prices do today. We tend to assume that all the consequences of an ageing society are problems for the old. Arguably, they are a deeper challenge for the younger generations, who will be tasked with trying to resolve, prioritise and fund them.

But this is only a narrow political perspective. The real impact, of course, will be personally and psychologically. Six years on from losing my father, and after a second child, half a decade of marriage, a global pandemic and writing this book, life's constant motion has created a sedimentary layer over my grief. But the pain remains palpable. Losing a parent hits people differently, and also differently at different stages of life. Friends who have gone through this loss have experienced all kinds of feelings, often all at the same time: rejection, as well as reconciliation and peace. And for those yet to go through it, it is one of the most dreaded inevitabilities of adult life.

Few admit how freeing it can be, though. Despite the grief and sadness, on a personal level, losing my father remade and matured me. And maybe that's a positive message that millennials need to imbibe in a culture defined by so much parental dependency.

So, How Much Is There?

In 2024, global property consultant Knight Frank claimed that millennials were poised to become the richest generation in history.[4] Well, *affluent millennials* that is. This was news to those battered and bruised by the consistent financial obstacles of the past fifteen years: firstly, the ripples of the 2008 crisis, then Brexit upheaval, then Covid, followed by the cost-of-living crisis and rising interest rates. Unsurprisingly, Knight Frank's claim was met with ridicule and derision by commentators.

I'm not convinced what value there is in telling even affluent millennials that there is money coming down the line, if anything it creates false expectation. As the journalist Harriet Walker surmised: 'The gulf in intergenerational wealth has turned my age group into so many Prince Charleses, greying as it awaits a birthright that comes with the worst price tag imaginable.' In this, she recognises too that she is one of the 'lucky infantilised ones, with generous parents who still help out with lifeline loans and take us on holiday'.[5]

Another journalist, Isolde Walters, admits she was only able to pursue a perilous career as a freelance writer because her father agreed to give her an 'inheritance in advance' to buy a flat in London. But when she read the headline that millennials were set to be the richest generation, her first thought was, 'What about the people who won't inherit?' Seeing it as 'confirmation that Britain has become an inheritocracy where only those with access to family money can hope to buy a home in the south-east', she noted that this is 'hardly something to celebrate'.[6] But while Walters is spot on, it is not a simple tale of winners and losers. Instead, it's an escalating scale of inheritance determined by unscriptable and uncertain factors.

So, what are the projections? Because they are just projections right now. The baby boomers have two main assets: pensions and housing, with both worth around £5 trillion to £6 trillion each. Most pensions, however, are not inheritable and will be potentially used up in old age. That still leaves £5 trillion to £6 trillion in asset wealth to be inherited. What the financial services industry likes to call the Great Wealth Transfer is not just something that affects the 1 per cent, nor the wealthiest 25 per cent. The issue of inheritance when our parents die will affect a significant number of families across Britain.

Of course, it is not the mere fact that families stand to inherit *something*, it is the *value* of that inheritance that matters. And because so much of the wealth is in property, the regional differences are profound. Those with parents living in London stand to inherit twice as much as those in the north-east. A Londoner's inheritance (linked to house prices) is estimated to be worth £440,000, whereas in the north-east it is £190,000. The latter is not an insignificant sum but obviously a great deal less.[7] But what is the likely value of our inheritance in comparison to our overall lifetime earnings? Millennial inheritances on average will be worth 16 per cent of our lifetime earnings (up from the 9 per cent for Gen X). There is, however, a significant divide here. For the top fifth of society, inheritance will boost their lifetime incomes by 29 per cent, but just 5 per cent for the bottom fifth.[8] That millennials will be the richest generation in history doesn't stack up across the income divide. And this data presumes just one inheritance. As we have seen, an increasing number of millennial middle-class couples may be fortunate enough to rely on two inheritances from different sides of the family.

Pointedly, when it comes to the issue of inheritance, there are layers of privilege. The Institute for Fiscal Studies has concluded that 'inheritances are set to increase inequalities in lifetime income between those with richer and poorer parents'.[9] In other words, if you think the Bank of Mum and Dad is dividing your friendship groups while you are in your thirties, it will be even more apparent and divisive when millennials are in their sixties. It will probably mean the difference between those who are able to retire and those who will have to stay working.

Be Nice to Grandma!

A few months after my father's funeral, my sisters, my mother and I found ourselves in an altogether more conventional scene: sat around our solicitor's office as our family lawyer read out my father's will. With few investments, no pension and no debts, there were no surprises. Full ownership of their properties went to my mother. And in this example is the major plot twist in the baby boomer inheritance story that seems obvious but few appreciate: before the great generational wealth transfer, there is often the great gender wealth transfer – to the widow. This is because most boomers are in heterosexual marriages and women still tend to outlive men by some 3.8 years.[10] Moreover, it is in most cases more tax efficient to pass wealth across the family tree than down it – i.e. interspousal inheritance is tax free.

It has been estimated that 60 per cent of the nation's private wealth will be in female hands by 2025, but a fair amount of this will be in baby boomer widows' hands, by inheriting their husband's wealth. It is a remarkable financial moment for a critical mass of privileged baby boomer women, many of whom gave up careers, paused work for children, worked part-time or have deficient or non-existent pensions.

Historically, older women, especially widows, have been the poorest members of society. In contrast, today they are one of the most affluent. The financial ascendance of wealthy baby boomer women is rarely commented on and yet just look at their impact on property: in 2021, women made up 48 per cent of the 2.6 million buy-to-let landlords in the UK.[11] Older women are now the ones gaining all those 'super-host' five-star ratings on Airbnb, representing 55 per cent of hosts globally.[12] And forget Gen Z crypto bros, it is this demographic that has seen a substantial rise in entrepreneurship – there has been a 132 per cent leap between 2007 and 2017 of women aged sixty-five and over in opening business accounts, the biggest surge of any age group.[13] All this points to an impressive 'third age' for baby boomer women. The writer Dolly Alderton once commented that she felt that despite the obvious cultural hostility to older women, her mother's generation were ageing better than baby boomer men. They were liberated from the physical pressures, harassment and sexism that comes with being a younger woman and were embracing this freedom. She felt that the opposite could be said of ageing men, who yearn for the freedoms that the patriarchy brought them when they were young. That women are somehow better adaptors to the ageing process (and more social beings) is one of the many reasons I'm glad that my father died before my mother.

In some families, however, Grandma is about to be, if she is not already, the chief financial officer. For some of these women, this is a reversal of a lifetime spent in financial dependency on the male breadwinner. This financial liberation for baby boomer women probably feels hard won and earned. For others, such as my mother, they were the breadwinner, who had their own financial independence and accumulated wealth, later inheriting their husband's assets and even more familial power. For some, they inherited from their own families, made their own wealth but now yield a considerable influence over the next two generations. There are also an increasing number of baby boomer female divorcees who lay some claim to their deceased husband's estate but who may have suffered financial hardship in the wake of the divorce. The dynamic of inheritance cuts differently for blended families, as we shall see, where the death of a patriarch may leave complex relations that disadvantage both the former and the current spouse.

I wanted to talk to a baby boomer woman who had experienced this tale of growing financial empowerment as a widow. Angela considers herself one of the lucky few. Now aged seventy-eight, she left school at fifteen, met her husband in her teens and managed to buy a house almost immediately in Hammersmith in the 1960s for just £2,000. Angela gave up work when she had her second child but returned to working in retail when her children were older. She and her husband moved up the residential ladder, first moving to Wimbledon Park and subsequently Wimbledon Village, one of the most expensive real estate locations in London.

Angela's life is a tale of social mobility and wealth accumulation through property and, as it turns out, freeholds: 'I have three of them that are due which will each cost about £50,000 to £60,000. My husband always said the leases will come good and he was right there.' Angela retired at sixty-seven, downsized and has bought an additional property to rent out. She inherited wealth from her husband when he died but also received a significant sum – £150,000 – from her 'great-aunt Mary' ('She wasn't my aunt, she was actually my mother's cousin's wife'). Angela also inherited a substantial sum from her oldest friend Brigette, who had no children, siblings or husband: 'She was what was known as a professional mistress back then.' Brigette gifted all her friends a sum; Angela received £300,000. 'I get quarterly reports from Brigette's financial advisor. It just seems to go up every year. The problem is that I don't think it is my money; I'm loath to spend it,' she says.

Angela currently gives her grandchildren a monthly 'Nan allowance' and enjoys taking the whole family on holiday. 'I just feel very lucky,' she says. I nod in agreement, slightly staggered by all the figures. Hers is a distinctly Thatcherite property-driven wealth tale, one that would be improbable now.

Angela's story also points to how inheritance often extends well beyond husband and wife. As chief carers, women are often the great beneficiaries in society. But this has not always been the case. In fact, it was only in the 1920s that legislation was passed to finally allow equal inheritance across families and for wives to inherit their husband's property. And in some families, the rule of primogeniture – that is, hereditary positions bypassing daughters and going to sons – still exists. When the 6th Duke of Westminster died in 2016, the rule of primogeniture meant that the title went straight to his third child, Lord Hugh, and not his elder sisters. This honouring of the male line still exists in some religious codes. According to the Halacha, Jewish law states that inheritance must be divided equally amongst the male heirs, who must in turn support any sisters.[14] Under sharia law, Muslim male children take 50 per cent more of the estate than female children, and only a fraction of the estate is left to the surviving spouse.[15] This in effect means that in many cases, Muslim families who follow sharia law are open to larger inheritance tax bills. Likewise, with polygynous marriages. Under the current law, those that take place abroad are recognised but not those that occur in the UK. That means there is no legal recourse under the British system for a 'second wife' to inherit anything if she was married to her husband here in, for instance, an Islamic or other religious ceremony.

Evidence points to a push back from South Asian women against the prevailing culture of male preference when it comes to inheritance. In one dispute that reached the High Court, an 83-year-old Sikh widow, Mrs Kaur, from the West Midlands, fought for the right to an inheritance from her husband of sixty-six years who had left her nothing from an estate worth £1 million. Her husband, who had wished to leave it 'solely down the male line' had left everything to his two sons and nothing to his widow and four daughters. The judge ruled that Mrs Kaur should get 50 per cent of the net value of the estate given that no provision had been made for her. Her lawyer, Jessika Bhatti, called for a change of attitude towards inheritance amongst the British Asian community, having been contacted by several women who had been disinherited. 'I am now beginning to understand that it may be a common practice,' she said.[16]

In the 2020s, Grandma, therefore, is set to hold considerable financial power. What will these women do with this leverage? There is evidence to suggest that our baby boomer mothers spend, invest and view their wealth very differently to our fathers. This generation of women are more likely than men to share their money with their family, to give it away in their lifetime and to be interested in environmentally friendly, socially conscious (ESG) investing than men. They are also more likely to lean on their children, especially daughters, for financial support and advice. In short, there is often greater financial openness with the matriarch.

'I've watched this family dynamic play out quite a lot,' says Samantha Secomb, CEO of Women's Wealth who has built a business offering better financial advice for women in an age when they are making, investing, gifting and inheriting more. 'The baby boomer women are inheriting and then, if they have a daughter, she, rather than the son, helps Mum with her finances. The daughter is already looking after Mum anyway, helping her with tech or doctors; the son tends to be too busy. The millennial daughter says things like, "I can't believe Dad invested in weapons," and takes one look at Mr Pinstripe Suit looking after her parents' money and says, "No thanks."'

Secomb points to the emerging female financial dynamic within the family and the reason why 70 per cent of widows reportedly ditch their financial advisors after their husband dies.

But this is a minority problem for the affluent; much more widespread is the economic infantilisation of the millennial generation. According to Secomb: 'I see a lot of millennial resentment, delayed parenthood, career frustrations and it's not their fault. I spend a lot of time trying to help my millennial clients heal from what I call their "baby boomer scars".'

'What are these generational scars?' I ask, convinced I had them.

'Their sense of failure for not getting on the property ladder,' she replies. 'I tell them it's not their fault. It's the parents. The boomers are part of the broken problem that is not serving their kids. Until Mum and Dad sell their four-bedroom houses – that, of course, they only need now so that everyone can come home for Christmas – and get into a two-bedroom place so everyone can shunt upwards, their kids will constantly be at a disadvantage … It's actually an impossible situation: millennials are relying on an inheritance, unable to get on the property ladder, and boomers are unwilling to give up on their castles. And however you fashion these new private old people's residentials as communities with mod cons like a cocktail bar and gym, boomers won't buy it. They don't want to downsize. They are living in financial fairyland and disadvantaging their kids. The problem is that any housing market where the new people can't get in any more has to accept that it is broken.'

Secomb was one of the most straight-talking people I'd spoken to on this subject. Her view was that one of the problems of inheritance and the property market more broadly was baby boomers' unwillingness to downsize. She's not alone. It has been estimated that 51 per cent of properties owned by baby boomers have at least two spare bedrooms. Some have suggested that the government should be offering incentives – such as reductions in stamp duty – to get baby boomers moving.[17] Some opponents have argued that this shaming of empty nesters – *The Times* has called them 'bedroom blockers' – amounts to age discrimination, and that it is their right to stay in the house they own and have paid for. There are also legitimate reasons for why so few are downsizing: a lack of decent alternatives, a desire not to move away from the community they know and plans to convert it into a multigenerational home for their kids and grandkids in the future.

'But aren't the empty nesters a diversion from the main issue?' I ask Secomb. 'The point is that given the money the boomers have in property, assets and pensions, aren't many millennials, however crude it seems, right to bank on some kind of inheritance?'

She laughs and then shifts into serious mode. 'I say: "Big mistake." Because I don't think the boomers are going to have much left.'

'Millennials Are Set to Be the Richest Generation in History'

That may have been the headline taken from the Knight Frank report in 2024, but in fact this research piece was not referring to an entire generation at all, rather a small minority classified as high-net-worth individuals (HNWIs – someone with $1 million investments) and an even smaller minority of ultra-high-net-worth individuals (UHNWIs – those with $30 million in investments). It was these folks who Knight Frank calculated would be passing down this $90 trillion, making their millennial offspring the richest generation in history.

The uber-wealthy live in an inheritocracy. Wealth generated

purely from inheritance now outstrips money made from entrepreneurship. Family offices managing these vast sums of money
doubled between 2008 and 2018.[18] Within these high-net-worth
families, women are considerably less likely to inherit wealth and
family businesses. Women make up around 11 per cent of global
UHNWIs, up 3 per cent in ten years but still very much a minority.[19] Arguably, the culture of economic infantilisation that Samantha
Secomb spoke of is even more evident within the uber-rich, but
so is the generational conflict on how to pass on this inheritance,
sustain family businesses and invest this considerable wealth. Unsurprisingly, this next generation of millennial heirs is prioritising
environmental sustainability and social impact investing more than
their predecessors. A wealth manager told me of one family where
the patriarch was leaving millions to each of his three children, but
he was reluctant to pass it on to his youngest son who wished to
donate much of this money to a men's mental health charity where
he was a volunteer. This caused some considerable tension within
the family, not least because the elderly patriarch struggled with the
idea that men's mental health was a cause worthy of millions of his
hard-earned wealth. The wealth that some global elite families have
amassed is unjustifiable, which is why many, including Thomas
Piketty, have called for a wealth tax as the only way that we can free
up our global economy from the inheritocratic dominance. But it
is also worth saying that there is a burden and a complexity to this
wealth that on a personal and familial level is utterly unenviable.

And this is probably the one thing that the global elite and the rest
of us share: disputes and difficulties when it comes to inheritance.
Whether we are talking about billions, millions or thousands, there
is inevitable tension between those who make the wealth and those
who are in receipt of it. 'The first generation builds it, the second

generation consolidates it and the third generation squanders it,' so the saying goes. There is, in fact, a variation of this proverb in most cultures, which tells you that the loss of wealth as it proceeds down the generations is the most human of stories. Ever wondered why many sons and daughters of bankers and lawyers end up doing art degrees?

The property market in the UK has created a lot of paper millionaires – those whose wealth has been generated not by hard work as such but an inflated market over thirty years. It is also true that this wealth will only be realised when it is passed down to offspring. These circumstances may create a very specific dynamic within families between the person who generated the wealth and the person who will be receiving it.

Steve Dyson, a financial advisor who has worked in the industry for forty years, tells me he sees a difference between families who have historical wealth (and therefore an understanding of how inheritance works) and the self-made, especially baby boomers from the 1980s, who perhaps are giving away wealth for the first time having never been significant inheritors themselves. In the case of the latter, it often comes with a reluctance to release it until they are advised they must. 'It is emotive,' Dyson tells me. 'The real issue is when to give it. If you give it too early, it tends not to be a good thing for the kids who don't know how to spend it wisely. If you give it too late, it's not a great thing for the parents who risk inheritance tax on their estate.'

'It seems like so much of this comes down not to your wealth bracket but the kind of parent you are? And how you view money?' I ask him.

'Yes, definitely,' he replies. 'You have to teach your kids to respect and appreciate money.' But the financial advice industry has played a considerable role, he tells me. 'It used to be that high-street banks gave advice, but in the '80s, with the rise of private pensions and investments, an advice industry grew up to serve that generation and it's very much still tied to the needs of that generation rather than those about to inherit it.'

But one millennial financial advisor I spoke to offered a more frank view: 'Lots of financial advisors are lazy and quite frankly expensive and shit. For many years, it has been an industry that often was money for old rope, where commission was charged in a growth fuelled environment.'

'How often do you see parents reluctant to discuss the issue of inheritance with their kids?' I ask him.

'Oh, it's a huge problem. They still don't trust their kids to inherit their money and hence don't want to pass on their hard-earned wealth. I had one elderly female client with a life expectancy of about six years. I finally got her to bring her son into the discussions. I told him that he stood to inherit around £350,000 on her death. He honestly had no idea. I had to advise him that unless his mother did certain things, the estate was looking at a 40 per cent inheritance tax bill. He looked at me in disbelief; he literally had no idea.'

But how will inheritance play out lower down the wealth bracket, for those who don't have the advantage of advice to invest their money and circumnavigate the tax system? The first problem is the lack of certainty around any likely inheritance. In fact, all talk of the Great Wealth Transfer may be generating false hope. One survey found that while the average amount beneficiaries expected to inherit was £110,000, the average amount they *actually* came to inherit was £54,000.[20] It is in expectation where the risk lies. One of my interviewees told me that she wasn't contributing to her pension currently as her budget was tight with two kids, plus she's confident there will be a substantive inheritance from her husband's family one day that will enable her to retire. I admire her for such unfailing faith in her marriage, but she also has maybe too much faith in any future inheritance.

I spoke to Elliot who, a couple of years ago, received a parental inheritance (of sorts), one that he had no idea was coming. His story, though, reveals the way in which passing down money can be shrouded in complex emotions and histories.

Elliot was born in east London but grew up in Kent. His mum worked in accounts while his dad was a postman, then worked for a bank. 'My mum and dad were also alcoholics,' he discloses. 'It was such a volatile environment growing up for my siblings and me.' His father lost his job and then became permanently unemployed, leaving his mother the sole breadwinner, working multiple jobs.

'We'd started out as a working-class family, became more suburban, living a middle-class life, but then we fell financially back into the working-class sphere with my mum trying to support three kids on about £20k a year.'

Elliot's difficult family situation was even more complex as he is queer but remained in the closet throughout his childhood: 'I was always the effeminate kid, but I played rugby to keep my dad happy. I was "straight passing" in front of the lads; I basically stayed in the closet until I was in my twenties.' Elliot only really feels he's come to terms with his sexuality in the last few years. 'I use the term "queer" … it feels inclusive, and the reclamation of a once defamatory word,' he clarifies.

Elliot left for university at eighteen and didn't go back home for ten years. 'I could have gone home, but I didn't want to. So, I just tried to survive as best I could.' Elliot had also come out to his mum by that point. 'The reaction wasn't great. But as soon as everyone else accepted it and told her they'd always known, she did too,' he says. Then when Elliot was twenty-nine, his mum got sick and passed away.

Unbeknownst to Elliot, she had taken out a life insurance policy before she had become ill. 'Honestly, I didn't know any money was coming. She ensured that it was in my name and not my dad's. So, when my mum passed, I received a lump sum of £125k. I split it equally between me and my two siblings. She just wanted to know that we would be left in an OK position.'

Elliot explains his confused emotions when it comes to the payout. 'The thing I find tricky is that she never really had much, and what she did have she gave to us, and in her passing she thought of us, she wanted to give us that bit of security. For all those years, she struggled.'

'What have you done with the money?' I ask.

'I haven't spent it. It is just sat in a high-yield investment account, and I do not touch it.' His upbringing has made him very wary of spending any money. Caution and fear define his attitude towards it.

Elliot now lives in Texas with his husband and dog. I ask Elliot how he feels now about looking after and losing his mother so young. 'I didn't think I would have to look after my parents that early on in my life. I loved my mum, but it was a really tricky upbringing. I did everything I could. My mum was my dad's sole carer and after she died, I had to assume that role, but I could feel my life being taken away. After some of the things he said to me when my mum passed, I was actually like, 'No, I am adult and so are you.' I wasn't willing to support him. I have pretty much relinquished any responsibility for anyone apart from myself, my dog and my husband.'

The process of probate and inheritance is much like buying and renovating a house. It is long, involving tax, lawyers and a lot of unexpected costs. Some find that after the loss of their parents, they are required to immediately sell the family home to pay the inheritance tax bill. If you fail to pay HMRC within the allotted time frame, interest begins to accrue. For the 'property rich, cash poor', this can be a real issue.

One of my friends has spent the best part of two years sorting out her deceased mother's finances and selling the family home. This does not include the previous three or so years she spent caring for her mother. Most millennials stand to inherit around the age of sixty-five, which I'd imagine is later than many would suppose but it will come at a critical time of life. Could it mean that in the 2040s and 2050s, we will see a sudden surge of affluent millennials retiring early on a decent pension they've essentially inherited rather than independently saved? Will we see those not yet on the housing ladder buying properties, or something more adventurous like retraining, travelling, starting a business? Or maybe something more boring like finally wiping out their forty-year mortgage? Or maybe we will see a surge of millennial divorces, women with newfound financial freedom extricating themselves from a man they've long fallen out of love with? Given nearly two-thirds of divorces are initiated by women, it is correct to presume women in this instance.[21] One of my friends who has recently become a divorcee believes the reason why she and her ex-husband were able to have such an amicable separation was that, although they had kids, they did not have a property together. She has several friends who have consciously chosen not to divorce because they are caught in a 'property-marriage trap'. Some millennials who fought so long to get on the property ladder are staying together not for the kids but for the house. That incentive may no longer be there when the inheritance comes.

There's no doubt that any windfall has the potential to affect millennial divorce in a way that it did not for our parents.

Just hear Nick's story. At forty-two, Nick finds himself navigating the sudden death of his father and the sudden death of his marriage. His father died unexpectedly, four years after his mother. 'I never thought about the inheritance; that money was for my dad to live out his last years,' he begins.

Nick has ended up inheriting a million pounds from his father's estate. It came as quite a shock, he tells me. 'We're a family where we have never inherited anything; in fact, deaths in our family have often cost us in terms of burials more than we've gained in inheritance!'

Given the vast majority of the estate was in the house and given the first million pounds of inheritance tax allowance was free, Nick's inheritance tax bill on his father's estate was only £8,000, 'which frankly is bonkers,' he adds.

Soon after his father died, and after fourteen years of marriage, his wife asked for a divorce. Nick understandably shares with me just the practical side: 'If not for Dad's inheritance being perfectly timed, we would have had to sell the marital home, downgrade our lives and make a complex situation miserable. As it is, I can give my ex-wife the marital home, I can give her my share of it, I can pay off her mortgage, give her a lump sum. I can buy a house. She's become a millionaire by divorcing me, which is fine, because she's the mother of my children.' Nick's inheritance has enabled them to leap over the biggest hurdle of any divorce: the financial settlement. 'This is the one time in my life that I really needed that money,' Nick explains.

'The timing of Dad's death was strangely perfect. If you look at my net worth, it stays level through what should be a catastrophic dip: a divorce. It gave me the option of paying off the marital settlement in one go, which means my ex-wife has no claim on my future earnings.'

Nick's circumstances are, of course, exceptional, but the surprise element around his father's estate and the amount of inheritance is certainly not. One area where inheritance is perhaps a little more certain and is already being felt is what is becoming known as BOGOG – the Bank of Grandma and Granddad. Inheritance is already skipping a generation and going straight to the grandchildren: Generation Z and Alpha (2011–present). Gillian Hepburn, who works in wealth management, told me of the considerable tax advantages of putting money in a trust for school fees or university, thereby relieving the grandparents and the parents of any inheritance tax on that gift and arguably a greater level of control on how that money is spent. What with holidays, childcare support, funds for clubs, lessons or university, all this amounts to a considerable investment in the grandkids and with it a degree of control over children that some partners may feel stifling or emasculating. It is also creating an opportunity inequality already within Gen Z and Gen Alpha that will mark their generation like it has millennials.

'Yes, it's all going to grandkids now,' Gillian confirms. One survey found that 42 per cent of grandparents were covering Gen Alpha's school fees while 75 per cent were paying for holidays as well as nursery or tuition fees or even a pension fund for their grandkids.[22] 'I've had this dynamic in my own family,' Gillian tells me. When Gillian's father died, her two twenty-something boys inherited a gift of money that came with her strict instructions: 'I sat them down and told them that they could have it now, but that Papa earned this money all his life and it mustn't be squandered. They had to invest it… and not in crypto. I wanted them to respect it.'

But within some families, the dynamic is the opposite. 'My inheritance is currently being drunk through a straw in a coconut in the Caribbean,' complained one millennial in the *Daily Mail*.[23] There is already an anachronym – SKIs (spending the kids' inheritance) – to describe those baby boomer parents who enjoy expensive exotic travel and renovation splurges supposedly to the detriment of their kids' future. As one millennial writer has noted, SKIs are the baby boomer equivalent of 'too much avocado on toast'. One 34-year-old explained that while she is on a low salary, is still renting and has not been on holiday for six years, her parents are exploring the world, own their own property and frequently buy new cars: 'The fact is their dream holidays are draining my inheritance … Do they want to go on holiday more than they want me to be able to have and bring up children?'

I imagine many would scream, 'Outrageous spoilt brat.' But her perspective is the result of an inheritocratic mindset, one that used to be confined to the aristocracy but today is evident amongst a wider population. One that sees inheritance as a right, not an unexpected privilege. To what extent is this millennial woman vocalising what others only whisper? Reportedly, two out of five millennials resent their parents' spending and 62 per cent of baby boomers think that their money is to be enjoyed now rather than left for an inheritance.[24] Many feel that they have already invested enough in their children in terms of education and property and feel that their offspring should be able to stand on their own two feet.

I spoke to Emma, thirty-one, from Southampton, who had strong views about accepting help from her parents and the expectations she and her husband have about a future inheritance from her parents and in-laws.

Emma was born in Kenya, the youngest of three daughters of a white British mother and a Kenyan father. 'He was a trailblazer: he was the first to go to university, at a time when only 1 per cent of people did. I am very proud of my father's story,' she tells me. Emma has twins and another child under five and works in an accountancy firm while her husband works in sport. Right now they are looking for some stability. 'We have always rented because we've moved around so much for my husband's work, but now we are ready to buy a house and settle somewhere. But it's proving a challenge,' she tells me in a burst of frustrated laughter. Unfortunately, they do not qualify as first-time buyers because of a house purchase her husband had made in a previous relationship. Emma has taken two lots of maternity leave, which has also affected their ability to save.

'When we first started looking, we had a conversation with my parents and because of our situation, I calculated that we needed to borrow £50k from them and I just decided that was too much … it just didn't sit right with me.' As the youngest daughter, Emma had found herself at a disadvantage compared to her sisters who are ten years older and who were able to tap into parental support at a time when houses were cheaper and her father was still working.

Emma tells me she is loath to ask her parents for any more money, especially given how much they have helped her throughout her life: 'My parents are now retired, and while they have a retirement fund, it is an ever-depleting resource. There's a sense that I'm taking away their retirement money.'

The contrast with her in-laws, she says, couldn't be sharper. 'My husband's family are quite well off, better than my parents in fact, but haven't helped in the same way. Not that we have any rights over their money, but they've got a different outlook. They are more like, "You will have to wait until we die before you can enjoy it," whereas my mum and dad are more like, "We want to see you enjoy it."' She admits that she finds herself panicking about the housing situation with house prices rising and rising. 'My worry is will we ever get there? First, we needed £20k, now it's more like £50k. Like I don't see how we're ever going to afford it.'

'Do you think about any future inheritance at all?' I ask her.

'My husband always says the sad reality is that both sets of our parents are in their seventies – in ten years' time, we're going to have more money than we know what to do with. Its morbid, but it's true.'

All the challenges around property have forced Emma to stop comparing herself to her parents. 'I almost feel like I'm in awe of my mum and dad because they did it on their own. And so I almost want to feel that same feeling of accomplishment of doing it on your own, but you have to bring yourself back down to earth and admit the conditions, the environment aren't the same. And therefore, it's not the same situation.'

Emma's story reveals the tension that many families feel when it comes to discussing the subject of inheritance and financial affairs with parents. The fact is that few families talk about what happens when the inevitable occurs. How many of us feel confident about broaching the subject with our parents, especially in families where it is still the oldies hosting at Christmas and paying for Sunday pub lunches (i.e. they remain the economic powerhouses within the family)? Revealingly, affluent Londoners are least likely to talk about inheritance, whereas the Welsh are reportedly the most adept at openly talking about family money. I suspect that this is not because the Welsh are naturally more open about talking about death and inheritance; rather, the more money involved, the more difficult it is to talk about.

Victoria Barber certainly understands the taboo of parental

inheritance, not only in her personal friendship groups but also in her professional work for TIME Investments. When I told her about the concept of the book, she immediately related: 'Oh, yes, I am in my early thirties, and I can totally see the "gift divide" amongst my peers. There are those who are being helped by Mum and Dad now and are planning weddings and kids, plus those who are still in shared accommodation. It affects everything from what restaurants we book to the type of conversations I am having with friends.'

But Victoria also has a good perspective on what will happen to all this parental wealth in the future: 'Today, a huge proportion of household wealth is sat dormant in property, which means families have to effectively plan for inheritance tax.'

'So, how are they doing that?' I ask.

'One major way is investing in companies that qualify for what is known as business property relief, which allows people to shelter assets from inheritance tax, while also fuelling investment in British industry, even smaller businesses. The AIM market, for example, is heavily reliant on business property relief.'

Victoria was referring to the fact that certain investments are inheritance tax free on the Alternative Investment Market (AIM – which features small companies rather than the bigger ones listed on the FTSE). The original aim of the Treasury was to aid British business, but the sums are now so huge there is a danger that they are propping up businesses that maybe should be allowed to fail.

One financial advisor privately suggested to me that although the Labour government was likely to close this loophole, the Treasury was wary because the AIM market is so dependent on this type of financing. 'When a financial advisor is recommending AIM investments, it is not solely based on the track record of certain companies but normally to dodge inheritance tax. It is completely legal, of course, but still.'

It is also happening with other areas exempt from inheritance tax such as agricultural land. A third of all farms recently sold in the UK were reportedly bought by private or institutional investors in large part to avoid inheritance tax, indirectly pushing up the price for smaller farmers wanting to buy land. The tentacles of our inheritocracy are entangled within various aspects of the British economy, chiefly by those wanting to pass on their estates without incurring an inheritance tax charge.

One obvious sign that we are living in an inheritocracy is the increasing political focus on inheritance tax. But it is telling precisely when this became a political issue. In 2007, when Prime Minister Gordon Brown was being urged by his advisors to hold a snap election, he ended up ducking it chiefly because the shadow Chancellor, George Osborne, delivered a speech to the Conservative Party conference pledging to raise the inheritance tax threshold to £1 million, thus pulling thousands of family homes out of the tax bracket. 'We will take the family home out of inheritance tax,' Osborne promised, and soon after, Brown shelved the election and his political future. Osborne was savvy enough to capitalise on the emotional weight and financial reliance on the family property. Arguably the Conservatives spent the next fourteen years in power not only sustaining but massively securing its value and their core voter demographic's wealth.

Inheritance tax receipts are set to net the Treasury billions in the next couple of years. Why is it then that some Tory MPs, and the *Telegraph* newspaper, have called for it to be abolished, while those on the left are arguing for it to be rapidly widened and loopholes closed?

'Inheritance tax is a really good headline grabber, that is my personal view anyway,' Victoria explains. 'It's emotive. Because it is a tax on assets that you've already paid tax on, especially if it's across multiple generations but also the implication of a restriction to pass down your wealth.'

The real problem is that inheritance tax currently does not really hit those with significant wealth. When the Duke of Westminster – the UK's richest man (and probably millennial) under forty – inherited his title from his father, he was not liable for inheritance tax because the estate is held in a trust. Trusts allow assets to be looked after by trustees on behalf of beneficiaries, with money staying in the trust, moving down generations through beneficiaries with nobody paying inheritance tax.

In the last year, the largest growth of families paying inheritance tax were in the north-east and the Midlands.[25] The number of inherited estates worth more than £1 million has increased by more than a third in five years, but the tax band hasn't changed, dragging families who haven't planned for inheritance into paying a tax on their estate.[26] But given only 4 per cent of estates pay inheritance tax, the major problem is how the current system encourages aggressive tax planning, shifting taxable income into other areas, notably grandchildren, the AIM market and agricultural land.[27] The most vulnerable to inheritance tax are often those whose family wealth lies in one valuable property and who are unable to access it before their parents pass away. As one financial advisor put it to me: 'The key thing is if you have a good financial advisor, you can always avoid inheritance tax. You shouldn't ever have to worry about it.'

So, should we reform it? When I interviewed Paul Johnson of the IFS, he put it succinctly: 'We need to create a society where inheritance matters less.' In his view, this means decreasing the rate of inheritance tax: 'Slash the rate and close the loopholes on farmland

and the AIM market. You will probably collect more as people will think about it less. We don't raise enough by international standards, so the hike arguably isn't justifiable.' Lord Willetts agreed: 'Right now, it is a very bad tax. A very high rate with loads of exemptions. It should be reformed and extended, not abolished. I think really the point here is that the tax on wealth is too low, whereas the tax on wages is too high. That so obviously disadvantages working people. And that is the starting point for any policy.' Amen to that.

'They've Left Me Nothing?'

When I was twenty-four, I got an administrative job in between my studies and one of the forms on my first day required me to put down the name of someone who would receive an insurance lump sum of my salary should I die while in the job. Forget my parents, siblings or friends. I ran through the contacts on my mental Rolodex and plucked the name of the man who at that precise moment in time lived 4,000 miles away, I'd known him for about five months, and I had quite an intense crush on him. I wrote his name and contact number on the form, tickled by the romantic idea of me dying, him receiving all this money, forever thinking fondly of my unrequited love (alternatively, as I suspect now, he would have found the whole thing a bit weird). These days, I'm not so reckless. I'm also at the not-so-enviable stage in life where I have just written my first will, and let's just say that man's name wasn't on it.

Naming beneficiaries on the account of your death feels like an odd process, but as a significant chunk of the great works of fiction attests, it is also fraught with conflict. One problem in the 21st-century asset-driven economy is that so few of us write a will.

Reportedly, more than half of UK adults do not have one. There is also a degree of mystery about the contents of wills. Reportedly, just 35 per cent of under-45s know how assets will be distributed in the wills of their nearest and dearest.[28] And 42 per cent have admitted that they have not told their partner or children about their will or where to find documents after death.[29] As someone who has dealt with probate herself, I feel compelled to shout loud and clear to you, reader: get this stuff sorted while your parents are alive and well. Because one of the sad inevitabilities in an inheritocracy is increasing family disputes.

It has been estimated that three out of four families are likely to experience a contested will or inheritance conflict in their lifetime. Between 2019 and 2021, attempts to block probate rose by 37 per cent.[30] And those are just the ones that go to court. Writing in *The Guardian*, Leo Benedictus has attested that 'for centuries, "freedom of testamentary disposition" – the right to put your money where you like – has been presumed by many Britons, but now it is crumbling at the edges'.[31] Why?

Aside from increasing wealth, the reason is that families are much more complicated today. The generation for whom divorce peaked are now entering their older years, with increasing numbers of blended families and complex inheritance obligations. Remarriages invalidate any previous wills and a stepchild who is not formally adopted may be disinherited. A family with children from a first marriage and stepchildren and children from a second marriage requires careful and transparent negotiation. One of the major reasons for disputes is the 'Cinderella tale': if an older father passes away and his surviving spouse is free to change the will at any time (unless they had a joint will), the partner can choose to entirely disinherit the children from his first marriage, leaving them disgruntled when they see their stepsiblings inherit everything. One survey found that one in five of those from blended families did not inherit anything like the wealth they expected.[32]

The UK, and for that matter the US, is unusual in giving as much freedom as it does to people making wills. In England and Wales, you can write a will to whomever you like, but in Scotland, France, Spain and Germany, the principle of forced heirship means a certain degree of the estate must be left to next of kin, thereby protecting their inheritance. Will rising disputes in this country lead to calls for a law that gives millennial offspring and subsequent generations a 'right to inherit'?

The truth is that in the UK, plenty of individuals prefer to give their money to good causes rather than family: £4 billion is left in wills to charities each year.[33] But even this has been an area for dispute. One daughter found herself in court with the RSPCA and other animal charities fighting for the £500,000 inheritance that her mother had given entirely to the charities. Her mother had even left an accompanying note leaving no doubt of her wishes: 'If my daughter should bring a claim against my estate, I instruct my executors to defend such a claim as I can see no reason why my daughter should benefit in any way from my estate.' Remarkably, after a twelve-year legal battle, the daughter was awarded £50,000.[34] If anything, the case proves that the real opponent in inheritance wars may not be other families but animals (and other causes) that have the potential to be the chief beneficiaries of the Great Wealth Transfer. Karl Lagerfeld's cat Choupette reportedly inherited $1.5 million from the fashion legend's estate. It's possible that soon this will not seem such an oddity and Choupette may be the first in a line of pet heirs.

Few, however, can perhaps relate to David Clarke, a millennial researcher from Liverpool who gave away a major chunk of his inheritance when his mother passed away. I wanted to speak to David, intrigued by his motivations in relinquishing what most people see as something that is rightly theirs and that has the potential to change their life. There are plenty of examples throughout history of millionaire heirs performing this kind of demonstrative philanthropic act or financial purging – ridding themselves of all their wealth – but David's case was different, the scale much more relatable and therefore that much more surprising.

'It was a pretty middle-class upbringing … but our life was quite stingy – there wasn't a lot of profligacy,' David tells me for context. David grew up in Gloucester and his family lived in a big house, his dad a civil servant and subsequently a chief executive of a charity. David inherited some money from his grandma in his teens, which helped pay for his university degree. Then in 2014, his mother died. At the time, David was living in London and on quite a small salary by the capital's standards of £25,000 per annum. But when his dad sold the family home, David found himself the beneficiary of a huge sum: £350,000. 'And I have basically spent several years trying to give away significant amounts of it,' he tells me.

'Wow, that is impressive, can you explain why?' I ask.

'I felt kind of crap about it. I'd had this feeling for a while that my fortunes have been on this slow path of divergence with the people I was at school with, simply because of money. It is total luck; it is the lottery of inheritance.'

I could relate to this, and I know plenty feel this breach, although David has translated his guilt into impressive action. He clarified: 'I'd done nothing to earn it. It put me in such an advantageous position compared to my friends who were still very much in house shares, struggling to make ends meet.'

But David didn't just write a cheque and give it away. He decided to set up a social experiment, establishing a committee of local people in his area to decide how to divide his inheritance.

'I was not only uncomfortable with inheriting all this money; I was also uncomfortable in deciding how it should be redistributed. So, I sent out 600 letters in my local area of Liverpool, I literally got on my bike and posted them. I invited anyone over the age of sixteen to register and attend a session to decide how my inheritance was spent. Most people thought it was a scam, that's why I also hired an independent facilitator to run the session. I gave a little speech at the beginning and sat at the corner watching it all play out ... I felt a bit like Willy Wonka, an eccentric who everyone was treating with a bit of scepticism. It was fascinating how involved they got and owned the decisions; they wanted the money to go to local causes above all.'

'So, what did your dad think?' I asked, impressed with not only his generosity but the thought and time that he had invested in the project.

'Well, it came as a bit of a shock to him initially and he wanted to make sure I knew what I was doing ... My friends, too, but as soon as they knew the details, they all thought it was pretty cool.'

Ultimately, the long-term aim of David's experiment is to get people talking about the distribution of wealth and particularly the role that voluntary citizenship assemblies can play in any redistribution.

'I support transfer of wealth through taxation, but people don't have much faith in dominant institutions. There is a role for voluntary initiatives like this,' he affirms.

I ask David how he sees his future: 'Well, on principle, I do not want to live a life based on any inherited wealth. I aim to get myself in a comfortable place economically.'

David's example and motivation were unique, but ultimately, they're a sign of an economy dominated by wealth and the draw we all contend with when it comes to the families into which we are born. Inheritance may feel more like an ever-justifiable right than a privilege as we clasp onto *any* signs that life might get easier in the future. And yet not only is it tied to the morbid condition of our parents dying; it is a drawn-out process with so many factors, time constraints and hurdles to render it a vague promise rather than any type of guarantee. One major mitigating factor potentially stands in the way of all this, of course, one that could derail even the tightest of future financial plans: the cost of eldercare both in terms of our time and our parents' money.

Chapter 8

Parenting Your Parents

I can't pinpoint the precise moment, but sometime during the pandemic, I began to feel old. I emerged from my Covid bunker ready to embrace the world again but with the stark realisation that the experience had aged us all, especially millennials. There were, of course, far more serious consequences to come out of this monumental global event, aspects of which we are only beginning to realise. But to many my age, this transition was most immediately palpable. I had taken the slow lane into adulthood but felt I was being fast-tracked to middle age.

Our sense of displacement as the purveyors of youth culture was real. Gen Z had stolen the mic and, worse still, started directing their youthful ire and mockery towards us – be it our skinny jeans or lol emojis. Somewhere between 2015 and 2019, millennials were the future. By 2020, it seemed as if our generation were suddenly on the wrong side of history.

I hear the collective 'doh' from anyone over fifty on this. That the disruptors become the disrupted is the natural order of things. But millennials' kidulthood years makes that switch into middle age even more pronounced when it does finally happen. Perhaps our digital lives are a factor here, too. In documenting the moment, time becomes fleeting. Our constant time-hop feed of memories thrust into view, our phone's regurgitation of life's showreel creates a temporal distance even before they've lodged as blurred memories in our minds. Whether it's pictures of my kids, garden or my face, the maturation is fast but feels faster because I can witness it frame by frame.

In my case, motherhood exacerbated this feeling, as did hitting a milestone age. I turned forty in lockdown with leaky boobs, greying hair and in a body I didn't recognise. Oh, and legal restrictions on when I could leave the house. I count myself extremely fortunate, but understandably, it was not a milestone birthday I felt like celebrating.

Another major realisation was that I was entering my 'sandwich' years, caught in the middle, looking after two generations within my family. I was confronted by this dual care role every time I walked down our narrow hallway and scraped my shin on either my daughter's pram or my mother's shopping trolley. If you are not yet in your 'sandwich years', you can get a sense of what is coming if you look to our Gen X elders. They are feeling the pressure from both sides, looking after young adults and ageing parents. They are the ones who are largely navigating the social care crisis and rocketing residential home fees right now, while at the same time facing the teenage mental health crisis or spiralling university or rental costs for young people. In important ways, as we shall see, the millennial experience of eldercare is projected to be even more complicated, intense and possibly even more expensive. Indeed, the foundations of our inheritocracy have been built on shaky ground – all that wealth could be spent on future care.

When I was in my twenties and early thirties, there was a time when I was an adult and I was fortunate to have both parents healthy, where our relationship was beyond the tetchy adolescent phase and had reached the semi-harmonious balance of respect and congeniality. But that phase can't last for ever. With my father passed and my mother now a widow, my sisters and I took ever-more responsibility for her needs, whether she wanted us to or not. To be clear, she is a healthy woman in her seventies, but there was a shift when she became a widow, as we assumed more control over her needs and health.

The pandemic proved the turning point in our relationship. I wasn't the only daughter or son who found themselves in March 2020 lecturing their indefatigable baby boomer parents, then classified as vulnerable by the state, to stay in and take the virus seriously. The coronavirus accelerated the care reversal process that inevitably happens within families; that tricky shift when the children start to parent the parents. 'I still think of my parents as the grownups, the ones who lecture me about saving for retirement and intervene in squabbles with my little sister,' wrote *New Yorker* contributor Michael Schulman at the time. 'It took a pandemic to thrust me into the role of the responsible adult and them into the role of the heedless children.'[1]

I treated any call or correspondence from my mother as an urgent priority. I remember one week early in lockdown, when my mother had sent me an email, quickly followed by a text message reminding me to read the email, then a voicemail which amongst other things was to check whether I had seen the email – and the text – all in the space of an hour. I immediately pulled up my inbox expecting something serious. It was a video of six ducklings being rescued from a drain on a busy US highway with an accompanying note: 'This is just lovely.' My mother had discovered the 'forward' button.

A false alarm. But it didn't prevent me from morphing into a 'helicopter mum' for my mother. Small things changed, then big things. We began to host her rather than vice versa, as she relinquished her decades-long role as the matriarch cook, one that felt especially poignant at Christmas. All the dreaded anxiety I once had about my father's health, I shifted on to my mother. This translated into constant badgering about doctors' appointments, probing questions about her mobility and diet. Our sibling WhatsApp group chat became mostly dominated by concern for Mum. Worried about her loneliness, I hooked her up on friendship dates with other friends' mums and thrust leaflets about community walking tours and over-sixties fitness clubs from the local library into her hand. Her reaction to all this was understandably mixed; sometimes she would be gracious, most of the time she told me to fuck off.

'We go out of this world just as we came in: in a nappy, being spoon fed,' my aunt likes to say. We may think that looking after our parents is similar to parenting our children, but this is a false comparison. When you have children, it is a full dunk immersion into round-the-clock care from the moment they are born with a (mostly) compliant being who can't yet answer back; but the narrative arc of motherhood is essentially about gradually letting go. When it comes to parenting a parent, it is the complete opposite. Parenting the parent starts innocently and only increases in intensity, sometimes over decades, involving someone understandably reluctant and often uncompliant. And all of this with someone with whom you have a complex emotional history.

To not include a chapter on looking after your parents when it comes to talking about the Bank of Mum and Dad would ignore how the generational contract, and frankly inheritance, works for most families. The link between care and inheritance is twofold:

firstly, because up until now we have spoken about the investment of time, care and money our parents have put into us. But how does modern culture, especially one built on over-parenting and parental investment, cope when it comes to reversing that process, and parenting the parents? That reversal will have to happen within boomer–millennial families, if it isn't already. Secondly, in the context of eldercare funding, there is a real threat that any promise of an inheritance for young people may end up being ploughed into social care costs. To return to financial advisor Samantha Secomb's prediction in full:

> I don't think the boomers are going to have much left. The fact is that the NHS can't deliver its cradle-to-grave promise to the boomers. They are going to have to finance later life themselves, and I'm not talking cruises but care here. The government can't afford to pay it, so the affluent ones will have to fund it themselves and many are not understanding that right now. The money in property now won't be there in twenty years' time.

So, although we may talk about the Great Wealth Transfer, it is often precipitated by the great transfer of responsibility and care and, as Secomb attests, the two are set to be inextricably linked. This chapter will explore the inevitable care load we assume for our parents as they age and their health falters. Not just caring in terms of their health and fatal illness, but the broad scope of responsibility from dealing with their loneliness and mental health as well as navigating state bureaucracy, tech, healthcare or banking on their behalf. If we need to start talking openly about the Bank of Mum and Dad, we need to start talking about caring for our parents, too.

That care process happens naturally in the majority (but not all) of families, and most of the time it happens willingly and lovingly. But it comes with complications and sacrifice, especially in an age where we are more individualistic, scattered, families are blended and lives are longer. For millennials, the call feels slightly more pressured, or certainly did in my case, because of the degree to which many of us have depended on our parents throughout the first half of our lives. To call it 'payback' would be crude, because the motivation, depending on your parental relationship, stems more from human instinct and love rather than obligation, but we cannot deny it's conceivably a burden too, especially for women. This chapter dissects what multigenerational living and eldercare will mean for millennials – the emotional complexities but also the financial costs.

Looking after the elderly in society, and not just our parents, is part of the fabric of human existence. Within some cultures and families, it is so ingrained as to go unquestioned. But there is little doubt that the responsibility for the elderly will intensify over the next ten years. Firstly, the boomers are hitting their 'care years', and they are not just living longer but also managing illnesses for longer. State structures are underfunded, their future uncertain; the financial and care burden will fall more on the family. This is already happening. Over 3 million people currently look after an elderly parent in the UK, that amounts to £162 billion worth of care, up a third since 2011.[2] Caring responsibilities are now a fundamental part of the poverty trap; the 2021 census data shows that unpaid care is most likely in deprived areas. In 2023, Age UK polled adults aged between forty and sixty and found that 61 per cent stated that they would struggle to manage eldercare financially.[3] In the US, the share of caregivers who are under forty-five has increased fivefold in two decades, incorporating parents, grandparents and extended family.[4]

As we have seen, baby boomers and Gen X have invested more

time and care in their kids over the past forty years, but their off-spring – millennials and Gen Z – will potentially spend evermore time and money on their parents in the next forty years, in what is rapidly becoming an ageing society. Will millennials and Gen Z, particularly those who have been grateful recipients of the Bank of Mum and Dad, be willing and able to reciprocate in terms of time and money? The answer is probably yes because, as I know from personal experience, when the time comes, you just do. But it is worth considering what this may entail. Curating the conditions for a decent end of life for our parents might not just cost us in terms of time but also, because of the complexities of modern old age, potentially any inheritance. If some millennials have had a dependent relationship on their parents in the first forty years of their life, does that mean that this dependency will naturally flip, as parents become dependent on their children? This was something that Lord Willetts wondered when I spoke to him: 'These days we spend less time on eldercare and increasing time on parenting. But I'm not sure whether that will be paid back. There is a sense that parents are building up moral capital with their children, but I'm not sure it will translate into care in later life.' His lack of certainty speaks volumes.

To a certain degree, this is an overwhelmingly female dilemma. Feminist Germaine Greer, now in her eighties, recently claimed that aged care is one of the most pressing feminist issues of our time.[5] Back when she was burning bras in the '70s, eldercare was not something second-wave feminists showed much interest in – perhaps now she should be setting fire to incontinence briefs. When we talk about the social care crisis or the ageing society, it's disproportionately older women that require assistance. Women outnumber men in care homes in a ratio of twenty-three to ten, while widows outnumber widowers over the age of eighty more than four to one.[6] The deliverers of this care are predominantly wives, daughters or daughters-in-law, or low-paid paid female carers, including many migrant workers, who often have their own caring responsibilities at home and abroad.

When my dad was terminally ill, he would often say he was glad he had three daughters and not three sons. Brutal, but the stats bear it out. It is overwhelmingly women who deliver care. In the US, up to 81 per cent of all caregivers, formal and informal, are women, and women spend 50 per cent more time giving care than men.[7] There are, in fact, nearly as many elderly husbands who care for their wives in the UK as vice versa, but evidence suggests that when there are daughters on hand, sons do less, with their wives often picking up the slack. According to one study from 2015, wives and daughters are three times more likely than sons to be primary care-givers to older parents.[8] It also comes at a huge financial cost for female carers: women are seven times more likely to be out of work due to caring commitments than men.[9] The gender pay gap is more and more a motherhood penalty, affecting women who take time out of the workforce to have children. But it could be that millennial women, both mothers and childfree women alike, are hit with the eldercare pay penalty when it comes to looking after our parents. Our eldercare responsibilities may prevent female workers from saving sufficiently for their own pensions, going for promotions or forcing them into a costly early retirement. Eldercare policies for employees are only now starting to be discussed within companies; very few have sufficient support structures in place.

Many Gen X women in their fifties currently care for their parents. As a generation, they have had greater work and career commitments than baby boomer women, and even more expensive dependent children (and they have less wealth). For millennials and Gen Z women, who are wedded to ideas about greater gender equality in terms of finances, careers and domestic responsibilities, the reality of the female eldercare burden may hit hard (if it hasn't already). So, while it's great that millennial fathers are changing more nappies than ever before, we need them to be just as willing to change as many catheters as necessary when the time comes. This is something that we, as a society, are perhaps beginning to recognise. According to a study of 2,000 people from across the UK, 84 per cent of women believe people need to rethink the role of women as the default carers in society – and, somewhat positively, this view is shared by 66 per cent of men.[10]

When thinking about inheritance, and the dynamic of an in-heritocracy, is Samantha Secomb right that the financial and time burden of care will not be done by female relatives at all but offloaded onto paid help? Secomb was adamant: '[Boomers] will have to use that money. Their millennial daughters won't do the care and frankly won't be able to take time off work to do the care and it costs so much, they'll be little left to pass on.'

This is why the most fortunate in an inheritocracy, as we have already seen, are those who have already received parental gifts, and why those expecting any kind of inheritance when their parents pass away are potentially vulnerable. 'The gifters not the will writers. The dream should be to live well and die poor. That's how the well off do it,' confirmed Secomb. One financial advisor told me that one of his elderly clients wanted to give as much of her money as possible before she needed care, 'so that the retirement home wouldn't get it'. Given the state of care funding, this attitude borders on the immoral, but it might be more widespread than we think. One financial advisor told me that when it came to considering care costs, his client base could be slotted into three camps: there are those who can afford to save for care and are doing so, which as we shall see is an eye-watering amount; then there are those who are deliberately whittling down their assets in savvy ways in order to preserve inheritance and will rely on the state to pay for their care; and finally there are those, the majority, with their head in the sand.

All Under One Roof

When my father passed away, I was in the fortunate position that my mother wished to gift some money to my sisters and me. It was the right time for my husband and me, too. In 2019, we were still renting and looking to buy our first property. We had a two-year-old and I was pregnant with our second child; we were ready to nest. We had accrued a small savings pot of our own and my husband's parents were able to help, too. We were the beneficiaries of what I call the triple financial privilege: able to realise a double parental gift plus dual incomes that generated enough to grow a deposit. If it had been our earnings alone, there is no way we could have afforded to buy a home in London. But once we started looking, we soon realised, even in our fortunate circumstances, we wouldn't be able to buy anything like the kind of place we imagined. I wanted to raise my children in the area I had grown up and be near my mother, but that was beginning to look impossible. Tooting had changed. As an option, my mother suggested that we buy her second property off her, the one she had bought in 1982 two streets from my childhood home, that I had lived in during my kidult years. We did and were able to renovate it in the process. Two months after the builders moved in, the world went into lockdown. Ten months later we were living in our new home with our son, new baby daughter… and my mother.

 In March 2021, after self-isolating for a year, my mother received her second AstraZeneca jab and moved into our spare room, which was also doubling up as my husband's office. My parents' house, for decades a crumbling wreck with no proper heating, was no longer appropriate for a woman in her seventies. The builders began converting her house and she moved in with me, my husband and two kids. She would stay for nearly two years.

 I feel it is important to first point out that she was an excellent house guest, but it was not without its challenges, ones that I think are worth dwelling on not least because they pose important questions for millennial female carers of parents. Firstly, there was a question of space. My mother would be ousted from the spare bedroom on mornings when my husband had to log on at some ungodly hour to another time zone. Most people had kids leaping into their lockdown Zoom calls; in our case, it was my mother shuffling out of shot in her dressing gown. Most of the time she stayed out of our way, never wanting to be a burden. Admirably, she would leave at 9 a.m. every day to go and sort out, in her words, 'all the junk your father collected over the years', returning after a full day's work at 6 p.m.

 Sometimes the dynamic was more *Absolutely Fabulous*. I was the draconian daughter telling off my bohemian mother for her deviancy, which, at seventy-seven, meant vaping in her bedroom. She inhaled furiously on a weighty contraption that looked like a hand grenade and made a noise like a small moped. I'd walk in and find her hiding under her duvet. 'I'm not!' she would protest, waving her hand while a sweet-smelling fog glided across the room.

 I remember one morning when I was particularly flustered, I

asked her if she would help a bit more around the house. I was very much in my 'mummy martyr' era, with a well-rehearsed stump speech on how I was drowning while managing two kids, a dual career marriage and emerging from a pandemic during which my business had collapsed. 'Oh, you know, stuff like unload the dishwasher, that would be a great help!' I lightly suggested, attempting and failing to not sound passive aggressive.

'You never did it when you lived with me,' my mother fired back.

I laughed. That's fair, I thought. Of course, from that moment on, she regularly unloaded the dishwasher.

Conversations would often drift into an intergenerational tussle of 'Who's Had it Harder?' My mother had started work at sixteen with few choices, been a working mum of three in a hostile environment for a female breadwinner. But she had also worked in an era when work really did finish at 5 p.m., where wages bought you more and when housing and childcare were affordable. In contrast, I had travelled, had unparalleled freedom and more parental support. But then I was working in an 'always-on' culture, expectations were higher, income didn't go as far and my trump card: I had just given birth in the throes of a pandemic.

Such conversations rarely fostered any mother–daughter solidarity; after a while we both resigned to buttoning it. The truth was that I was in the most chaotic part of my life, and guilty of revelling in that fact, whereas she, who had done it all before in very different conditions, found it hard to hark back. Most importantly, of course, she had also just lost her husband, her partner since she was twenty; a breach I could never truly understand. It wasn't about loading the dishwasher, or even who had had it harder; we were both struggling with the gradual but inevitable role reversal between mother and daughter.

Eighteen months in, I came to realise that I, as a millennial woman, was finding it difficult for a very specific reason. I have been bred in a liberated but selfish society, one that gave my generation, and especially someone of my education, race and gender, an unparalleled degree of agency in my career, relationships and finances. And for the first time in my life, I felt trapped. The restrictions that come with marriage and kids were one thing; Covid lockdowns were another. But my mother living with us felt like a step too far. In part, it was the speed at which all this had happened. I'd had a slow meandering path into traditional adult responsibility, and then a fast track into the dual responsibilities of motherhood and multigenerational living. That is not to say that I wasn't accepting, more that I found it harder to transition and manage, perhaps more than earlier generations of women where caring expectations were more pronounced.

There was only one answer: therapy.

You may be reading this thinking, 'You ungrateful spoilt daughter.' Perhaps. But at least I'm honest. Contemporary female expectations around eldercare are one of the great unspoken subjects in our society, not unlike, nor unrelated to, the overreliance on parental support. Nor am I trying to elicit sympathy here. I just want to understand why this most natural of familial states, taking gradual responsibility for one's parents and moving my mother in, especially after she had just granted us a financial gift, proved such a challenge.

When I relayed my multigenerational set-up to my female peers, it was often met with a shudder and look of dread, especially, it must be said, from those who didn't have siblings. It was often followed by sentiments like, 'I know it's coming, and I don't know what we are going to do' or 'I've only just moved out of the family home; I can't bear the thought of my mother moving in.' My childfree queer friend, who is an only child, conveyed the panic the clearest when she joked: 'It scares me enough to want to marry a rich cis [man].' All these reactions sounded a lot like denial. Maybe it's because we don't like to think of these things happening. Still, I believe that when they do, most naturally adjust.

And yet the reaction from my male peers was noticeably different, often an acceptance with far less paranoia and angst. Why this gender divide? The writer David Goodhart has contested that this 'angst' about care is particularly common amongst 'highly educated women who are less socialised into caring roles [than their mothers] and often want the same autonomous, career-focused lives as highly educated men'.[11] That feels a bit crude to me, but there is some truth to it. The ones who were least enthused by my situation were my highly educated friends, often affluent dependents on the Bank of Mum and Dad, but possibly unwilling to admit precisely how much. The ones who understood it without reservation were either culturally attuned to filial duty, had no access to the Bank of Mum or Dad, were already living in multigenerational homes or were reliant on their parents for childcare. Speaking to the *Metro* newspaper in 2021, London resident Bushra Shaikh put it admirably:

> My values don't allow me to turn around and disregard the very people who have raised me. Our parents deserve to know that they always have a home with any of us. What that will look like in the future is subject to individual circumstances, but both my mum and dad will be cared for by us.[12]

It's worth saying that even if the responsibility of parental care is wilfully accepted, or accepted cultural tradition, it does not necessarily follow that it is free from frustration and difficulty. For others, though, it is less clean-cut. If we're living in a society where parental financial dependency is protracted, caring has become denigrated (or at least not as respected as work) and we've been bred and parented into hyper-individualists, is it any wonder that 21st-century women have complex feelings around care? Tellingly, the main type of care our generation has championed is self-care.

There are parallels here with the millennial view of motherhood. We grew up with a warped opinion that procreating too young was not only a social ill (all that derogatory rubbish about teenage mothers) but a massive curtailment of freedom and opportunity, likely to halt any career. This is why we became obsessed with timing it right and, I suspect, one of many reasons why many of us have embraced the concept of being 'childfree'. But our rejection of, struggles with or slower journey into motherhood may also stem from the fact that we have been so little socialised in it. We grew up being told we could do anything that a man could. But we weren't taught what *only women could do*. You don't need to be an aspiring 'trad wife' to see the truth in this.

I am a perfect representation of Goodhart's 'highly educated women unsocialised in care'. I had hardly held a baby until I held my own. It is difficult to overstate how different this was from my mother's and grandmother's experience. At my antenatal classes before the birth of my first child, I was more than a little embarrassed when I struggled to put a nappy on the toy baby, and it slid off as soon as I lifted the doll. My husband, on the other hand, who had grown up in a large family on a tiny island off the coast of Cornwall, where they breed young and a lot, came top of the class. My lack of education was made most apparent when it came to breastfeeding. It's a process that feels genuinely alien to a generation of women who are child-rearing later in life. They have exercised so much control over their bodies and up to that point, most have had few real-life encounters with breastfeeding until they find themselves, like I did, in a dark room in the middle of the night with blistering red nipples, crying in pain and exasperation, pleading with my body and baby *just to latch*. 'I've got three degrees, but I can't feed my baby,' was a thought that often ran through my mind – a life lived with the wrong priorities. Similarly, the same can be said in this age-segregated society about growing old and eldercare, not only our expectation or our skills base but also what it entails.

This is subject tackled in Emily Kenway's searing millennial memoir *Who Cares*, in which she recounts the story of looking after her terminally ill mother in her thirties. Kenway writes openly and honestly about the responsibility and the burden: 'I absolutely hated losing my freedom to care. I craved desperately a weekend when I could do exactly as I pleased, when I could know for certain that I wouldn't suddenly be at a hospital.' Kenway's realisation is that as a woman, the freedom she pined for was in fact 'a category error, because I had never truly been free to begin with. I just didn't realise it.' Gender equality is a mirage – in fact, for our generation, it has come to mean a double burden: 'women work *and* care'. In Kenway's view, contemporary womanhood is simply a process of waiting for that 'unfreedom to wake' in the form of care for babies and parents. In a rather drastic conclusion, Kenway is clear: 'We stay faithful to our emancipated idea of the family, only realising when it's too late that this structure we thought was our safety net is instead a cage.'[13]

But Kenway's picture is a resoundingly depressing one that borders on the notion that we should be autonomous beings free from familial obligation. There is less emphasis on the purity of love between children and parents, however emotionally complex. There is something especially profound and beautifully human about the kind of love that you execute as one of your parents dies, one that extends well beyond duty and into the realm of the spiritual. It is different for the receiver, of course; dying is essentially humiliation and this is only softened by being surrounded by people who love you. And rarely is it your 'chosen family' (bar partner) who are willingly there at the end, feeding and cleaning you. Kenway views millennial female independence as a fraud, a mask we wear for a while (depending on our choices). But do we need to see it in such stark terms? Until the age of thirty-six, I had basically only been responsible for feeding and taking care of myself. I have now been in the caring part of my life for seven years, becoming a mother and stepping up as a daughter. And while it has been the most challenging, compromising and difficult years of my life, it has also given me the most meaning and brought much-needed shape, motivation and clarity to parts of my identity forged during the 'freedom' years. After all, isn't proximity to life and death the most identity-forming of experiences?

Kenway is spot on in one regard, though – there is a fundamental tension for our generation. On the one hand, millennial women, especially professional women, have been socially conditioned out of our caring roles, and yet the lingering construct of a patriarchal society means that women are still obliged to do most of the care. There is a justifiable disconnect here. Kenway's rage is reflective of a generation who have been given more independence than our forebears and are therefore *rejecting* the notion of female sacrifice even more than the women who came before us. But there's a central paradox for women living in a 21st-century inheritocracy: we are individualists, but in many instances our freedom has been funded or enabled by parental support and wealth. Unexpectedly, you could say that modern women are even more defined by familial obligations than our mother's generation, whom the second-wave feminists sought to free from precisely these constraints.

All this, I suspect, is a legacy from the sort of mashed up feminism we ingested. Somewhere between left-wing and corporate feminism, we were fed the idea that education and career equalled freedom, we could (and should) do anything a man could and domestic responsibilities were a restriction only to be entered into under certain conditions, ideally with a progressive conciliatory partner. Within families, care has not only been side-lined, denigrated and outsourced, usually to low-paid female workers; we have also disbanded the wider village and the welfare state that eased the female burden. The great hope for our generation is that men help kick down the patriarchy and pick up some of the slack. In child-rearing, there is evidence that this is happening – but whether the funding, social acceptance and willingness from men is there in respect to eldercare remains to be seen.

Lots of millennial men see fatherhood as bringing much-needed meaning to masculinity in the twenty-first century; I hear few men saying that about looking after their parents. Women will also have to recognise that modern feminism has not always served us well, nor has it presented us with all the answers. What we do know is that the debate around familial care will be as important as any debate about inheritance or housing for the millennial generation. The gender relations rule book was ripped up by us and our parents; we are in flux as to what the new rules should be for our kids.

Thirty-six felt quite young to lose my father; thirty-nine felt too young to be housing my mother. Tellingly, I found solidarity when I spoke to older women in their fifties about my predicament. There was an immediate awareness, either from personal experience or from friends, of what caring for a parent entailed. They exhibited far less fear, less selfishness, but they were also at a different life stage to me. Many had kids that were older. And almost all were in a different financial dynamic with their parents, having often been much less reliant. Quite often these women were paying for care themselves or carrying the financial burden of multigenerational living. It was surprising, though, how many of these women made a point of (naïvely, I felt) telling me that they were determined not to be the same burden on their children.

In recent years, multigenerational living has been on the rise, which is logical given housing and care costs. Today, granny annexes are increasingly popular, although this set-up makes up a tiny percentage – just 2.1 per cent – of households.[14] Multigenerational homes enable a family to fold their wealth into one pot, thereby diluting some inheritance complications. Most prefer to live nearby than in the same house. As much as we like to think we are a transient and transactional culture today, it is estimated that most Brits settle just under forty miles from where they grew up, often near parents.[15] There are some signs that first- and second-generation immigrant families in the UK, especially from South Asia, are in fact becoming *less* multigenerational, not more. The real rise, of course, has been in the numbers living alone.

Within multigenerational households, evidence suggests that young children benefit most of all, generating a capacity to build stronger relationships and greater emotional resilience.[16] I saw this in my own children, who gained significantly from living with Grandma; she could provide them with the time, patience and concentration that I, as an overloaded working parent, couldn't always muster. With one of the most expensive childcare systems in the world, the average costs of nursery at £212 a week, it is little wonder that millennials are starting to prioritise multigenerational living or relocating to be nearer family. You only need to look at the number of grandmas (and it is mostly grandmas) in playgrounds and libraries running after pre-schoolers to realise who has picked up the care tab for dual-income households: 42 per cent of grandparents help regularly with the school run, and do so willingly, with 41 per cent believing it is their role as a parent to help in any way they can.[17] But as much as bringing great joy, it is also a great responsibility. I know one grandma who has relocated *away* from her family, overwhelmed by the care expectations when she is in her seventies. In Spain, the 'burned-out grandma' phenomenon was seen as so widespread that in 2010 unions urged them to refuse their duties and go on a childcare strike.[18] As women have babies later, grandparents are now comparatively older, so it's no wonder that 31 per cent of grandparents say they are unable to help due to ill health.[19]

In a multigenerational home, however, the expectation is that the care burden is shared. The old look after the young; and when the time comes, the young reciprocate. With three generations living under one roof, care is more likely to be evenly distributed than in any other set-up. Grandchildren do a surprising amount of eldercare (especially if they were co-raised by their grandparents); 10 per cent of British family caregivers are grandchildren.[20] Husbands tend to step up more within multigenerational homes as well, which is why I suspect women tend to be more in favour of them than men.[21]

You Just Resent It in the End

As we were leaving the hospital having received his terminal diagnosis, I remember my father saying, almost under his breath, 'Don't worry, I'm going to make this short. You've all got better things to do.' It was as if he was making a promise to himself as well as us. In his final weeks, it was something that he kept repeating despite us wishing he wouldn't. This was my father taking control of the cancer. But it was also someone who, as an only child who had nursed his mother, father and aunt in their final years, knew the reality of what was coming. As it turned out, my father needed round-the-clock care for four months – a relatively short amount of time in an era defined by prolonged life and complex terminal care. If retirement years are your 'third life' (after education and employment), then we are seeing the evolution of our 'fourth life stage' where care, family and finances become critical. I wanted to talk to someone who had been a carer for a number of years to understand the impact that such responsibility can have on their life.

Carol is from Wales. A baby boomer at sixty-four, she spent fifteen years looking after her elderly mother before she eventually passed away in 2017. 'I never left home, technically,' she tells me, starting her story. One of three, Carol had had a varied career. She finished school at sixteen and went to work for a utilities company before training in sewing and then becoming a pet sitter. Her dad passed away when he was just sixty, leaving her widowed mother: 'As I still lived at home and didn't have children, it was I rather than my siblings who looked after her.' As her mother's health started to deteriorate, Carol found that she became a full-time carer: 'It is an awful thing to say but I got trapped. Although I had a brother and sister nearby, I was the one still at home. I looked after my mother for fifteen years, and two of those years she was bed-bound. Mentally she was OK, but physically she couldn't really move, and it was so hard, but I couldn't abandon her.'

In her final years, Carol's mother required a hospital bed, and she was fortunate that the local council helped to pay for some in-home additional support: 'I couldn't physically look after her. She fell a lot and I had to have help.'

I asked Carol about the mental stress of those fifteen years. A 2021 survey conducted during Covid of more than 10,000 caregivers found that 70 per cent said that they had experienced issues with their mental health, from chronic stress to suicidal thoughts.[22] Recent studies have also found that caregiver distress and depression is often a precursor to physical illness.[23]

Carol agreed. 'It is the emotional toll, yes. The role reverses, you become the mother and she is the child. There's no let up. You have to do everything for them, wash their hair, teeth, meds. You need a medical degree, to be honest.'

Carol was highlighting that with more care being encouraged in the home, there is even greater expectation on the carer and what they administer. In a recent poll, 27 per cent did not feel qualified to give the level of aid needed.[24] I could relate to this. When my father was ill, we were fortunate that my sister is a doctor. She helped on the medical side of things but also, critically, advocated on his behalf with the NHS, hospice and social services.

When I ask Carol how she now sees those years, she pauses and takes a sharp intake of breath. 'To be honest, you just resent it in the end. She was my mum, and I loved her, but it is a lot to put on someone,' she says, in what feels like a generous understatement. The unequal load caused tensions between her and her two siblings. 'My sister helped, but my brother not so much. I was resentful towards my brother. I remember being out with my best friend, only out down the road for a meal, and I looked up and my brother was standing there, and he said, "You've got to come home. I have had a call from Mum, she's had a fall, and I can't go, we've got dinner booked." Well, I thought, why can't you deal with her? You know men, they don't want to get involved in mucky things. I was able to say to my sister, right, I need to have a break. Thankfully, I did get a reprieve.'

Carol's experience chimes with the work done by social worker Elaine Brody in the 1960s. Brody identified that in most families there is a 'burden bearer' – a single member who carries most of the responsibilities even when there were others who could share them.[25] Today, these are often, but not always, women. They are also often those with the least demanding careers, who are the most financially or time capable, who live the closest or who are childfree. Increasingly, with families now smaller, international and blended, rarely is the load shared equally between offspring. When it comes to inheritance, though, Carol and her siblings split it equally even though there was an obvious imbalance in who had looked after their mother. In Carol's case, this caused little resentment, but in many families, it does.

At sixty-four, Carol is starting a new exciting chapter in her life. 'I was actually packing boxes before you called,' she tells me with an enthusiasm that is infectious. After years as a carer and several years with her partner but living apart, Carol is moving to the east coast of England to be with him. 'He's been very patient. After sixty-four years in Wales, I'm moving. There's so much to do!' Carol and her partner are buying a home together, which has only been possible due to the inheritance Carol received from the sale of her mother's house as well as some additional inheritance she received from two friends: 'I feel like this is a beginning of my life. I didn't think I would ever afford to buy, and I am now living my dream having cared for my mother for so many years. Now my partner and I can finally have a life together.'

I ask Carol whether she is thinking about her own social care costs given what she experienced with her mother: 'I won't earn enough to put some aside. Now I'm just going to live for the moment.'

'I don't blame you!' I instinctively reply.

But given Carol's experience, I asked her whether she thought that younger generations would make the same sacrifice when the time comes?

'I'm not sure. I think that is a good point. Just looking at the young today, they are so self-obsessed. Everything must be perfect. How would they cope with people who are ill? It is so unpredictable. Perhaps I'm being unfair. I just don't think young people will sacrifice their lives like I did.'

Maybe Carol is right, but it's not just younger generations. New research found that 40 per cent of the UK wouldn't consider letting a parent move into their house, despite 28 per cent worrying about their parents' safety.[26] When the time comes, most families muddle through but often only bite the bullet when things reach crisis point.[27] Overall, 81 per cent of families say they are reluctant to talk about care options with their elderly relatives.[28]

I tentatively ask Carol what feels like a crude question: 'So, as someone who has given so much time to care and is now in receipt of an inheritance, do you connect the two? If so, do you have any advice to younger generations thinking about both?'

Before I could finish my question, she leapt in to answer: 'You cannot guarantee the inheritance. It is not a right. I think it is justified that social care comes before inheritance. What else can you do? You have to be cared for.'

But was Carol right about young people being more self-obsessed and less willing to help their parents? This felt like the kind of sentiments that older generations have been saying about young people since time immemorial, and yet the rise of individualism, as we have seen, is undeniable. Carol expressed the torn emotions, the sense of duty and love but also the resentment that accompanies this sacrifice over many years. This is complicated by the emotional history that you share with this person; looking after a parent is very different from looking after a spouse, friend or any other relative. Many offspring find themselves caring for people they do not like.

Carol was fortunate in one respect: she and her siblings lived near their parents. In a more dispersed world, for many this is not the case. Indeed, ageing parents was one of the top reasons cited for moving back to one's country of birth or family origin.

But what was it like on the other side of that care dynamic? I needed to talk to someone who worked in the home care sector, an industry that is much maligned and misunderstood and one that operates on predominantly female labour, serving families and clients who need care in their homes.

Sammy could never concentrate in class. She was always told she was too social, talked too much. In maths, she was made to face the wall because she was deemed too much of a distraction. There were some lessons she didn't bother going to. She grew up in the Black Country: 'We were always playing in the street; it was a big family and we all hung around together.'

Sammy left school after her GCSEs and studied for the health and social care BTEC at college. She found it easy: 'It was all a bit basic. I did very well because I've just got a lot of common sense.' Sammy has worked in domestic social care for sixteen years and is now an award-winning registered manager in charge of an entire team of home-help carers in the East Midlands. She looks after some of her clients for a few weeks, some for years. One of them, an ex-Harley-Davidson rider, has been on her books for nearly a decade. Sometimes her team can spend a couple of hours in the person's home; sometimes it's only fifteen minutes. 'You're going into people's homes; you don't know what you are finding,' which is why she is very picky about who she hires: 'You can have such turnover in social care, but I won't just hire anybody. I always give the people that are willing to learn the chance. Moulding them, this is the way it's gotta be done. I'm looking for common sense.'

These are skills Sammy finds lacking in younger generations: 'It's completely changed. They just want money; a lot don't want to learn. They've literally been mollycoddled, and you have to teach them how to make a piece of toast without burning it. And eggs, people struggle so much with having to cook eggs, they literally don't know how to boil an egg, and God forbid if you ask them to do poached! I have a lot who are shy and who can't communicate with the clients. You might be the only person the client sees all day; you need to be able to connect with them.'

I wanted to know how Sammy thought families were dealing with the growing care responsibilities of elderly relatives.

'You've got some families who are really good, some families who don't do anything. We've got a history of elderly parents being abused, especially financial abuse.'

A major part of Sammy's job is raising safeguarding issues, but in her view many of these situations arise because the family carer does not understand the patient's medical diagnosis or behaviour. That is why Sammy's company now offers free training to educate family carers on these complex conditions. She is trying to help them be better carers for their loved ones. She also sees families struggle to navigate a complex and overburdened state system as well as over-caring and exhaustion. Giving temporary respite to carers is one of the chief ways her team helps families, in essence recreating the community that she grew up with. But Sammy recognises that as a manager she is in an impossible juggling act trying to help family carers but also managing her own teams under a system that is creaking: 'Councils are broke, bills are going up, people can't afford care, but then you have to put the rates up as the professional carers have to be paid a decent wage.'

But in an environment where you are pressured to take on more and more, Sammy prides herself in providing a humane service not driven by solely profit and efficiency. 'I think it's about being honest; I don't take on what I know I can't achieve. I am not going to deliver a bad service. I don't want all the complaints. I will say that openly to social workers.'

I wanted to know whether Sammy saw home care as predominantly one where the women in the family carry most of the responsibilities. Her answer surprised me: 'I see more men stepping up now, not just husbands but sons. We have several who will do the cooking and the cleaning and sometimes we are just going in to do the personal care or clean. Actually, I see a lot more men stepping up than women. We used to have a lot more women; you used to have the wife ring up, but more and more it is the son.'

I was admittedly sceptical about Sammy's assertion that more men were stepping up on the care front until I spoke to Stu. When I call, Stu immediately lets me know he's on a come down from a three-day bank holiday bender. It started with a pub quiz and ended in a hot tub, although at thirty-four he insists it was very tame; Monday, he spent hungover, planting strawberries in his garden. Stu lives with his long-term girlfriend and his parents on their property in Sussex. He is also primary carer to both his mum and dad. But it wasn't always like this. His dad left school at twelve and in Stu's words 'basically never stopped working' – he was a tradesman who over four decades built an impressive property portfolio. 'My dad was the definition of non-stop. He thinks the rest of the world should work as hard as him,' Stu tells me with a tone of disapproval. By the time Stu was born, his parents had done well enough to send both him and his sister to independent school: 'Everyone there was from hard-working families, business owners who had done well. I mucked about a lot, but sport was my saviour.' Stu wasn't really pressured to go to university by his parents: 'My dad wanted me to get to work as fast as possible. My mum was more supportive; I think she would support me even if I was going to jail. She's just like that.' Stu tried working for his father's firm, 'but we really didn't see eye to eye'. After several odd jobs, Stu left to travel around North America; his parents matching anything he had saved.

After hitchhiking and living like a nomad for two years, Stu received a phone call from his dad telling him to come home. His mum had taken a turn for the worse. She had originally been diagnosed with MS when Stu was ten. 'I remember being in this room in hospital and someone telling me about her illness, and I was like "No, she hasn't, Mum's fine."' By the time that Stu returned from his travels, things had become more serious. 'I read up on how I could help her, but you can't do a lot but just be a family member. It's one of those cruel diseases. There's no real medication, just care.'

Stu's life changed dramatically in 2019 when his dad had a massive stroke. 'Everything fell really fast, really hard,' he tells me. 'I shifted into organise mode, probably too much, organising a counsellor and swimming for mum, physio for both, cooking three meals a day to ensure they were eating properly.' Stu not only became chief carer for his parents but also took over the family business, which by that time had matured into multiple properties and shops. 'My dad was like, "I've got no bloody choice, he's got to run it" … So, me taking over the business has come with much resentment. He doesn't agree with my decisions because I'm coming with more of a modern outlook and he's very old guard. Dad still thinks he will get better and go back to being the boss, but he won't.'

'It's a lot to take on,' I say.

'Yeah, I want to look after my parents, I want to be a good son. How can you do that though without sacrificing your own time and life? There's so much I want to do and unfortunately time is starting to run out. I want to go and travel Japan, do a chef's course, live in a camper van. That balance is the thing I struggle with every day. And it isn't just me battling with that because I have a partner and there are things that she wants to do, she has aspirations. We talk about things we want to do, and we don't really do any of that, because I am constantly having to do something for someone else. It's also why I don't really want kids.'

'That's impossible to juggle,' I say. 'So, how has it affected your relationship with your parents?' I ask him.

'Well, the last three years have been intense, and I've had to take a step back for me and for them. I had a serious conversation with my mum not long ago and she said I don't want to do any of this any more. And it kind of dawned on me that maybe I'd got too pushy-pushy, they were resenting me for doing too much for them.' Stu was speaking of the complex emotions that fluctuate between carer and cared-for over time, as challenging as any financial or physical burdens.

Stu is now aiming for greater balance; he insists that weekends are for himself and his partner, and he's also thinking what happens in the medium term. 'When my dad had a stroke, I remember walking out of the hospital and saying to myself, "I'm going to give them seven years." So, on the day those seven years are up, I'm going to start making plans for what I want to do, irrelevant to where they are at, irrelevant to how they are feeling, it has to be me. Otherwise, I'll be here till I'm fifty.'

'You've got a year and a half left,' I calculate.

'Yep, I'm already putting things in place. I'm organising stuff, people have keys, all that. I remember a friend saying something once that stuck: "They chose to have kids; you didn't choose to have parents. Don't get caught looking after them too much, you'll just get caught not doing what you want to do." I've remembered that.'

I just had one more question, which seemed especially pertinent given Stu was now running the family business. 'So, do you think about inheritance?'

He immediately responded without pondering: 'To be honest, not really. At the end of the day, I know the money is there, I've never thought about it. If it wasn't and we were just dealing with care, the lack of money really would be an issue.'

Who Will Pay?

In the 1980s, economists at Harvard found a rather depressing connection between money and elderly care. Examining the data from thousands of families, they discovered that parents with higher transferable wealth received considerably more phone calls and visits from their children. Those who were given the most attention of all were rich and sick and had two or more kids.[29] Make of that what you will.

Now let's assume that this is not how or why most of us will address the care needs of our parents. Equally, though, it would be ignorant not to consider the costs of care and its likely impact on inheritance. The current decision facing governments of whether to channel public funds to the young or old may soon be the decision facing many private families: to pay for care or pass the wealth down.

To put this debate into context, consider there are currently approximately 400,000 residents living in care and nursing homes in the UK. We may not yet be in the situation they have in Japan where nappies for older people outsell nappies for babies, but an ageing population inevitably means increasing demand for residential homes and palliative care services. Of those 400,000 residents today, almost half pay for their own care, with the rest supported by state funding. Currently, it costs about £800 a week for a residential care home and £1,078 for a nursing home, around £56,000 a year – more expensive than Eton – with the average period for a stay in a nursing home 2.2 years. That totals around £125,000 on average – impossible for most families to pay without releasing existing savings or assets. But even *that* is considered an underestimate by those paid to calculate these things with certainty. One financial advisor told me that on average, the cost for the best care for his affluent clients would be more like £70,000 per year (the price of which is going up faster than most house prices). He also estimates that to err on the side of caution, you should calculate requiring this care for five years. This totals £350,000, and if we are saving for a couple then that is £700,000. In total, he advises clients to think about setting aside a million pounds for care costs, which includes any additional private healthcare needs. This seven-figure sum may sound extreme, but you can now see why his industry is assuming that all that money belonging to baby boomers in property is the only way that future care bills can be secured. One financial advisor told me: 'It's something my industry talks about a lot. I don't think the wealth transfer will be as much as people think, care costs will increase at such a rate, the government haven't got the appetite to solve that. We probably won't see anything like the real returns we have seen in investments and housing over the past ten years in the next ten, so I'm not convinced by the trillions of pounds of inheritance that people talk about.'

Anyone with wealth of just £23,250 must pay for their own social care – this threshold has not changed since 2010, meaning that more and more poorer families have been dragged into this bracket. Local council assistance is means tested, taking into consideration any capital (savings and assets) and any income. Care is initially paid for by existing savings and then subsequently from the sale of the house.

The fees vary across different parts of the UK, where responsibility for social care provision is devolved. What that means in practice is that it is a postcode lottery. But it is also an illness lottery. I don't think my father ever once considered himself fortunate to have terminal cancer, but, in this context, he was. Unlike the NHS, where you are treated for free whatever the illness, however long, when it comes to social care those with complex needs requiring long-term care are inevitably disadvantaged. Even within care homes, there is an additional cost for someone with dementia. To be blunt, the lottery of death plays as much of a role as the lottery of birth in an inheritocracy.

Very often the only possible route for paying for this care is liquidating the family home. This is a politically charged and emotive issue. Consider the fact that the two election clangers so far this century have come over the potential jeopardising of the family home. The first, as we saw in Chapter 7, was in 2009 when Gordon Brown dithered calling the election having been outsmarted by George Osborne over the inheritance tax threshold. The second, more recently, was in 2017: Theresa May's blunder over the so-called dementia tax. Billed as the Conservatives' proposal to solve the social care funding gap, it focused on care not inheritance, but it targeted the same demographic of homeowners and seemingly posed the same threat: loss of the family home.

In an illustration of just how politically charged this topic became, the Conservatives paid for a Google advert to appear at the top of the page when users searched for 'dementia tax' in response to growing attacks on the policy. The Conservative Party was forced into an embarrassing U-turn, scrapping it together. May's successor, Boris Johnson, confirmed that he had an 'oven-ready' plan for dealing with social care when he entered Downing Street two years later. But the dementia tax debacle ensured that social care funding became the policy that elected officials were happy to kick down the road. The political choice facing Westminster is whether the wealthy elderly should pay for their own care by releasing private and property wealth. If they do, it will potentially mean less inheritance for their offspring and in turn may achieve what Paul Johnson of the IFS says is the vital challenge: 'to make inheritance matter less'. Importantly, it will ensure that younger taxpayers do not carry the huge burden of elderly care.

But it is surprising how little is said about this dilemma, not just by politicians but by older people themselves. A few years ago, I interviewed a series of affluent baby boomer women to talk about their attitudes and aspirations around money. One thing stood out: a complete denial about social care and an unwillingness to consider that it was something that they wanted to save for or spend their money on. These were not young women but women in their sixties and seventies, many of them widows. One woman who was gearing up for retirement offered a contradictory and confusing view: 'My mum died in her fifties. I just assume that elderly care won't be an issue for me. It's reckless, I know, but I feel too young to be thinking about it.' She was sixty. All these women I spoke to were affluent and could afford to plan long term. Those in less financially secure positions are understandably thinking even less about social care. But there is little guarantee they can rely on the state.

We are, as has often been said, sleepwalking into a care crisis, one which inheritance culture is making worse. Could it be that some parents are still prioritising their kids rather than their own long-term needs? Anecdotally, financial advisors tell me that the realisation about one's mortality tends to hit around seventy-five – it is only then that people start thinking seriously about funding their 'fourth life'.

Most striking was how many of the women I interviewed said they did not want to be a burden on their children. Many were in favour of assisted dying, rather than going into a home. I can also count at least five friends whose mothers have quietly said to them in all seriousness that they would choose assisted dying over years in care. This is not as flippant as it sounds: many of them have seen relatives and parents in the care system. Their perception is that it's a life half-lived at great expense, to say nothing of their fears of being a burden. Public attitudes, too, are changing around assisted dying – two-thirds of Britons support new legislation – and Parliament is currently debating it.[30] A pre-planned death will look very different in terms of wills and inheritance and is something that younger family members will find especially challenging to navigate.

I have been trying to track down Dean for a couple of weeks now, but it speaks to how busy and complicated his life is right now that it's taken a while for us to find the time to talk. Dean, thirty-nine, works full-time, has a severely autistic son and is also looking after both his terminally ill parents.

His dad was a royal engineer for a while and then a truck driver, while his mum was a bookkeeper for small businesses in the area they lived. Dean's parents divorced when he was two, but they both moved out of London to the same area, Clacton-on-Sea. His mother bought a house she owns outright, and his dad did the same. 'My parents have two properties worth around £280k each,' he explains.

When Dean was three, his mum was in a serious car accident. She recovered but has needed a walking stick and then a Zimmer frame most of her life. 'She was a single disabled mum and really her problem is that she's never taken help from anyone,' he tells me, revealing the tension of caring for someone who doesn't really want to be cared for. In recent years, his mother's health has deteriorated to such an extent that she is often in and out of hospital. 'She's fractured her pelvis three times in the last eighteen months.' Dean describes the difficulties of not only navigating the NHS but also trying to tame his mum's now misguided sense of her independence. 'She's even dismissed the home carers. If I could describe her, she's a cross between Thatcher and Hitler, a very strong independent woman!'

But at the same time, Dean has also had to contend with the deterioration of his father's health. Three years ago, his father was given six months to live, but he has confounded the medical experts. 'He wants to die,' Dean confides. Currently, his father is in a care home with around-the-clock care that costs £70,200 a year. Dean tells me that it is at the expensive end of the market, but his father's medical needs are such that he requires it. At the moment, the major challenge Dean has is ensuring the care bills are paid: 'If we don't pay his fees, they will put a charge on his house.'

'So, how are you funding it, if not through his property?' I ask, confused.

Dean talks me through the family maths of social care, which has seen his father eat through all £70,000 of his savings. With his pensions and local authority support, this continues to leave a shortfall of £3,000 a month.

'So, who is paying that?' I wondered.

'I am,' Dean replies. Dean has sold his flat, moved into his father's house and managed to get a pay rise. All of which means, at a stretch, Dean is able to fund the shortfall in his father's fees.

'That is impressive, but why not just allow the sale of his house?' I ask, genuinely bemused.

'Because it's my dad's dying wish that he leaves his son something. He reminisces about the house all the time and he doesn't want it sold to pay for his care.' Dean's father wants to pass his house down to his son, at any cost.

Dean was so dismayed by the system and confused by the economics that he started doing some investigative work into the company that runs his dad's social care home. 'I couldn't understand why somewhere like Clacton, a place where the property prices are so low, was charging the top rate for care? So, I've looked into the company that ran my dad's care home. Turns out they only have a 50 per cent to 60 per cent occupancy rate and most in there are state funded. So, it's *losing money*.' Dean was alluding to the fact that in the care business, there is a two-tier system, 'and if you've got assets, they will strip you of them'.

'Do you think you will face the same challenge with your mother?' I wondered.

'My mum definitely doesn't want to go into care. We've had that conversation about her going to Switzerland and booking into Dignitas. She's already planned for her own funeral, given me her passwords and bank PIN codes. She's told me that when she kicks the bucket, I must fulfil my duty,' Dean says with a degree of resignation.

'How does that make you feel?' I ask, conscious that such a process is more complicated for those left behind than those seeking peace.

Dean's response makes sense: 'She talks about it all the time, which means I'm kinda desensitised to it. She places a value on her own independence; she wants to do it her way. She's not relied on anyone her whole life.'

Before he signs off, Dean expresses his frustration and anger with a care system that seems to disadvantage those who have worked hard and done what they were told to do. 'In this country, you've got people in what's called the squeezed middle, those who don't meet the threshold of government support but who haven't got the net wealth to fund it. They are the ones who are getting screwed over.'

It was hard not to agree with him.

Dean's family dilemma reveals the challenge of assuming that property wealth can just pay for care. We may have billions of pounds in wealth caught up in property in the over-65s and a looming black hole in care funding, but it is not as simple as saying that one solves the other.

There is a tendency to talk about the trillions of baby boomer property wealth as 'trapped wealth' – like it just needs releasing, be it for care, downsizing, gifting or inheritance. But to many of that generation, who were raised on the notion of a property-owning democracy and who have seen the value of their home rise exponentially, their home is not trapped wealth. Far from it: it is status, freedom and the rewards of hard work. The realising of that generation's dream. I recall what one of my interviewees, Londoner

Alex Smith, had said to me about how his dad, who had bought his north London townhouse for a low-price tag, enjoyed seeing the seven-figure valuation on a piece of paper. 'It means something to him,' Alex said. Many retirees are relieved and delighted to own their own property outright. How many retirees would be happy to go into debt or downsize their home to fund social care or even get their kids on the housing ladder? They've spent their entire lives paying off their mortgage; it goes against everything they've been told. But can we really expect the under-45s to shoulder the burden of social care in addition to funding public pensions and the NHS for older generations? This is how the tale of intergenerational un-fairness will continue to play out in the next twenty years or so.

The truth is, of course, that there are no easy answers to the conundrum of care and its relation to family wealth, not least be-cause many of us see inheritance as a right of any family. Part of the answer may lie in reframing the conversation about inheritance entirely: from an expectation to something much more uncertain. Most millennials believe that the state pension is unlikely to be around by the time they come to draw it; it could be we need to attach the same indifference to inheritance. To return to the words of Samantha Secomb once again, 'I get so many clients complaining to me, "What about my inheritance?" and I always reply, *it never was your inheritance.*'

My sense is that for all the inequality, discord and advantages we have unpicked over the past seven chapters, the fairness of our inheritocracy will eventually reach crunch point not over the costs of higher education, nor over young people's ability or not to get on the housing ladder, but over how we fund social care for the old.

Epilogue

For most of my life, I have considered myself a hard worker – driven by a hunger that often veers into the unhealthy. The kind that makes me stay up all hours of the night writing books, attached to my laptop at weekends, always on. I've taken great pride in the fact that I worked very hard through my exams, degrees and into my career. I was the first one in my family to graduate. I made my way up into the professional class through sheer graft. I improved and elevated myself through a route I'd always believed in: hard work, academic success, qualifications. This is the narrative I told myself as I, and many others, grew up in what we thought was a meritocratic society.

In truth, I've come to see this as a wilful misreading not just of my own history but of the way adulthood evolved in the twenty-first century. Not the working hard bit, that was true for us all in the digital age. Nor in the importance of education or the value of a degree, which I still believe in. But it obscured a critical fact: the grand underlining narrative of my life and any achievements was largely down to the fact that I could financially rely on my parents, and it must be said, especially my breadwinner mother. This granted me unparalleled fun and freedom as a woman, a lengthy and rewarding education, an extended kidulthood, the luxury of living in London rent-free, a fast track into adulthood and eventually the necessary help to buy a home. When it came to my identity, it was always my meritocratic achievements or my parents' working-class roots that I put front and centre, and not any inheritocratic dynamics.

I'm aware that as I write this, this all sounds incredibly naïve. But the thing that puzzles me most is why I could not openly admit this sooner. Perhaps because I was comparing my life to many of my middle-class friends. I always struggled financially, I worked from a young age, I had student loans, I got into debt, I was broke throughout my twenties. The truth is, though, I always had the safety net of home and the launch pad of Mum and Dad.

When it comes to wealth, it is always relative. I self-identified as someone socially mobile, distinct from those with established wealth who I was meeting more and more as my career veered in a professional direction, those who had had a smoother path through private education, multiple financial gifts and monthly allowances. My inheritance was only realised on my father's death.

The subtitle of this book is 'It's Time to Talk About the Bank of Mum and Dad' because the fact is we are *really* bad at talking about it. Whether it's manners, guilt or embarrassment, those of us whose parents have helped us tend to keep quiet about it. This book sought to understand why but also argues that we must talk about the Bank of Mum and Dad. Throughout our lives, most of the political narrative has focused on denigrating those who were dependent on the state, while far less attention was paid to highlighting a more widespread development: the increasing number dependent on their parents. We shy away from talking about the Bank of Mum and Dad with our friends, within society and, especially, with our parents. It amazes me how few millennial offspring feel confident in broaching the subject with their parents; maybe because they feel infantilised by their support, maybe because we didn't learn basic financial literary in school, maybe because we don't feel it's our place to initiate the conversation, even though our mute button is storing up all sorts of trouble for when our parents get ill or pass away. It's a taboo topic that causes embarrassment and tension amongst friends, too. According to our YouGov survey, 38 per cent of under-45s would not be comfortable talking about the extent of parental support they've received, with those in higher income brackets even less comfortable talking about it. In this era of comparison culture, in which we all feel rotten about ourselves, it is genuinely helpful, especially if you are a mother, I think, to talk about how much of a leg up and help you have had. It is a taboo at a political level, too, which has led to short-sighted policies around inheritance tax, education, care funding and, of course, house building in the UK. Our silence on this issue means we are failing to confront the fact that our economy has for too long prioritised wealth over wage, old over young, understandably pushing those families that could into supporting their loved ones but generating an exceptionally unfair and warped system in the process. It's a dynamic that also massively disadvantages those who don't have an account at the Bank of Mum and Dad.

The silence is especially, and perhaps understandably, more prevalent amongst men than women; the latter, in fact, have arguably gained more in an inheritocracy. The rise of BOMAD is a major factor in the crisis of masculinity and, more positively, in the increasing prominence of progressive millennial fatherhood.

Our failure to talk about it isn't just because the British think it's rude to talk about money. The truth is that we were fed a different story: a meritocracy not an inheritocracy. We were promised by politicians, parents and teachers that if you followed the education path, you would be rewarded. Many of us built entire identities around our profession and our approach to work. To say you are a nepo baby is not only deeply embarrassing; it feels fundamentally untrue – but is it? We mock Brooklyn Beckham for his gilded path into photography books and cookery TV shows but dare not admit how our own CVs have been shaped by similar forces.

You need an education more than ever before, but it will come far easier if parental wealth helps you acquire one. Middle-class millennials may cling to the belief that they've worked hard, but it's mostly been about self-preservation – *maintaining* the life our parents had if we can. I am proof of that; it was only through my mother's help that I was able to stand still and *remain* in the area that I had grown up.

Those who gained most from educational meritocracy were those whose path was lubricated through family funds, be it through personal tutors, extra-curricular activities, university fees and rent paid, master's funded. For older millennials, there was a certain level playing field in education, but as catchment areas tightened and tertiary costs soared, educational experience and success has focused evermore around parental wealth. This is why we are seeing so many middle-class parents elbowing to get their children onto degree apprenticeships but also so many disadvantaged students working so many hours during their degrees and being left disillusioned by the level of debt.

In the 2020s, the real beneficiaries are those who can draw on three privileges: firstly, an education to command a decent salary. Secondly, access to the Bank of Mum and Dad in terms of a timely gift, notably for a house. And thirdly, the combining of wealth through marriage. And after that lies the great unknown, the potential of a double inheritance when the time comes. As we have seen, for the middle classes, marriage (and divorce) has taken on new currency in the inheritance economy.

One of the paradoxes in our inheritocracy is the way in which it not only disorientates those who think they should be doing better – those high earners and the highly educated with no parental wealth – but it also forces us to recalibrate some lazy assumptions that still exist in this country about class. In an inheritocracy, we cannot assume that those doing 'well' are in certain professions or went to private school. Or Oxbridge. Or whose parents went to university or were homeowners. But as my millennial profiles show, nor can we assume that meritocracy and social mobility are dead in this country. In the case of Sean or Cole, a good education, financial savviness and a good employer can be pivotal in overcoming challenging circumstances. But tellingly, both Cole and Sean see themselves as extremely lucky and are aware of how exceptional their stories are. So, too, the interviews here from first- or second-generation immigrant families offer tales of social mobility through education within the context of profound economic obstacles. In speaking to millennials about their life stories, I wanted to not only demonstrate why it is important to talk about parental support but fundamentally to show the myriad of stories, experiences and differences across the UK. Too often any mention of parental wealth is confined to status wars within the middle classes relating to house prices, school selections, even holiday destinations. Yet as these narratives attest, every family has a story that is intimately intertwined with Britain's 21st-century inheritocracy, whether they are a beneficiary or not.

Inheritance may be a taboo subject, but it is also one that more often than not stems from love and the desire to help, rather than callous economic injustices. The majority of the British public support the right to pass down wealth to the next generation. They recognise, even if some politicians don't, that it is too reductive to say our inheritocracy is good or bad. It requires more nuance. Families are complex. We need to accept there is an inequality not only in terms of access, amount and timing of parental support but also in terms of financial savviness, investment opportunities and advice. It is not simply a two-tier system between those who have access to the parental ATM and those who don't. There are layers of family financial privilege – the gift of time, extended shelter as well as money – and it's conditioned as much by where you were born as to which family you were born into. Whether you have come from a single-parent family, your parents stayed together, passed away prematurely or remarried, these will all have an impact on your financial destiny. Another great determinant will be how your parents see out their later years and whether they need expensive care.

And so, it is time to talk about the Bank of Mum and Dad for the very simple reason that their generation are beginning to pass away and pass on that wealth. Intergenerational unfairness – boomers versus millennials, millennial victimhood – has been the conversation for the past fifteen years. But cracks in that dichotomy are apparent as the money starts to trickle down. That demographic bulge of the baby boomers, the great privileged generation of the twentieth century, will continue to squeeze public finances in terms of pensions and NHS costs well into the mid-twenty-first century.

At the height of the Thatcher decade when millennial babies were in their infancy (or yet to be conceived), Chancellor Nigel Lawson predicted that Britain would soon become a 'nation of inheritors'.[1] Thirty-six years later, Britons agree with him. A survey conducted by YouGov exclusively for this book found that 63 per cent think that Britain is a place where your parents define your opportunity

and, crucially, 71 per cent of under-45s believe it. As French economist Thomas Piketty has shown, and the most recent data attests,
in the twenty-first century, the wealth inheritors are doing better
than the wealth creators. That gap is only predicted to widen over
time. But what this book has sought to address is the wider culture
of inheritance that exists beyond the 1 per cent, an examination of
how *all* families have been forced into closer economic reliance at
a time when both the market and the state have become reduced
or dysfunctional. In such circumstances, it is easy to say that our
inheritocracy represents a return to the nineteenth century, with
modern-day family tales mirroring the novels of Dickens, Eliot and
Austen. We live again in a world where wills, deaths, marriages and
inheritances are the narrative thread on which great dramas were
based. While many of us may experience shades of these narratives,
there is one crucial difference today: the position of women. We are
seeing the great rewriting of the gender rule book for our generation in terms of family finances, care and responsibilities. We have
to finish what our mothers started.

The truth is that inheritance is a huge societal issue that affects
everyone. It is therefore a debate that deserves to go well beyond
tinkering with inheritance tax thresholds. David Willetts shared
some healthy advice with me on that front:

There is a reluctance on the right to deal with any of this, while the
left is coming at it from the point of tax: what is the correct balance between taxing income or capital? The question we should
start with is not 'Do you want your child to have a wonderful
world to live in?' but 'What kind of world do you want them to
live in? In a mobile society or an inheritance society? In a functioning society with an enlivened economy or a gated community

protected from dysfunction?' As that is frankly the choice with this unequal level of wealth.

As we have seen, the 21st-century inheritocracy was built on the opportunities of the twentieth-century meritocracy, especially in respect to its education and housing. But we are living in a new century where the promises of the old have been found wanting. Twenty years into the twenty-first century and an altogether different timeline is crystallising: tech hysteria and low birth rates; political disruption and an ageing population; and climate crises and global power plays. If baby boomers are the privileged generation, then millennials are the restless in-betweeners, with a foot in both centuries. Like the Edwardians before us, millennials have been straightjacketed by the conventions of a former age, even though these middle-class trappings (tertiary education, mortgage, career, even retirement) are now becoming less relevant and more contested. We've allowed the promises of the last century to define us. Future generations will not do this.

When I sat down with my dad in the living room of his childhood home to record our family history, I considered how my father, knowing that his life was coming to an end, was seeking to slot his life into that timeline. In this book, that's exactly what I've tried to do for mine.

Notes

Chapter 1. Inheritocracy: The Family Tree

1   'Living longer: changes in housing tenure over time', Office for National Statistics, February 2020
2   'Housing wealth held by over 65s hits record high', Savills, https://www.savills.co.uk/insight-and-opinion/savills-news/346692-0/housing-wealth-held-by-over-65s-hits-record-high-of-over-%C2%A32.6-trillion--according-to-research-by-savills
3   Pascale Bourquin, Robert Joyce and David Sturrock, 'Inheritances and inequality over the life cycle: what will they mean for younger generations?', Institute for Fiscal Studies, 26 April 2021
4   'Employee earnings in the UK: 2023', Office for National Statistics, November 2023; UK House Price Index, HM Land Registry, December 2023
5   Liz Moor and Sam Friedman, 'Justifying inherited wealth: Between "the bank of mum and dad" and the meritocratic ideal', *Economy and Society*, 2021, vol. 50, p. 620
6   'Passing on the Pounds: the rise of the UK's inheritance economy', Kings Court Trust, February 2017
7   'Cerulli Anticipates $84 Trillion in Wealth Transfers Through 2045', Cerulli Associates, January 2022, https://www.cerulli.com/press-releases/cerulli-anticipates-84-trillion-in-wealth-transfers-through-2045
8   Thomas Piketty, *Capital in the Twenty-First Century*, Harvard University Press, 2017, p. 29

Chapter 2. The Backstory: The Making of the Boomers and the Origins of Inheritocracy

1   'Boom and bust? The last baby boomers and their prospects for later life', Centre for Ageing Better, November 2021
2   'Older people in the private rented sector', National Housing Federation, 29 November 2023, https://www.housing.org.uk/resources/older-people-in-the-private-rented-sector
3   Tom Wolfe, 'The "Me" Decade and the Third Great Awakening', *New York Magazine*, 23 August 1976, pp. 26–40
4   *People*, 9 June 1975
5   Carl J. Öhman and David Watson, 'Are the dead taking over Facebook? A Big Data approach to the future of death online', *Big Data & Society*, 2019, pp. 1–13
6   'Smartphone Screen Time: Baby Boomers and Millennials', Provision Living, 1 March 2019, www.provisionliving.com/blog/smartphone-screen-time-baby-boomers-and-millennials/
7   US Centers for Disease Control and Prevention data presented at the European Congress

of Clinical Microbiology and Infectious Diseases, April 2024, https://gis.cdc.gov/grasp/nchhstpatlas/charts.html

8   John Curtice, Elizabeth Clery, Jane Perry, Miranda Phillips and Nilufer Rahim, 'British Social Attitudes: The 36th Report', National Centre for Social Research, 2019

9   Chris Horrie, 'Grammar schools: back to the bad old days of inequality', *The Guardian*, May 2017

10 Richard Hoggart, 'IQ plus effort = merit', *The Observer*, 2 November 1958, p. 21

11 Peter Mandler, *The Crisis of Meritocracy*, Oxford University Press, 2020, p. 2

12 'Inherited wealth is making a comeback. What does it mean for Britain?', *The Economist*, 27 April 2019

13 M. Bond and J. Morton, 'Trajectories of Aristocratic Wealth, 1858–2018: Evidence from Probate', *Journal of British Studies*, 2022, vol. 61, issue 3, July 2022, pp. 644–75

14 Carl Emmerson, 'Would you rather? Further increases in the state pension age v abandoning the triple lock', Institute for Fiscal Studies, 27 February 2017

15 David Willetts, *The Pinch: How the Baby Boomers Took Their Children's Future – And Why They Should Give It Back*, Atlantic Books, 2011, p.108

16 Andrew Grice, 'Labour and Tories Target the "baby boomers"', *The Independent*, 20 October 2006

17 Gemma Francis, 'First time buyers average age has risen by seven years since the 1960s, survey finds', *The Independent*, 7 March 2018

18 'Defined benefit pension schemes', UK Parliament Work and Pensions Committee, 26 April 2023, https://committees.parliament.uk/work/7369/defined-benefit-pension-schemes

19 Amy Edwards, *Are We Rich Yet? The Rise of Mass Investment Culture in Contemporary Britain*, University of California Press, June 2022

20 Ibid., p. 44

21 Will Dunn, 'The end of the housing delusion', *New Statesman*, 1 February 2023

22 'Millions of middle-class families fall into inheritance tax trap', *Daily Mail*, 22 September 2006

23 'Brown's inheritance tax grab', *This Is Money*, 17 August 2004, https://www.thisismoney.co.uk/money/news/article-1507604/Browns-inheritance-tax-grab.html

24 'English Housing Survey Headline Report, 2022–23', Department for Levelling Up, Housing and Communities, https://assets.publishing.service.gov.uk/media/657c3ff691864e001308bdba/2022-23_EHS_Headline_Report.pdf

Chapter 3. Education, Education, Education: The Illusion of a Meritocracy

1   Paul Bolton, 'Oxbridge "elitism"', House of Commons Library, 25 May 2021

2   Tony Blair, Labour conference speech, 1999

3   Paul Bolton, 'Education: Historical Statistics', House of Commons Library, 28 November 2012

4   'Participation Rates in Higher Education: Academic Years 2006/2007–2017/2018', Department for Education, 26 September 2019

5   Malcolm Harris, *Kids These Days: Human Capital and the Making of Millennials*, Little, Brown & Company, 2018, p. 7

6   Gordon Brown, Trades Union Congress speech, May 2000

7   Killian Mullan, 'A child's day: trends in time use in the UK from 1975 to 2015', *British Journal of Sociology*, April 2018, vol. 70, issue 3, pp. 997–1,024

8   Sandra L. Hofferth, 'Changes in American children's time – 1997 to 2003', *Electronic International Journal of Time Use Research*, January 2009, vol. 6, issue 1, pp. 26–47

9   Harris, *Kids These Days*, p. 6

10 Tom Fryer and Steven Jones, 'How do Admissions Professionals use the UCAS personal statement?', Higher Education Policy Institute, June 2023

11 Richard V. Reeves, *Dream Hoarders: How the American Upper Middle Class is Leaving Everyone Else in the Dust, Why That is a Problem, and What to Do About It*, Brookings Institution, 2017, p. 44

12 Gavan Conlon, Pietro Patrignani and Iris Mantovani, 'The death of the Saturday job: the decline in earning and learning amongst young people in the UK', UK Commission for Employment and Skills, 16 June 2015

13 Santander Mortgages research, August 2017, https://www.santander.co.uk/about-santander/media-centre/press-releases/one-in-four-parents-have-had-to-move-house-to-be-within

14 Carl Cullinane and Rebecca Montacute, 'Tutoring: The New Landscape', Sutton Trust, March 2023, https://www.suttontrust.com/our-research/tutoring-2023-the-new-landscape/

15 Reeves, *Dream Hoarders*, Chapter 1

16 'Widening Participation in Higher Education', Department for Education, 13 July 2023, https://explore-education-statistics.service.gov.uk/find-statistics/widening-participation-in-higher-education#releaseHeadlines-tables

17 'Education at a Glance 2022', OECD, 3 October 2022, https://www.oecd.org/en/publications/education-at-a-glance-2022_3197152b-en.html

18 Jon Marcus, 'How Britain Is Encouraging More Men to Go to College', *The Atlantic*, 2 May 2016, https://www.theatlantic.com/education/archive/2016/05/british-universities-reach-out-to-the-new-minority-poor-white-males/480642/; HESA data, 2021–22, https://www.hesa.ac.uk/news/19-01-2023/sb265-higher-education-student-statistics

19 'School league tables: Boys behind girls for three decades', BBC News, 6 February 2020

20 Nazia Parveen, 'Students from northern England facing "toxic attitude" at Durham University', *The Guardian*, 19 October 2020; Lauren White, 'A Report on Northern Student Experience at Durham University', 30 September 2020

21 Anne Helen Petersen, *Can't Even: How Millennials Became the Burnout Generation*, Chatto & Windus, January 2021, p. 12

22 'One in 10 students in England "rich enough to avoid big debts"', *The Guardian*, 15 January 2019

23 Emma Yeomans, 'Parents protest as lecturer strikes deny children their degrees', *The Times*, 17 August 2023

24 'English Studies Provision in UK Higher Education', British Academy, June 2023

25 Eliza Filby, 'As the middle classes rush to degree apprenticeships, poorer British kids miss out', *City AM*, 9 May 2023

26 Jon Ungoed-Thomas, 'Martin Lewis: "We must stop calling it a student loan"', *The Observer*, 13 May 2023

27 Tom Richmond and Eleanor Regan, 'No train, no gain: An investigation into the quality of apprenticeships in England', EDSK, November 2022, https://www.edsk.org/wp-content/uploads/2022/11/EDSK-No-Train-No-Gain.pdf

28 'One in eight young people without degrees work in graduate jobs', Office for National Statistics, 18 September 2018

29 'ISE Recruitment Survey 2023', Institute of Student Employers, October 2023, https://ise.org.uk/page/ISE_Recruitment_Survey_2023

Chapter 4. Rise of the Kidults: How Inheritocracy Corrupted Adulthood

1 Jonn Elledge, 'Boomers' generosity to their kids is warping British society', *New Statesman*, 4 February 2023

2 BuzzFeed and Publicis research, September 2018, https://www.thedrum.com/opinion/2018/09/27/buzzfeed-bets-its-future-being-the-home-adulting-advice

3 'Rapporto annuale 2024: La situazione del Paese', Istituto Nazionale di Statistica, 15 May 2024

4 'More adults living with their parents', Office for National Statistics, 10 May 2023

5 Julie Lythcott-Haims, *How to Raise an Adult: Break Free of the Overparenting Trap and Prepare Your Kid for Success*, Pan Macmillan, 2015

6 Piers Morgan's Royal Television Society Cambridge Convention Q&A, 26 September 2019, https://rts.org.uk/article/watch-full-sessions-rts-cambridge-convention-2019

7 Petersen, *Can't Even*

8   Anne Helen Petersen, 'How Millennials Became the Burnout Generation', BuzzFeed, 5 January 2019

9   '2013 Intergenerational Fairness Index: Young People's Prospects Worsened in Past Year', Intergenerational Foundation, 18 June 2013

10 Rachel Connolly, 'How did rich millennials become the voice of generation rent?', The Guardian, 13 August 2020

11 'Pilot', Girls, HBO, 15 April 2012

12 Joe Hickman, 'How are parents planning on saving for their children?', Wealthify, 3 March 2022, using data from December 2021, https://www.wealthify.com/blog/saving-for-children

13 'Parents Expect their Children to Become Financial Grown-Ups at the age of 29', Sainsbury's, https://www.about.sainsburys.co.uk/news/latest-news/2016/19-09-2016a

14 'Fewer than one-in-three people expect to benefit from Britain's big inheritance windfall', Resolution Foundation, 3 February 2022

15 Alice Kantor, 'Why I refused to lend money to my parents', Financial Times, 6 September 2019

16 '£8.2 billion borrowed from Bank of Mum and Dad during pandemic', OneFamily, 24 May 2021

17 Bee Boileau and David Sturrock, 'Bank of mum and dad drives increasing economic inequalities in early adulthood', Institute for Fiscal Studies, 13 February 2023

18 Kate Hughes, 'Bank of mum and dad fuels financial inequality – with more than property', The Independent, 12 January 2022

19 Bee Boileau and David Sturrock, 'Who gives wealth transfers to whom and when? Patterns in the giving and receiving of lifetime gifts and loans', Institute for Fiscal Studies, 13 February 2023

20 'Families and Households in the UK: 2020', Office for National Statistics, March 2021; 'Profile of the older population living in England and Wales in 2021 and changes since 2011', Office for National Statistics, 3 April 2023

21 David Harrison, 'It's the modern girls' night out – mums go too', The Times, 15 March 2015

22 First Choice survey, April 2019, https://swnsdigital.com/uk/2019/04/multi-generational-holidays-are-now-popular-amongst-brits/

23 'Company recruiters see a rising level of parental involvement in collegiate job searches', MSUToday, 24 April 2007, https://msutoday.msu.edu/news/2007/company-recruiters-see-a-rising-level-of-parental-involvement-in-collegiate-job-searches

24 '(Say wha???) The CEO who writes her employees' parents', Fortune, 28 January 2014

25 Amanda Barroso, Kim Parker and Richard Fry, 'Majority of Americans Say Parents Are Doing Too Much for Their Young Adult Children', Pew Research Center, 23 October 2019, https://www.pewresearch.org/social-trends/2019/10/23/majority-of-americans-say-parents-are-doing-too-much-for-their-young-adult-children/

26 Rob Carrick, 'Parents financially supporting thirtysomething kids? It's happening', Globe and Mail, 28 February 2019

27 'Early Adulthood: The Pursuit of Financial Independence', Merrill Lynch and Age Wave, April 2019, https://globalcoalitiononaging.com/wp-content/uploads/2019/04/merr9555_EarlyAdulthoodStudy_v05a_pages.pdf

28 Barroso, Parker and Fry, 'Majority of Americans Say Parents Are Doing Too Much for Their Young Adult Children'

29 John Burn-Murdoch, 'Home ownership in Britain has become a hereditary privilege', Financial Times, 14 July 2023

30 'Millennials have paid £44,000 more rent than the baby boomers by the time they hit 30', Resolution Foundation, 16 July 2016

31 'Bank of Mum and Dad: Key to driving Britain's housing market recovery?', Legal & General, August 2020

32 Lisa Adkins, Melinda Cooper and Martijn Konings, The Asset Economy: Property Ownership and the New Logic of Inequality, Polity, 2020, p. 14

33 'The Bank of Mum and Dad', Legal & General, August 2017
34 Sarah O'Grady, '"Parent landlords" set to double to 1.4 million in the UK', *Daily Express*, 6 October 2016
35 'The Bank of Mum and Dad', Legal & General, 2016
36 'The Bank of Mum and Dad', Legal & General, 2017
37 Ibid.
38 'The Bank of Mom and Dad', Legal & General, February 2019
39 Laurence Troy, Peta Wolifson, Amma Buckley, Caitlin Buckle, Lisa Adkins, Gareth Bryant and Martijn Konings, 'Pathways to home ownership in an age of uncertainty', Australian Housing and Urban Research Institute, March 2023
40 'Generation Buy', HSBC, 2017, https://www.hsbc.com/-/files/hsbc/media/media-release/2017/170227-hsbc-beyond-the-bricks-press-release-generation-buy.pdf
41 'Early Adulthood', Merrill Lynch and Age Wave

Chapter 5. Soft Boys, Henrys and Deanos: Why Class Sits Differently for Millennial Men

1 Instagram account: @beam_me_up_softboi
2 Peter Turchin, *End Times: Elites, Counter-Elites and the Path of Political Disintegration*, Allen Lane, 2023, p. 7
3 Noah Smith, 'The Elite Overproduction Hypothesis', Noahpinion, 26 August 2022, https://www.noahpinion.blog/p/the-elite-overproduction-hypothesis
4 Across the working-age population, STEM graduates earned, on average, £3,000 more than LEM (law, economics and management) graduates and £7,000 more than OSSAH (other social sciences, arts and humanities) graduates. 'Graduate Labour Market Statistics: 2015', Department for Business, Innovation and Skills, April 2016
5 Smith, 'The Elite Overproduction Hypothesis'
6 'Investing in Our Talent's Future', Advertising Association, January 2023; Niamh Carroll, 'Employment in marketing and advertising has fallen 14% in three years', *Marketing Week*, https://www.marketingweek.com/employment-marketing-advertising-down-14-three-years/
7 Alexandra Turner, 'UK local newspaper closures: Launches in digital and print balance out decline', *Press Gazette*, 7 October 2022
8 Mark Spilsbury, 'Diversity in Journalism', National Council for the Training of Journalists, May 2022
9 Peter Turchin, 'Political instability may be a contributor in the coming decade', *Nature*, February 2010
10 Keir Milburn, *Generation Left*, Polity, 29 March 2019
11 Smith, 'The Elite Overproduction Hypothesis'
12 John Burn-Murdoch, 'Millennials are shattering the oldest rule in politics', *Financial Times*, 29 December 2022
13 Laura van der Erve, Sonya Krutikova, Lindsey Macmillan and David Sturrock, 'Intergenerational mobility in the UK', Institute for Fiscal Studies, September 2023
14 Ben Ansell, 'Generation Games', Political Calculus, 2 January 2023, https://benansell.substack.com/p/generation-games
15 Sebastian Payne, *Broken Heartlands: A Journey Through Labour's Lost England*, Macmillan, 2021
16 Owen Jones, *Chavs: The Demonization of the Working Class*, Verso Books, 2012
17 Acutely aware of the narrowness of a sample that would be drawn to the BBC website, the researchers accompanied it with additional fieldwork to ensure a social range.
18 'The Great British class calculator', BBC News, https://www.bbc.co.uk/news/special/2013/newsspec_5093/index.stm
19 Mike Savage, *Social Class in the 21st Century*, Pelican Books, 2015
20 'Billionaire Ambitions Report 2023', UBS, November 2023, https://www.ubs.com/global/en/family-office-uhnw/reports/billionaire-ambitions-report-2023/download.html

21 *Fortune*, 25 June 2006
22 Guy Standing, *The Precariat: The New Dangerous Class*, Bloomsbury, 2014
23 'Schools, pupils and their characteristics: Academic Year 2023/2024', School Census Statistics, 6 June 2024, https://explore-education-statistics.service.gov.uk/find-statistics/school-pupils-and-their-characteristics

Chapter 6. Milestones, Marriage and Mating: Why Inheritocracy is a Feminist Issue
1 'The One Where They All Turn Thirty', *Friends*, air date 8 February 2001
2 Sylvia Ann Hewlett, *Baby Hunger: The New Battle for Motherhood*, Atlantic Books, 2002
3 Amy Beecham, '"I'm terrified of wasting my life": why women in 2023 are experiencing so much time pressure', *Stylist*, October 2023, https://www.stylist.co.uk/life/women-time-pressure-wasting/834142
4 Nell Frizzell, *The Panic Years*, Bantam Press, 2021
5 Megan Agnew, 'Meet the queen of the "trad wives" (and her eight children)', *Sunday Times*, 20 July 2024
6 Petersen, *Can't Even*
7 'Marriage and civil partnership status in England and Wales: Census 2021', Office for National Statistics, 22 February 2023
8 Kim Bansi, '"I'm more in touch with my femininity": the South Asian women defying cultural expectations and moving out of the family home', *Stylist*, 2021, https://www.stylist.co.uk/life/south-asian-women-family-home-moving-out/628523
9 Rebecca Liu, 'The Making of a Millennial Woman', *Another Gaze*, 12 June 2019, https://www.anothergaze.com/making-millennial-woman-feminist-capitalist-fleabag-girls-sally-rooney-lena-dunham-unlikeable-female-character-relatable/
10 Ibid.
11 John Carvel, 'Women "will own 60% of UK's wealth within two decades"', *The Guardian*, 22 April 2005
12 'Women and the UK economy', House of Commons Library, 4 March 2023
13 'Higher education student numbers', House of Commons Library, 2 January 2024
14 'The Gender Pay Gap', House of Commons Library, 10 November 2023
15 'More adults living with their parents', Office for National Statistics, 10 May 2023
16 'Women lead mortgage revolution', *This Is Money*, 3 November 2004
17 Savills data for FT Adviser In Focus, 8 September 2021
18 US Census Bureau data analysed by lending marketplace LendingTree, 2023
19 Olivia Petter, *Millennial Love*, Fourth Estate, 2021
20 Robert Trivers, 'Parental investment and sexual selection', *Sexual Selection and the Descent of Man*, 1972
21 American Medical Association data as cited by Peter Coy, 'Studies Show How Cupid Isn't Fair', *New York Times*, 13 February 2023
22 Tanya B. Horwitz, Jared V. Balbona, Katie N. Paulich and Matthew C. Keller, 'Evidence of correlations between human partners based on systematic reviews and meta-analyses of 22 traits and UK Biobank analysis of 133 traits', *Nature Human Behaviour*, 31 August 2023
23 Coy, 'Studies Show How Cupid Isn't Fair'
24 'Ethnic group, England and Wales: Census 2021', Office for National Statistics, 29 November 2022
25 'Opinion on relationships/marriages to different social classes in Great Britain 2017', Statista, https://www.statista.com/statistics/778782/opinion-on-different-social-class-relationships-great-britain
26 Louis Theroux interviews Germaine Greer, S2 E7, *Louis Theroux Podcast*, 5 March 2024
27 Laura Gardiner, 'The Million Dollar Be-Question', Resolution Foundation, December 2017
28 'Families and households in the UK: 2021', Office for National Statistics, 9 March 2022

29 Melissa S. Kearney, *The Two-Parent Privilege: How the decline in marriage has increased inequality and lowered social mobility, and what we can do about it*, Swift Press, 2023

30 Richard V. Reeves, *Of Boys and Men: Why the modern male is struggling, why it matters, and what to do about it*, Swift Press, 2022

31 Richard Fry and D'Vera Cohn, 'Women, Men and the New Economics of Marriage', Pew Research Center, 19 January 2010

32 'Childcare and early years survey of parents', Official Statistics, 27 July 2023, https://explore-education-statistics.service.gov.uk/find-statistics/childcare-and-early-years-survey-of-parents/2022

33 Harriet Walker, 'The partner every woman should have: a doesband', *The Times*, 11 May 2023

34 Consumer Intelligence survey, November 2019, cited in Amelia Murray, 'Joint bank accounts are becoming "obsolete" as younger couples marry later in life and turn to online services to split shared finances, survey finds', *Daily Mail*, 2 November 2019

35 Ibid.

36 Victoria Waldersee, 'Four in ten men in heterosexual relationships feel a responsibility to be the "main breadwinner"', YouGov, 1 November 2018, https://yougov.co.uk/society/articles/21513-four-ten-men-heterosexual-relationships-feel-respo

37 Katie Bishop, 'Women breadwinners: Why high-earners compensate at home', BBC Worklife, 7 April 2022; Rosemary L. Hopcroft, 'Husbands with Much Higher Incomes Than Their Wives Have a Lower Chance of Divorce', Institute for Family Studies, 1 June 2023; American Sociological Association, 'Men more likely to cheat if they are economically dependent on their female partners, study finds', *ScienceDaily*, 18 August 2010

38 'Women still doing most of the housework despite earning more', UCL, 21 November 2019

39 Bishop, 'Women breadwinners'

40 Marriage Foundation, August 2021, https://marriagefoundation.org.uk/wp-content/uploads/2021/08/MF-briefing-note-on-prenups-FINAL.pdf

41 Gwyneth Rees, '"They're becoming an integral part of getting married": Why prenups are no longer just for celebrities', *iNews*, 13 January 2023

42 Matt Rudd, 'Will you marry me darling? (If so, please sign this contract)', *The Times*, 24 October 2010

Chapter 7. Will Millennials *Really* Be the Richest Generation in History?

1 'Burying Traditions: The Changing Face of UK Funerals', Co-op, August 2019, https://assets.ctfassets.net/iqbixcpmwym2/5v6n2gA1yGR5BCDRJ4kNKu/93696c8e8e2f9e260795c941fa96c6c9/3876_1_Funeralcare_Media_pack_artwork_SML_v4.pdf

2 Cassandra Rutledge Newsom, Robert P. Archer, Susan Trumbetta and Irving I. Gottesman, 'Changes in Adolescent Response Patterns on the MMPI/MMPI-A Across Four Decades', *Journal of Personality Assessment*, 2003, vol. 81, issue 1, pp. 74–84

3 'Burying Traditions', Co-op

4 'The Wealth Report 2024', Knight Frank, https://www.knightfrank.com/wealthreport

5 Harriet Walker, Isolde Walters, Chris Stokel-Walker and Charlie Gowans-Eglinton, 'I'm part of what will be the richest generation ever? You must be joking', *The Times*, 29 February 2024

6 Ibid.

7 Arun Advani and David Sturrock, 'Reforming inheritance tax', Institute for Fiscal Studies, 27 September 2023

8 Bourquin, Joyce and Sturrock, 'Inheritances and inequality over the life cycle'

9 Ibid.

10 'National life tables: UK', Office for National Statistics, 11 January 2024

11 Ludlow Thompson report, July 2021

12 'Women Hosts made over £6k a year to help offset rising cost of living', Airbnb, 8 March 2023

13 Barclays Bank survey, 2017, cited in Moya Sarner, 'Meet the women launching startups in their 50s: "I took a deep breath and jumped"', *The Guardian*, 28 August 2017

14 'Rabbi I Have a Problem: Should I split my estate equally between my children?', *Jewish Chronicle*, 1 December 2013

15 Matthew Evans, 'Sharia law compliant wills and inheritance tax', Hugh James, 13 November 2018, https://www.hughjames.com/blog/sharia-law-compliant-wills-and-inheritance-tax/

16 'Lawyer calls for change to female inheritance traditions', BBC News, 24 February 2023

17 'As Younger People Struggle to Get on the Housing Ladder, the Majority of Homeowners Aged 65+ Have TWO or More Spare Bedrooms', Zoopla, 1 December 2023, https://www.zoopla.co.uk/press/releases/as-younger-people-struggle-to-get-on-the-housing-ladder-the-majority-of-homeowners-aged-65-have-two-or-more-spare-bedrooms/

18 'Billionaire Ambitions Report 2023', UBS, December 2023

19 'World Ultra Wealth Report 2022', Altrata, November 2022

20 'Great British Retirement Survey 2023', Interactive Investor, October 2023

21 ONS statistics showed women petitioned for 62 per cent of divorces in England and Wales in 2019. Maya Oppenheim, 'Divorce enquiries to legal firms soar by 95% in pandemic with women driving surge in interest', *The Independent*, 8 May 2021

22 'Saltus Wealth Index Report', June 2023; quoted in Ed Pyke, operations director at tour operator Simpson Travel in Amanda Hyde, 'Do wealthy parents owe their grown-up children a free annual holiday?', *The Telegraph*, 27 July 2023

23 'My inheritance is being drunk through a straw in a coconut in the Caribbean! Am I selfish for resenting my boomer parents for burning through money that should be mine?', *Daily Mail*, 19 March 2024

24 Carmen Reichman, 'Most babyboomers willing to spend kids' inheritance', *FT Adviser*, 12 January 2018

25 Robert Lea, 'Inheritance tax brings in record £7.5 billion', *The Times*, 23 April 2024

26 Charlotte Gifford, 'More families feud over wills as millionaire inheritances rise', *The Telegraph*, 14 July 2022

27 Arun Advani and David Sturrock 'Reforming inheritance tax: Green Budget 2023 – Chapter 7', Institute for Fiscal Studies, 27 September 2023, https://ifs.org.uk/publications/reforming-inheritance-tax

28 'Changing Family Structures: The will writing industry in 2018', Kings Court Trust, 2018

29 'The National Wills Report: The Culture of Will Writing in the UK 2023', National Will Register, April 2023

30 'Attempts to block probate rise 37 per cent in two years', *Financial Times*, 11 August 2022

31 Leo Benedictus, 'Disinheritance and the law: why you can't leave your money to whoever you please', *The Guardian*, 31 July 2015

32 Censuswide, May 2023, https://censuswide.com/news-consumption-habits/

33 'Another record-breaking year for legacy income, but short-term challenges ahead', Legacy Futures, 20 November 2023, https://dashboard.legacyfutures.com/another-record-breaking-year-for-legacy-income-but-short-term-challenges-ahead/

34 Helen Weathers, 'The dirty tricks used to stop a daughter overturning her estranged mother's will', *Daily Mail*, 24 March 2017

Chapter 8. Parenting Your Parents

1 Michael Schulman, 'Convincing Boomer Parents to Take the Coronavirus Seriously', *New Yorker*, 16 March 2020

2 'Unpaid care in England and Wales valued at £445 million per day', Carers UK, 3 May 2023

3 Age UK, June 2023, https://www.ageuk.org.uk/globalassets/age-uk/documents/reports-and-publications/reports-and-briefings/health--wellbeing/age-uk-briefing-state-of-health-and-care-july-2023-abridged-version.pdf

4 Jaeah Lee, 'The Agony of Putting Your Life on Hold to Care for Your Parents', *New York Times*, 28 March 2023

5   Ella Hunt, 'Germaine Greer says feminism is ageist and the aged care sector is under attack', *The Guardian*, 8 March 2015

6   Just Group, 20 February 2024, https://www.justgroupplc.co.uk/~/media/Files/J/Just-Retirement-Corp/news-doc/2024/four-times-as-many-widows-as-widowers-aged-80-plus.pdf

7   Nidhi Sharma, Subho Chakrabarti and Sandeep Grover, 'Gender differences in caregiving among family – caregivers of people with mental illnesses', *World Journal of Psychiatry*, 2016

8   Jan Michael Bauer and Alfonso Sousa-Poza, 'Impacts of Informal Caregiving on Caregiver Employment, Health, and Family', *Journal of Population Ageing*, 2015, vol. 8, pp. 113–45

9   'Jobs and recovery monitor: Issue #15: gender and pay', Trades Union Congress, March 2023, https://www.tuc.org.uk/sites/default/files/JobsandRecoveryMonitor_GenderandPay23.pdf

10 Home Instead survey, February 2024, https://www.homecareassociation.org.uk/resource/home-instead-survey-uncovers-family-carer-crisis.html

11 David Goodhart, 'The duty of care', *The Critic*, July 2023

12 Natalie Morris, '"I feel guilty for not doing better in life to support them": Will you move your elderly parents in with you?', *Metro UK*, 19 October 2021

13 Emily Kenway, *Who Cares: The Hidden Crisis of Caregiving, and How We Solve It*, Wildfire, 2023

14 'Families in England and Wales: Census 2021', Office for National Statistics, 10 May 2023

15 Gemma Francis, 'Brits will live in 11 different homes in their lives – but settle near where they grew up', *Mirror*, 26 October 2020

16 Gemma Burgess and Kathryn Muir, 'The Increase in Multigenerational Households in the UK: The Motivations for and Experiences of Multigenerational Living', *Housing Theory and Society*, August 2019, vol. 37, issue 3, pp. 322–38

17 'One in Four Seniors Move Closer to Family to Help Out', McCarthy Stone, 13 July 2023, https://www.mccarthyandstone.co.uk/articles-and-news/friends-and-family/one-in-four-seniors-move-closer-to-family-to-help-out

18 Emma Jacobs, 'Grandparents left holding the baby', *Financial Times*, 20 April 2016

19 'One in Four Seniors Move Closer to Family to Help Out', McCarthy Stone

20 Julie Hicks Patrick, Laura E. Bernstein, Arianna Spaulding, Bianca E. Dominguez and Carly E. Pullen, 'Grandchildren as Caregivers: Adding a New Layer to the Sandwich Generation', *International Journal of Aging and Human Development*, June 2022

21 'Under One Roof', Legal & General, https://www.legalandgeneral.com/insurance/over-50-life-insurance/under-one-roof/

22 Morbidity and Mortality Weekly Report, 18 June 2021, https://www.cdc.gov/mmwr/volumes/70/wr/mm7024a3.htm

23 Richard Schulz and Paula R. Sherwood, 'Physical and Mental Health Effects of Family Caregiving', *American Journal of Nursing*, September 2008, pp. 23–7

24 Home Instead survey, October 2019, cited in Morris, '"I feel guilty for not doing better in life to support them"'

25 Elaine M. Brody and Geraldine M. Spark, 'Institutionalization of the Aged: A Family Crisis', *Family Process*, March 1966, vol. 5

26 Morris, '"I feel guilty for not doing better in life to support them"'

27 Home Instead survey, February 2024

28 Home Instead survey, October 2021

29 Richard Davies, 'How to make inheritance an incentive', *The Economist*, 13 October 2016

30 Ipsos Assisted Dying polling, July 2023, https://www.ipsos.com/en-uk/2-3-britons-think-it-should-be-legal-doctor-assist-patient-aged-18-or-older-ending-their-life

Epilogue

1   *The Times*, 1 July 1988

Acknowledgements

I'm a nosy person. I always skip to the acknowledgements page first when I pick up a book. It will tell you more about the author than the actual text, even in a memoir. In that vein, these acknowledgements say one key thing about me: I outsource A LOT. I relied on an embarrassing level of support to produce this book but also to keep my life and family functioning.

My first thanks must go to two people without whom this manuscript would not have materialised. Firstly, my writing coach Jack Ramm, who steered me with patience and just the right amount of challenge and encouragement over the course of two years. Secondly, my 'second brain' Emma Fagg, who managed to have an answer to every question I posed (however esoteric) and met every deadline I set her. I am also exceedingly grateful to Nathan Boroda, who was pivotal in the early stages, especially in getting me to understand the national story, and Ollie Herniman and Beatrice St Pier. Thank you to the brilliant Julita Waleskiewicz for sourcing interviewees so speedily as well as Abigail Carberry and Ceri Roberts. Likewise, to Émilie Chen for deploying all her creative powers in producing such an arresting front cover. Biteback have been the perfect and patient publisher, while thanks must go to Harriet Dunlea at Carver PR for bringing such enthusiasm and commitment to the project and to Gavin Ellison at YouGov for his guidance with the polling.

There are some people who you meet that genuinely change your life. My agent, Katy Cole, whom I first met the week before my father died, is one such person. She brings me nothing but good news and is a model of female entrepreneurship, working motherhood and human positivity that I constantly seek to emulate. Thanks too to all those at Amplify, especially Phoebe Blair, for keeping me 'posting' and posted throughout this ordeal.

Within my team, thanks must go to Christina, the praetorian guard of my diary for whom nothing is ever too much, who prevented me from saying 'yes' to everything and managed to afford me the time (and often physical space) to write this book. And to Harriet Lilley, my chief executioner and frankly everything I'm not, who joined my team just at the right time, freeing me of the mental load of running a business and enabling me to knuckle down and write.

Thank you to all the clients and audiences over the past few years, for all the insightful questions, remarks and sharing of stories. And all the team at Mission, especially Mark Lund, who over lunch one day convinced me to write this book.

As much as this is a memoir, the most enjoyable part of this was telling other people's stories, so sincere thanks must go to all the interviewees for giving me their time and sharing their lives with such intimacy, honesty and commitment. All interviewees are anonymised, but so much of what they said will stay with me for a long time. I am so very grateful to Lord Willetts for offering vital feedback on the manuscript.

I am also grateful to all those public figures who gave up their time to speak to me: Victoria Barber, Steve Dyson, Nell Frizzell, Gillian Hepburn, Paul Johnson, Helen McCarthy, Alan Milburn, Seb Payne, Mike Savage, Samantha Secomb, James Sefton, Alex Smith, Otegha Uwagba and a few within the wealth management industry whose honesty meant they wish to remain anonymous.

I ignored my friends for the best part of twelve months while I wrote this, but I am also incredibly indebted to my 'chosen family' for providing much-needed inspiration and an intellectual springboard, especially Ali Alizadeh, Charlotte Appleyard, Mike Ayres, Tom Cahn, Sarah Jones, Vicki Lawrence, Martin Lovegrove, Jimmy McLoughlin, Will Nash, Rowan Pelling, Charlotte Riley, Mickey Sheen, Paul Wicks, Katherine Wilson and especially Ela Lee for her sage advice, inspiring example and blunt but perfectly pitched comments on the final draft.

Thanks to Elvis and Zoltan for keeping me moving during a mostly sedentary twelve months and Emily Jenkins for critical moments of calm. To Carolyn for ensuring this book went smoother than the last one and MC Taylor for ensuring this book was more 'me' than the last one. And Rosie for being the third parent in our house and ultimately the most stable, consistent and good humoured of us all.

Thank you to my sisters for their guidance and grounding, always on hand to bring me back to the Filby-ways. And to the entire May clan for all your love, wine and support. And of course, my mother, who days from the deadline went through the manuscript scrupulously to ensure her reputation was kept intact. I consider myself fortunate to be able to tell her story and for her to read it; this book is dedicated to her. I consider myself lucky to have grown up in a household with a female breadwinner and a stay-at-home father – the best conditioning for adulthood in the twenty-first century. I unashamedly wrote my first book to make my father proud; this book he would never read, but his spirit, humour and gusto is evident throughout.

Finally, the ultimate thanks must go to Christian, a definite 'doesband' who kept me well fed, clothed and our kids well-loved throughout this process, as well as editing the book with enthusiasm and sensitivity. But that's the easy stuff. I am most grateful to him for his calm and kindness in those difficult moments when I descended into panic, self-pity or over-analysis and for keeping me going whenever I was derailed. You are truly the best man I know. Thank you for indulging me in this. To my children, thank you for your patience, encouragement and independence while Mummy wrote her 'big story'. I promise I won't write another one for a while.